Fa...

of the

Arab

Spring

From Revolution
to Destruction

Christopher L. Brennan

ProgRESSive
Independent Media.
ProgressivePress.com

2015

Fall of the Arab Spring
From Revolution to Destruction
© Christopher L. Brennan

First print edition, revised and released Jan. 22, 2016,
by ProgressivePress.com, San Diego, Calif.
List Price: $14.95. Length: 56,000 words on 204 pages.
ISBN: 1615772448, EAN: 9781615772445
Cover design by Jose Ernesto de la Torre and John-Paul Leonard.

Library of Congress Subject Heading
Arab Spring, LC: JQ1850.A91, Dewey 956

BISAC Subject Area Codes
POL059000 POLITICAL SCIENCE / World / Middle Eastern
POL045000 POLITICAL SCIENCE / Colonialism & Post-Colonialism
POL062000 POLITICAL SCIENCE / Geopolitics
HIS001030 HISTORY / Africa / North
HIS031000 HISTORY / Revolutionary

Was the "Arab Spring" that recently swept the Middle East an authentic grass roots movement for democracy, or just another set of US-sponsored "Color Revolutions," aimed at toppling non-compliant rulers? Mainstream media portray it as a wave of spontaneous uprisings by impatient youth against old-line dictators, but *Fall of the Arab Spring* shatters this myth. With Egypt and Libya as case studies, it exposes the Arab unrest as a US-engineered destabilization, targeting nationalist resistance to Western and Israeli domination.

We see how the "Arab Spring" fits into history, and explore the tactics used. There is a world tendency to shift away from US hegemony to a system of multiple centers of power. To stave this off while buttressing Israel, Washington manufactured the "Arab Spring." Avoiding GW Bush's crude and direct approach, the Obama team leaned on less direct means, a synergy of soft and hard power: so-called smart power. Through alliances with ambitious regional powers, NATO states, and naive local proxies, ranging from idealistic secular youth to Islamist extremists, they unleashed regional conflagration. Disguised by lofty romantic platitudes, the outcome was the breakdown of societies, civil war, terrorism, and the mass flight of refugees from chaos and bloodshed.

TABLE OF CONTENTS

PART ONE: INTRODUCTION. METHODS OF IMPERIALISM

Another possibility, which could even be precipitated by fundamentalism, is what has of late become fashionable to call "Lebanonization." Most of the states of the Middle East—Egypt is an obvious exception—are of recent and artificial construction and are vulnerable to such a process. If the central power is sufficiently weakened, there is no real civil society to hold the polity together, no real sense of common national identity or overriding allegiance to the [nation-state]. The state then disintegrates—as happened in Lebanon—into a chaos of squabbling, feuding, fighting sects, tribes, regions and parties.[1]
— Bernard Lewis

Lebanon's total dissolution into five provinces serves as a precedent for the entire Arab world including Egypt, Syria, Iraq and the Arabian peninsula and is already following that track.[2]
— Oded Yinon

From 2011 to around early 2014, the so-called "Arab Spring" encompassing the MENA (Middle East and North Africa) region came to the forefront of international political affairs. In the words of Sergei Lavrov, Russian Foreign Minister, it was "frequently referred to as the most remarkable episode in the international life of the new 21st century." The authoritarian regimes of the Arab world have been fragile systems. This is especially true more recently in their relationship with burgeoning youthful populations. Arab historian Said K. Aburish argues that these various regimes all lack modern

---

[1] Bernard Lewis, "Rethinking the Middle East," *Foreign Affairs*, Fall 1992, http://www.foreignaffairs.com/articles/48213/bernard-lewis/rethinking-the-middle-east

[2] Israel Shahak, "'Greater Israel': The Zionist Plan for the Middle East. The Infamous 'Oded Yinon Plan.' Introduction by Michel Chossudovsky" June 14, 2014, http://www.globalresearch.ca/greater-israel-the-zionist-plan-for-the-middle-east/5324815

political legitimacy—from Saudi Arabia and the Gulf states to Egypt, from military cliques to monarchies.[3] This lack of modern political legitimacy—coupled with decades of political repression, world economic crises, and unresolved grievances such as the unmitigated oppression of the Palestinian people—creates potential for massive political awakening. This dynamic was particularly pronounced because of the region's marked demographic youth bulge. Historically, youth cohorts are receptive to new ideas, eager to challenge the status quo, and active in times of political crisis. Indeed, it was the age 25 and under demographic that spearheaded the MENA mass protests. Using what is referred to as "civilian-based power," Western powers exploited and guided this massive potential for political awakening to advance Western and Israeli geopolitical imperatives. These eruptions were followed closely by covert and overt military intervention.

This study examines modern imperialism vis-à-vis the so-called "Arab Spring." This widespread Arab upheaval takes place in the context of a period when the restructuring of the world order—from *unipolarity* (uncontested world hegemony) toward *multipolarity* (multiple centers of world power)—converges with aggravated economic breakdown. This provides the lens from which this study is viewed. This analysis is, by no means, all-encompassing, nor does it have pretensions to be. Its focus is the underlying themes, methods, and most prevalent aspects of the MENA uprisings. Particular focus is given to Egypt and Libya as highly instructive case studies. Egypt demonstrates an effective utilization of "civilian-based power," while Libya provides one of the most palpable displays of the empire's ruthless stewardship of the "Arab Spring" to smash a recalcitrant Arab state.

In his study *The Sorrows of Empire*, author Chalmers Johnson, professor emeritus of the University of California, San Diego, categorizes modern imperialists into two groups: "[T]hose who advocate unconstrained, unilateral American domination of the world (couched sometimes in terms of following in the footsteps of the British Empire) and those who call for imperialism devoted to

---

[3] Said K. Aburish. *A Brutal Friendship: The West and the Arab Elite*, (New York: St. Martin's Press), 13.

'humanitarian' objectives.... The complex issue at the heart of liberal imperialism is 'humanitarian intervention' ... 'the responsibility to protect' "[4] as a pretext for military intervention.

"Liberal imperialism" has continued to evolve. A more novel method for modern imperialism includes the use of the "color revolution." Adherents of this method, such as Peter Ackerman of the Albert Einstein Institute (AEI) and Carl Gershman of the National Endowment for Democracy (NED) (See Part III), argue unfriendly regimes can be toppled by mobilizing swarms of discontented adolescents, via mass communication media such as SMS, Facebook and Twitter. Illustrating its appeal to the Obama team, this later tactic of "civilian-based power" was utilized as the initial driving force of the so-called "Arab Spring," and was later superseded by direct military intervention and America's newest unconventional model of warfare.

Despite evidence to the contrary, the mainstream narrative — predominantly accepted by both mainstream corporate and most alternative media — is that the wave of uprisings against the status quo autocratic Arab regimes were entirely organic. Additionally, a narrative sometimes found in alternative media is that these uprisings were initially organic, but were subsequently hijacked or diverted by the West and Gulf state monarchies. The latter narrative is given credence through the West's direct military intervention to topple Muammar Qaddafi's government in Libya. As we shall see, both of these notions are specious. The idea that romantic Arab youth activists alone initiated the attempt to topple their autocratic regimes is a myth. The objective of this book is to shatter this prevailing mythology.

In truth, the so-called "Arab Spring" that swept through the MENA region was a wave of destabilizations sponsored by Washington and launched through "civilian-based power" techniques. It was American imperialism of the most modern form. With the onset of *multipolarity* — with many of Washington's vassals looking to resurgent power centers such as Moscow and Beijing — the

---

[4] Chalmers Johnson, *The Sorrows of Empire: Militarism, Secrecy, and the End of the Republic.*(New York: Metropolitan Books), 67.

US moved pre-emptively for "regime change" against the independence of enemy states and erstwhile clients. Additionally, the "Arab Spring" offensive was given impetus by the imperative to accelerate the regional process of what Bernard Lewis, perhaps the most influential British Arabist, termed "Lebanonization" as a self-fulfilling prophecy.[5] This refers to the far-reaching balkanization, societal breakdown, and explosion of sectarian conflicts following the attenuation or collapse of the state—the model of Somalia.

For the casual outside observer, especially those imbibing the corporate controlled media's narrative, the complex and covert nature of the destabilization meant its intrinsic imperialism was not immediately discernable. The initial lack of overt military offensives gave the empire's use of "civilian-based power" the appearance of meritorious organic grassroots movements for change.

While it is important to acknowledge and support the aspirations of peoples toward accountable and democratic forms of governance, it is unacceptable to interfere in the internal affairs of sovereign states during this process. This principle is enshrined in the charter of the United Nations and that of natural law. In a non-Hobbesian world it would be recognized that is not for any state to dictate another's government for their own selfish aggrandizement or hegemonic interests. It would be recognized that every nation has the right to determine its future independently, without outside interference. Alas, rather than this notion as a guiding principle, the Post-Cold War era unleashed a state of uncontested world hegemony by a single power: the United States. In this single world power framework its own interests and ideology are regarded as paramount.

Although it is commonly thought to have gradually faded following World War II, imperialism continues via neo-colonialism.[6] The actions of the West, with its leading state the US at the forefront, have followed an imperialist tendency throughout the MENA uprisings. As we shall see, the West's ongoing involvement in the

---

[5] See Israel Shahak, "Plan for the Middle East." Introduction by Michel Chossudovsky

[6] Many "post-colonial" states are seemingly independent, but in reality have limited sovereignty. Via economic, military, and institutional means, they are subject to control by hegemonic powers.

"Arab Spring" is part of a larger offensive to maintain the status quo of Western and Israeli hegemony. This was done—not through the crude and direct means of the Bush II regime—but more indirectly and via a sustained synergy of hard and soft power: so-called "smart power." This was supplemented and spearheaded through the techniques of the "color revolution." This approach can be aptly labeled "imperialism on the cheap." It has been the defining foreign policy strategy of the Obama presidency.

The excessive reliance on "hard power," overt military and economic means to project power, during the George W. Bush presidency, generated widespread discourse on its imperial nature.[7] In contrast, the presidency of Obama was rarely, if ever, characterized in similar terms in its early stage. On the contrary, it was often branded as a radical departure from the aggressive tendencies of the Bush II regime. "Soft power" is defined as "the ability to obtain the outcomes one wants through attraction rather than using the carrots and sticks of payment or coercion."[8] After President Bush put US standing in a compromised position—with allies antagonized and a military and populace demoralized—the American establishment opted to shift to a more emphatically "soft power" approach, as advanced by theoreticians such as Joseph Nye, Jr., and Zbigniew Brzezinski of the elite Trilateral Commission. The new strategy rejected an outright bellicose use of "hard power," the proclivity of the second Bush administration. Instead, hard power was used more selectively and from the standpoint of "leading from behind." This means encouraging allies (or vassals) to engage in

---

[7] See, for example, Michael Cox. "Empire, Imperialism and the Bush Doctrine." Review of International Studies 30, no. 4 (2004): 585-608. http://search. proquest.com/docview/204970875?accountid=12387; Lewis H. Lapham, *Pretensions to Empire: Notes on the Criminal Folly of the Bush Administration* (New York: New York Press), 2007; Madeline Bunting "Beginning of the end: The US is ignoring an important lesson from history - that an empire cannot survive on brute force alone." *Guardian*, http://www.guardian.co.uk/world/2003/feb/03/usa. comment ;Johnson, *Empire*, 322-323.

[8] Harvard professor Joseph Nye in the *Huffington Post*, "Barack Obama and Soft Power," June 2008, http://www.huffingtonpost.com/joseph-nye/barack-obama-and-soft-pow_b_106717.html

geopolitical initiatives for the US, which provides necessary military aid covertly.

During the MENA uprisings, as the Trilateral Commission's Joseph Nye, Jr., former Assistant Secretary of Defense, had suggested even before Obama was elected, the US used "a smart strategy that combines hard- and soft-power resources—and that emphasizes alliances and networks that are responsive to the new context of a global information age." Or, as articulated by Obama State Department apparatchik Susanne Nossel, a strategy of "enlisting others on behalf of U.S. goals, through alliances, international institutions, careful diplomacy, and the power of ideals." [9] This encapsulates US strategy to topple and destabilize non-compliant states during the "Arab Spring."

Reacting to a waning American empire and a need to ensure the security of Israel, this synergy of "soft power," alliances,[10] and "hard power" came to characterize US strategy. In Libya—where direct military intervention took place—humanitarian imperialism was carried out with these as guiding principles. This study will outline the synergy between this array of methods including the use of information and irregular warfare. In the process, it will examine the current imperialist system and the pursuit of its perpetuation via the so-called "Arab Spring."

---

[9] Susanne Nossel, "Smart Power," *Foreign Affairs*, March-April 2004, http://www.foreignaffairs.com/articles/59716/suzanne-nossel/smart-power

[10] Additionally, aside from allied states, there is the use of "civilian-based power" via the "color revolution" method, relying on idealistic liberal youth. Irregular warfare by proxy, using illegally armed gangs as in Libya and Syria, represents another extension of the shift to alliances and indirect warfare.

PART TWO: CONTEXT. MULTIPOLARITY AND THE CRISIS OF EMPIRE

Will the coming world order be the American universal empire? ...The coming world order will mark the last phase in a historical transition and cap the revolutionary epoch of this century. The mission of the American people is to bury the nation states, lead their beheaved [sic] peoples into larger unions, and overawe with its might the would-be saboteurs of the new order who have nothing to offer mankind but a putrefying ideology and brute force. It is likely that the accomplishment of this mission will exhaust the energies of America and that, then, the historical center of gravity will shift to another people. But this will matter little, for the opening of new horizons which we now faintly glimpse will usher in a new stage in human history.... For the next 50 years or so, the future belongs to America. The American empire and mankind will not be opposites, but merely two names for the universal order under peace and happiness. *Novus orbis terrarium.*[11]
— Robert Strausz-Hupé (1957)

To provide context for the "Arab Spring," analyzing the roots of imperialistic tendencies is a core component of this study. It will shed light on some of the underlying causes, dynamics, and background of modern imperialism. In many ways, the current impulse towards imperialist adventures is the culmination of decades of financial calamity, deindustrialization, and a deteriorating military and political situation in the United States, the leading state of Western civilization. Ultimately, this deterioration stems from an increasingly oligarchic and impoverished society, which has been unable and too apathetic to circumvent the prevalent oligarchic dynamism.

Even prior to the Arab uprisings, eminent historians posited civilization has been in crisis for some time. Such an example is provided by legendary historian Carroll Quigley of Georgetown University. In his study *The Evolution of Civilizations* Quigley posits

---

[11] Robert Strausz-Hupé, "The Balance of Tomorrow," *Obris: A Quarterly Journal of World Affairs* Volume 1, Number 1 (1957): 26. Viewed onsite by the writer at the Foreign Policy Research Institute in Philadelphia, PA.

this civilizational crisis began sometime around the year 1890.[12] Quigley advances the existence of seven cycles which all civilizations undergo: (1) mixture, (2) gestation, (3) expansion, (4) age of conflicts, (5) universal empire, (6) decay, (7) and invasion.[13] After an "instrument of expansion" becomes an institution, posits Quigley, it no longer generates innovation for productive activities needed to sustain civilization. If this institution, and the ruling class with a vested interest in it, is not either reformed or circumvented, civilization begins to decline and enters an "age of conflicts."

This is the period civilization undergoes today. It is characterized by a declining rate of expansion, increasing class conflicts, growing irrationality, pessimism, and frequent and increasingly violent imperialist wars, with violence becoming an appealing solution for all problems to the ruling class.[14] Morally and intellectually unjustifiable war becomes endemic, with untenable pretexts for engaging in destructive imperialist adventures. Imperialism becomes more palatable, albeit updated in keeping with the modern era of platitudes and illusions.

The collapse of empires has long been accompanied by large-scale wars. In the present context, the accelerating political, financial, and economic decline of the unipolar world order has driven Western elites towards imperialist wars and destabilizations—using myriad pretexts. Prior to the onset of the MENA uprisings, power began to redistribute into a multipolar framework. The "vassals" of the American empire began to rebel. Increasingly, they began formulating independent foreign policy—driven by the imperatives of their own nation states. They looked to rival centers of power such as Moscow and Beijing for economic and political assistance and cooperation. The imperialist offensive in the midst of the "Arab Spring" was, *inter alia*, a reaction to this tendency.

ECONOMIC AND FINANCIAL CRISIS

Coupled with the geopolitical decline of the US, the imperialist reaction is related to an ongoing economic crisis. The MENA

---

[12] Caroll Quigley, *The Evolution of Civilizations: An Introduction to Historical Analysis*, (Indiana: Liberty Fund, 1979), 404.
[13] Ibid., 146.
[14] Ibid., 150-51.

uprisings transpire within the context of world economic dislocation. The Russian based think tank Strategic Culture Foundation noted: "There has hardly been a time in the past, except the eve of WW I and WW II, when global economic, environmental and social crises would be so interrelated and so linked to psychological problems of humankind." [15] As posited by Quigley, imperialist wars and destabilization become palatable solutions for the ruling class when existing institutions cannot solve societal crises. [16] In the present context, economic depression helped push Western elites towards destabilization and war.

Far from a novel phenomenon, there have been ongoing world economic crises, accelerating the decline of US power. The world economic and financial system has experienced pronounced dislocations since around the 1990s. [17] These disruptions have recently become more marked since the world banking panic of 2007-08, after the bankruptcy/panic run on investment firm Lehman Brothers, extending to major multinational institutions. As Wall Street continues unrepentantly to pursue purely short-term speculative enterprises, the US economy is altered in the direction of a volatile financial casino economy.

Notably, pressure towards the demise of the dollar as the world's reserve currency—a sinew of US primacy—is an ominous symptom

---

[15] Konstantin Gordeev, "Managing the Breakdown of World Order," Strategic Culture Foundation, May 17, 2012, http://www.strategic-culture.org/news/2011/05/17/managing-the-breakdown-of-the-world-order.html

[16] Quigley, *Evolution*, 152-53.

[17] For example: 1990, the bankruptcies of Drexel-Burnham-Lambert, Canadian real-estate speculator Campeau Corporation; the collapse of the junk bond market; 1992, the crisis of the European Rate Mechanism; 1994, the world bond market crisis involving Orange County, California and Barings bank; 1995, Japanese bond market crisis along with Dawa Bank losing $1.1 billion in bond losses;1997, the "Asian contagion" hitting Indonesia, Thailand, Philippines, Malaysia, Hong Kong, Singapore, coupled with a world stock market panic; 1998, the Russian monetary crisis and default; 1998, insolvency of Long Term Capital Management. See also Tarpley, "Financial Crises and Panics 1987 – 2003," in *9/11 Synthetic Terror*, 5th ed., p. 117-18.

Fall of the Arab Spring

of the international economic crisis and US decline. Since the 1944 Bretton Woods conference, world trade is generally conducted in US dollars, including Eurodollars based in London. Many raw materials and especially oil are quoted in US dollars. Major oil importers price their oil in dollars. This creates artificial demand for the dollar, which would otherwise find fewer buyers, as the US has drastically reduced its emphasis on physical production for export on the world market.

Author William Clark makes the case that Saddam Hussein's decision to begin pricing oil in Euros—as opposed to dollars—was among the motivations for the second Iraq war. After Hussein began to price oil in Euros in 2000, a goal emerged to prevent an OPEC momentum towards the Euro as an alternative currency for oil transactions.[18] He cites an anonymous expert:

> The Federal Reserve's greatest nightmare is that OPEC will switch its international transactions from a dollar standard to a euro standard. Iraq actually made this switch in Nov. 2000 (when the euro was worth around 80 cents), and has actually made off like a bandit considering the dollar's steady depreciation against the euro. (Note: the dollar declined 17% against the euro in 2002.) The real reason the Bush administration wants a puppet government in Iraq—or more importantly, the reason why the corporate-military-industrial network conglomerate wants a puppet government in Iraq— is so that it will revert back to a dollar standard and stay that way.

He concludes that after Saddam began pricing oil in Euros, his expulsion was made fait accompli:

> Saddam sealed his fate when he decided to switch to the euro in late 2000 (and later converted his $10 billion reserve fund at the U.N. to euros)—at that point, another manufactured Gulf War became inevitable under Bush II. Only the most extreme circumstances could possibly stop that now and I strongly

---

[18] William Clark, "The Real Reasons for the Upcoming War With Iraq: A Macroeconomic and Geostrategic Analysis of the Unspoken Truth," Center for Research on Globalization, February 17, 2003, http://globalresearch.ca/articles/ CLA302A.html

doubt anything can—short of Saddam getting replaced with a pliant regime.

The now discredited assertion Iraq possessed of weapons of mass destruction—with 350 unfettered UN inspections—gives this argument more credence. What is more, by President George W. Bush's own admission, "…the reality was that I had sent American troops into combat based in large part on intelligence that proved false."[19] What intelligence the Bush neocon team did have however, was accurate regarding Iraq's vast oil reserves, and the "petrodollar" connection of oil to the fate of the dollar.

Today, like Saddam, the Chinese and others have signaled an intent to diversify away from the dollar.[20] This puts the US in a more tenuous position. As pointed out by Brad Setser, formerly of the National Economic Council, the large dollar holdings of the Chinese, for example, make the US vulnerable. In a Council on Foreign Relations study *Sovereign Wealth and Sovereign Power: The Strategic Consequences of American Indebtedness*, he calls attention to China's voluminous US debt holdings, which constitute an "underappreciated strategic vulnerability." A precipitous large-scale sale of U.S. debt or dumping of dollar holdings could drive the US treasury market into disarray, drive up interest rates, and wreck the dollar.[21] While this is an unlikely scenario, because China would hurt itself in the process, it nonetheless shows an economic vulnerability.

---

[19] Michael Kinsley, "Bush on Bush," *New York Times*, December 20, 2010, http://www.nytimes.com/2010/12/19/books/review/Kinsley-t.html?pagewanted=all

[20] See Roger Baeting, "China's Foreign Exchange Shifts From US to EU," International Business Times, March 2, 2012, http://www.ibtimes.com/china%E2%80%99s-foreign-exchange-shifts-us-eu-419548 ; Daniel McDowell, "China Turns to BRICS to Globalize Yuan," World Politics Review, March 15, 2012, http://www.worldpoliticsreview.com/articles/11735/china-turns-to-brics-to-globalize-yuan

[21] Brad Setser, *Sovereign Wealth and Sovereign Power: The Consequences of American Indebtedness*, September, 2008, (New York: Council on Foreign Relations: Council Special Reports), 28.

ONGOING DEINDUSTRIALIZATION

The ongoing dollar crisis is coupled with a widespread deterioration of the physical economy through deindustrialization. A study by the International Monetary Fund (IMF) in 1997 observed: "All advanced economies have experienced a secular decline in the share of manufacturing employment—a phenomenon referred to as deindustrialization."[22] The IMF paradoxically concludes this to be a positive development, vaguely defining it as a corollary of "the industrial dynamism" existing in developed economies. In reality, the process of deindustrialization is not due to an inherent "dynamism." It is the result of political decisions, favorable to US multinational corporations, and unfavorable to American workers and the rest of the economy as a whole.

Contrary to the IMF's report, the ongoing process of deindustrialization of the United States and Western world is a vulnerability typifying its decline. "Ever since the industrial revolution," "the economic inequality it produced" has been a "cardinal source of friction in world politics," Chalmers Johnson observes.[23] Indeed, since the coming of the industrial age, the world's preeminent powers have been the foremost industrialized countries: the US and Great Britain. The deterioration of a nation's industrial might translates into a decline of its power. For example, as Germany overtook Britain industrially, it also increased its position as a world power. As a result, this precipitated British anxieties and intense Anglo-German geopolitical rivalry. Similarly, China's meteoric rise will entail an increased ability to project power. This points to a correlation between international power and advanced industrialized economies. In fact, noted international relations theorist Paul Kennedy argues, in *The Rise and Fall of the Great Powers* (an influential work in China), economic power is followed naturally by military power. Geopolitical strategist Zbigniew Brzezinski also argues US economic supremacy is among the sinews of its primacy.[24] In the case

---

[22] "Deindustrialization: Causes and Implications," 1997, International Monetary Fund, http://www.imf.org/external/pubs/ft/wp/WP9742.PDF
[23] Chalmers Johnson, *Blowback: The Cost and Consequences of American Empire* (New York: Henry Holt and Co., 2004), 144.
[24] Zbigniew Brzezinski, *The Grand Chessboard: American Primacy and its Geostrategic imperatives*, (New York: Basic Books), 24.

of Japan, a highly industrialized economy, its military power is limited voluntarily. With its legacy of empire, defeat and unconditional surrender, it became a vassal of the United States, which purports to be a protective bulwark against threats from Russia, China, and North Korea.

Civilizations are based on a surplus of agriculture and other production. This is the core of economics. Investment in innovative modes of stimulating these activities is a necessary component for any civilization's sustainability. [25] Consequently, a dominant civilization must maintain high levels of industrial production and agriculture. By this measure, the US has substantially faltered. It emerged from the Second World War as the most advanced industrialized country, with the world's largest economy, the result of years of effective economic dirigisme and a mixed economy.

In the 1970s the tendency towards the pursuit of a "post-industrial" society gained momentum, however. According to the adherents of this ideology, society was excessively productive; there was not enough work to keep the burgeoning labor force busy. In 1973 Daniel Bell, Professor of Sociology at Harvard University, explored the emerging tendencies of this societal trend in *The Coming of the Post-Industrial Society: A Venture in Social Forecasting.*[26] He posited this alleged tendency as fait accompli, arguing in "the next thirty to fifty years" it will be a main feature of society in the US, Japan, Soviet Union, and Western Europe. [27] Instead of capital investment in productive activity in plant and equipment, its main feature was the creation of a "knowledge society," with a focus on technical dynamics. Menial industrial labor was better suited to developing countries, while the West would focus on leisure and the "knowledge society." This prevalent outlook served as apologia for corporate capital accumulation and aggrandizement. For the masses of wage-earning Americans this has been an onerous development. Rather than leisure or a "knowledge society," the vast majority of Americans have worked harder and longer hours. Rather than a pre-

---

[25] Quigley, *Evolution*.
[26] Daniel Bell, *The Coming of the Post-Industrial Society: A Venture In Social Forecasting*, (New York: Basic Books, 1973).
[27] Ibid., x.

eminent "knowledge sector," increased reliance on the retail and financial sectors has resulted in lower wages and longer hours for American workers. Wal-Mart, America's largest employer, pays less than a third of the level of wages and benefits autoworkers received.[28]

US industry is a shattered hulk today—a relic of its former glory. In the words of economist William Wolman, it maintains an increasingly volatile "Blanche Dubois economy" largely "dependent on the kindness of strangers."[29] Its industrial base and physical economy have been dramatically attenuated, creating an economy largely dependent on the vicissitudes of the US dollar. This is coupled with a largely moribund infrastructure on the brink of thermodynamic collapse.[30] The crisis of deindustrialization has only been tempered by the military-industrial complex, which is sustained by state capitalism and a militaristic interventionist foreign policy. With other nations seeking to diversify from the US dollar, weakening its position, the American military and covert destabilizations increase in significance as enforcers of dollar preeminence. Faced with this state of affairs, war and imperialism are palatable solutions to elites.

UNIPOLARITY DIMINISHES

Coupled with the ongoing economic crisis, the key dynamic is a transitioning world power structure. The world is in the process of historical change from *unipolarity* back towards *multipolarity*—from

---

[28] See Ravi Batra, *The Myth of Free Trade: The Pooring of America*, (New York: Touchstone).

[29] "America's 'Blanche Dubois Economy,' " Bloomberg Business Week, May 19, 2005, http://www.businessweek.com/stories/2005-05-19/americas-blanche-dubois-economy

[30] The United States reputedly has perhaps the most decaying infrastructure in the Western world. In 1981 the Council of State Planning Agencies issued a report on the deteriorating condition of US public works, titled *America in Ruins*. The findings were that in the US, "public facilities are wearing out faster than they are being replaced. The deteriorated condition of the basic public facilities that underpin the economy presents a major structural barrier to the renewal of our national economy." In 2009 the American Society of Civil Engineers gave the US a near failing D-rating for infrastructure.

one center of power and authority to multiple centers. Doubtless, there have been many aspirants to unipolar world power throughout history — termed in early times as "universal monarchy." Never before, however, has a single entity achieved truly global hegemony. "Not since Rome has one nation loomed so large above the others," one theoretician observes.[31] Unlike Rome, US hegemony exists in a globalized planet, where all stretches of the globe are within reach.

The momentum for US supremacy was shaped following World War II, with the guiding principles for the "American Century" formulated by George F. Kennan, State Department Director of Policy Planning.[32] In 1948 he outlined the future of US foreign policy objectives:

> ...we have about 50% of the world's wealth but only 6.3% of its population. This disparity is particularly great as between ourselves and the peoples of Asia. In this situation, we cannot fail to be the object of envy and resentment. Our real task in the coming period is to devise a pattern of relationships which will permit us to maintain this position of disparity without positive detriment to our national security.

Today there is no evidence of deviation from Keenan's thesis,[33] and since the collapse of the Soviet Union, the US has become "the first and the only truly global power." In the pages of *Time* magazine, neoconservative pundit Charles Krauthammer proclaimed, "America bestrides the world like a colossus... The unipolar moment will surely last at least for a generation." Meanwhile *Fortune* magazine declared in 1999, "There's every reason to think the upcoming 100 years will prove to be yet another American century."[34]

---

[31] Joseph S. Nye, Jr., "U.S. Power and Strategy After Iraq," *Foreign Affairs,* July/August 2003, http://www.foreignaffairs.com/articles/58997/joseph-s-nye-jr/us-power-and-strategy-after-iraq
[32] Tom Athanasiou, "Ecological Decay and, Eventually, War," Peace Review, (Sep 1999): 379-386.
[33] Ellen Brun and Jacques Hersh, "Faux Internationalism and Really Existing Imperialism," *Monthly Review,* April 2012, 63, 11.
[34] Norman Solomon, *War Made Easy: How Presidents and Pundits Keep Spinning Us to Death* (Hoboken, NJ: John Wiley & Sons, Inc., 2005), 28.

But despite these bold pronouncements, this position as the sole global hegemon, which has characterized the last 20 years of history, is being replaced by a more multipolar world. As noted, the limited longevity of Anglo-American preeminence was foretold by Robert Strausz-Hupé, founder of the Foreign Policy Research Institute, (credited with popularizing the word "geopolitics" in the US), when he declared in 1957 that "the next 50 years or so the future belongs to America."

It is increasingly becoming recognized that within the next few decades the world system will be entirely multipolar, and US influence will wane. The US National Intelligence Council, in a report titled Global Trends 2025: A Transformed World asserts that by "2025, the international system will be **a global multipolar** one with gaps in national power."[35] [Emphasis in the original]

Currently, America's unipolar decline is a prominent subject of debate in Anglo-American policy circles.[36] During the 2010 Aspen Ideas Festival, Harvard professor and prolific author Niall Ferguson issued a stark warning on the increasing prospect of the American "empire" collapsing. This portent is, according to him, due to the rising level of debt.[37] Analysts such as neo-conservative Robert Kagan of the Brookings Institution have contended that US primacy is undiminished, and the idea of American decline is a myth. America, as long it sets its mind to it, can retain its current position.[38]

---

[35] "Global Trends 2025: A Transformed World," US National Intelligence Council, November 2008, www.dni.gov/nic/NIC_2025_project.html

[36] See, for example, Robert O. Keohane, "Hegemony and After," *Foreign Affairs*, July/August 2012,
http://www.foreignaffairs.com/articles/137690/robert-o-keohane/hegemony-and-after# or Joseph Nye, Jr., "The Future of American Power," *Foreign Affairs*, November/December 2010,
http://www.foreignaffairs.com/articles/66796/joseph-s-nye-jr/the-future-of-american-power

[37] Brent Gardiner-Smith, "Historian Warns of Sudden Collapse of American 'Empire,' " Aspen Daily News, July 6, 2010,
http://www.aspendailynews.com/section/home/141349

[38] Robert Kagan, "Not Fade Away: The Myth of American decline," The New Republic, January 11, 2012
http://www.tnr.com/article/politics/magazine/99521/america-world-power-declinism

In contrast, Charles A. Kupchan of the Council on Foreign Relations argues Kagan's thesis is "broadly wrong." "Power is undeniably flowing away from the West to developing nations," and "the worst thing to do is to pretend it's not happening." Kupchan warns against "an illusory strategic complacency: There is no need to debate the management of change when one denies it is taking place." Instead, "it is time for thrift: Washington should husband its many strengths, be more sparing with military force, and rely on judicious diplomacy, to tame the onset of a multipolar world."[39]

This restructuring of the world system contributes to the current impulse for imperialist wars and interventions. The Russian-based think tank, Strategic Culture Foundation, observes: "US strategy proceeds from the assumption that losing the global primacy is unacceptable to the country. The linkage between global leadership and the XXI century prosperity is an axiom for the US elites regardless of political details."[40] It makes the case that the ongoing economic and political turbulence, along with rising *multipolarity*, requires war for US elites. Foreign policy elites—accustomed to decades of unipolar domination—are aghast that resurgent upstarts such as Russia, which they saw fade and nearly collapse, act more assertively on the world stage.

Historically, world power realignment and rivalry are often accompanied by large-scale hostilities. This is especially true with the waning and collapse of empires. Thucydides illustrated this principle over 2,400 years ago, reflecting on the rivalry of Sparta and a rising Athens. Viewing the structural stress engendered by the shift in the balance of power between these two rivals, he found: "It was the rise of Athens, and the fear that this inspired in Sparta, that made war inevitable." Anglo-German rivalry—with a declining Britain and a

---

[39] Charles A. Kupchan, "The Decline of the West: Why America Must Prepare for the End of Dominance," *The Atlantic,* March 20, 2012, http://www.theatlantic.com/international/archive/2012/03/the-decline-of-the-west-why-america-must-prepare-for-the-end-of-dominance/254779/#.T2jBv98_fpE.twitter
[40] Viktor Burbaki ,"Why the US needs a War," Strategic Culture Foundation, April 1, 2012, http://www.strategic-culture.org/news/2012/01/04/why-the-us-needs-a-major-war.html

rising Germany — was crucial in the coming of the First World War.[41] Britain feared that Germany's growing economy, armed forces, pursuit of "political hegemony and maritime ascendancy" was an existential threat to "the independence of her neighbours and ultimately the existence of England." Consonant with Robert K. Massie's voluminous treatise *Dreadnought: Britain, Germany, and the Coming of the Great War*, Henry Kissinger, adherent of realpolitik, observes, "once Germany achieved naval supremacy ... this in itself — regardless of German intentions — would be an objective threat to Britain, and incompatible with the existence of the British Empire."[42]

Similarly, the decline of the Spanish Empire and Hapsburg monarchies, contrasting with a rising France, played a role in the Thirty Years' War, with Richelieu in France adopting the guiding principle to "arrest the progress of Spain." Subsequently, the decline of French supremacy was accompanied by the War of the League of Augsburg, the War of Spanish Succession, and the Seven Years' War. These conflicts laid the groundwork for eventual British supremacy.

Regardless of any prevailing bonhomie between two peoples and states, the framework of great power realignment often has its own momentum. Indeed, a recent study of power politics shows that in twelve out of sixteen cases where a ruling power is confronted with a rising power, the results were war.[43]

In regional dynamics, multipolar systems are more diverse, fluid, and therefore more unpredictable.[44] John Mearsheimer, proponent of the "offensive realist" school of international politics, argues that in a

---

[41] See Robert K. Massie, *Dreadnought: Britain, Germany, and the Coming of the Great War*, (New York: Ballantine Books, 1991) for a thorough treatise of Anglo-German rivalry vis-à-vis their respective navies, a sinew of British world hegemony Britain would not allow to go contested by upstart Germany.

[42] Graham Allison,"The Thucydides Trap: Are the U.S. and China Headed for War? " *Atlantic*, September 24, 2014, http://www.theatlantic.com/international/archive/2015/09/united-states-china-war-thucydides-trap/406756/?utm_source=SFFB

[43] Ibid.

[44] Michael Sheehan, *Balance of Power: History and Theory* (New York: Rutledge), 197

state of unbalanced *multipolarity* (i.e., when states compete regionally, with one of them having the potential to dominate the others), the likelihood of war increases.[45] Professor of international politics David Calleo noted, "The international system breaks down not only because unbalanced and aggressive new powers seek to dominate their neighborhoods, but also because declining powers, rather than adjusting and accommodating, try to cement their slipping preeminence into an exploitative hegemony." [46] This tendency persists in the MENA region.

Accordingly, in the present historical context, emerging *multipolarity* is a twofold impetus for aggression: first, it incites an impulse for maintaining the existing regional power structure by American power circles, who have a vested interest in the current framework; second, the decline in *unipolarity* creates a power vacuum, which regional powers such as Iran, Turkey, Qatar, Saudi Arabia and its allies compete to fill. This is augmented by US policy which encourages these actors to undertake a more forceful role against enemy states, effectively perpetuating American hegemony by outsourcing, by recruiting regional powers to fill the power void against rivals. Mearsheimer continues: "Buck-passing is a threatened great power's main alternative to balancing... to get another state to bear the burden of deterring or possibly fighting an aggressor while it remains on the sidelines."

Particularly in the Middle East, the creeping death of *unipolarity* exacerbates competition between Iran and Saudi Arabia, two rival and antagonistic powers. For example, in the case of Syria—a majority Sunni Arab country allied with Persian and Shiite Iran— Saudi Arabia, a conservative Arab Sunni power, sees itself well-poised to bring Syria into its sphere of influence. As part of the emerging "Cold War" between the two, the Kingdom of Saudi Arabia seeks to undermine the Iranian position, with Iran having the same in mind. Likewise, a rising and ambitious Turkey, encouraged by the US, seeks regional preeminence, with dreams of an Ottoman imperial revival coloring its strategic thinking. Rhetoric about human

---

[45] Mearsheimer, *Tragedy*.
[46] Quoted in Johnson, *Blowback*, 224.

rights is opportunistically used by these powers—themselves no paragons of human rights—to advance their ambitions.

Since attaining uncontested global supremacy, the US has explicitly declared its intention to maintain its position. Following the fall of the USSR, the US was left as the world's sole superpower. The first Bush administration boldly declared the US was the foremost power in the world, and meant to remain so. Bush's declaration of a "New World Order" was a euphemism for the new Anglo-American unipolar world order. As an axiom, and on a bipartisan basis, US foreign policy apparatchiks, and the American establishment, consider retaining American world supremacy and leadership imperative. Successive American administrations have regarded America as the world's "exceptional" or "indispensable" nation. In a policy statement written in 1992, the Department of Defense boldly asserted how "America's political and military mission in the post-cold-war era would be to insure that no rival superpower is allowed to emerge in Western Europe, Asia or the territory of the former Soviet Union."[47] The paper explicitly made clear:

> Our first objective is to prevent the re-emergence of a new rival, either on the territory of the former Soviet Union or elsewhere, that poses a threat on the order of that posed formerly by the Soviet Union. Second, in the non-defense areas, we must account sufficiently for the interests of the advanced industrial nations to discourage them from challenging our leadership or seeking to overturn the established political and economic order. Finally, we must maintain the mechanisms for deterring potential competitors from even aspiring to a larger regional or global role.[48]

This bold pronouncement is known as the "Wolfowitz doctrine," whose eponymous chief architect is Paul Wolfowitz, the Under Secretary of Defense for Policy at the time: "The U.S. must show the

---

[47] Patrick E. Tyler, "U.S. Strategy Plan Calls For Insuring No Rivals Develop," *New York Times*, March 3, 1992, http://www.nytimes.com/1992/03/08/world/us-strategy-plan-calls-for-insuring-no-rivals-develop.html
[48] Ibid.

leadership necessary to establish and protect a new order that holds the promise of convincing potential competitors that they need not aspire to a greater role or pursue a more aggressive posture to protect their legitimate interests." In other words, Bush's "New World Order" would not be challenged by any actor on the world stage. Specifically vis-à-vis Russia and the former Soviet sphere, Wolfowitz added: "We continue to recognize that collectively the conventional forces of the states formerly comprising the Soviet Union retain the most military potential in all of Eurasia." Russia presents the biggest military challenge to continued US preeminence.

The September 2002 Bush national security strategy reiterated adherence to the unipolar position, asserting the US should check rising powers and maintain a commanding presence in the global balance of power. This was illustrated palpably by his brutal Iraq war adventure. "The basic and generally agreed plan," observed Anatol Lavien, formerly of the Carnegie Endowment for International Peace, in 2003, "is unilateral world domination through absolute military superiority... since the collapse of the Soviet Union." [49] This commitment has not changed. It continues to undergird many foreign policy decisions of the Obama administration. As late as 2014 President Obama affirmed his conviction in American "exceptionalism" [50] —that is, America's indispensability and its right and duty to lead. Obama's subsequent Arab Spring offensive would demonstrate this commitment writ large.

THE BRICS CHALLENGE

Russia—given latitude to recover after the Soviet Union's fall by the US pivot to wars in the Middle East—has acquiesced at times, but often presents a vociferous challenge to America's unipolar "New World Order." The Russian position has been articulated and

---

[49] F. William Engdahl, *A Century of War: Anglo-American Oil Politics and the New World Order*, (Ann Arbor: Pluto Press), 267.
[50] "Remarks by the President at the United States Military Academy Commencement Ceremony," Whitehouse.gov, May 28, 2014, https://www.whitehouse.gov/the-press-office/2014/05/28/remarks-president-united-states-military-academy-commencement-ceremony

spearheaded by Vladimir Putin, Russia's undisputed leader since the post-Soviet period. Speaking at the 43rd Munich Conference on Security Policy, Putin provided the most incisive critique of the post-Cold War unipolar world order. Calling the American unipolar model "unacceptable," he remarked:

> The history of humanity certainly has gone through unipolar periods and seen aspirations to world supremacy. And what hasn't happened in world history?

> However, what is a unipolar world? However one might embellish this term, at the end of the day it refers to one type of situation, namely one centre of authority, one centre of force, one centre of decision-making.

> It is world in which there is one master, one sovereign. And at the end of the day this is pernicious not only for all those within this system, but also for the sovereign itself because it destroys itself from within.

> I consider that the unipolar model is not only unacceptable but also impossible in today's world...

> And with which results?

> Unilateral and frequently illegitimate actions have not resolved any problems. Moreover, they have caused new human tragedies and created new centers of tension...

> Today we are witnessing an almost uncontained hyper use of force - military force - in international relations, force that is plunging the world into an abyss of permanent conflicts. As a result we do not have sufficient strength to find a comprehensive solution to any one of these conflicts. Finding a political settlement also becomes impossible.

> We are seeing a greater and greater disdain for the basic principles of international law. And independent legal norms are, as a matter of fact, coming increasingly closer to one state's legal system. One state and, of course, first and foremost the United States, has overstepped its national borders in every way. This is visible in the economic, political, cultural, and educational policies it imposes on other nations. Well, who likes this? Who is happy about this?

And of course this is extremely dangerous. It results in the fact that no one feels safe. I want to emphasize this -- no one feels safe! Because no one can feel that international law is like a stone wall that will protect them. Of course such a policy stimulates an arms race.

I am convinced that we have reached that decisive moment when we must seriously think about the architecture of global security.[51]

Because of this critique of the unipolar world order, and fear of Russian resurgence, Putin has become one of the most vilified world leaders in US officialdom and its mainstream media echo chamber, at times reaching hysterical proportions.[52]

In this increasingly dynamic epoch, it is being recognized that Moscow, Beijing, and other rising powers such as the BRICS grouping (Brazil, Russia, India, China, and South Africa) do pose a challenge to the American international order. The greatest mistake of the Bush administration, according to Democratic vice-presidential candidate Joe Biden on the 2008 campaign trail, was its failure "to face the biggest forces shaping this century: The emergence of Russia, China and India's great powers."[53] Secretary of Defense Leon Panetta twice in a two-month period warned that the US is facing challenges from rising powers such as China and India in Asia in the 21st century. "We have got the challenges of dealing with rising powers in Asia. We have got the challenge of, you know, dealing with countries like Russia, rising countries like India and others," Panetta remarked to PBS News Hour. "All of that represents the kind of challenges that we are going to have to deal with in this world of the

---

[51] "Transcript: Putin's Prepared Remarks at 43rd Munich Conference on Security Policy." washingtonpost.com.
http://www.washingtonpost.com/wp-
dyn/content/article/2007/02/12/AR2007021200555.html
[52] See Stephen F. Cohen, "Stop the Pointless Demonization of Putin,"
Reuters: the Great Debate, May 7, 2012, http://blogs.reuters.com/great-
debate/2012/05/07/stop-the-pointless-demonization-of-putin/
[53] Umberto Pascalli, "Joe Biden: Russia, China, India: 'The Real War,'
" Center for Research on Globalization, http://www.globalresearch.ca/joe-
biden-russia-china-india-the-real-war/

21st century."[54] In 2007, British historian Max Hastings posed the question: "would we have to fight Russia in this century?" He concluded that "the notion of Western friendship with Russia is a dead letter... We may hope that in the 21st century we shall not be obliged to fight Russia. But it would be foolish to suppose that we shall be able to lie beside this dangerous, emotional beast in safety or tranquility."[55] More recently, in the 2012 election season, Republican presidential candidate frontrunner Mitt Romney characterized Russia as America's "number one geopolitical foe." A virulently anti-Russian position has, for a long time, been a staple of neocon strategic thinking, which continues to retain influence in Washington.

While Russia has been the most vocal and assertive, China is seen by many as the logical primary strategic challenger to American global supremacy. Author Martin Jacques even argues that China will reshape and *dominate* the coming global system. In his work *When China Rules the World: The End of the Western World and the Birth of a New Global Order*, he argues that although its first steps toward global preeminence are economic, eventually China's political and cultural influence will be even greater. "China's impact on the world will be at least as great as that of the United States over the last century, probably far greater," is the conclusion Jacques reaches.[56] Mearsheimer concurs that "the United States and China are likely to engage in an intense security competition with considerable potential for war."[57] A Department of Defense white paper notes, "China is steadily assuming new roles and responsibilities in the international community... China's rise as a major international actor is likely to stand out as a defining feature of the strategic landscape of the early

---

[54] "Panetta on Pentagon Budget: 'Cutting Almost $500 Billion Is Not Chump Change,' " PBS Newshour, January 5, 2012,
http://www.pbs.org/newshour/bb/military/jan-june12/panetta_01-05.html
[55] Max Hastings, "Will We have to Fight Russia This Century?" *Dail Mail*, June 05, 2007, http://www.dailymail.co.uk/news/article-459919/A-blundering-Bush-Tsar-Putin-question-century-fight-Russia.html#ixzz1vTupCVA5
[56] Martin Jacques, *When China Rules the World: The End of the Western World and the Birth of a New Global Order*, (New York: Penguin Books, 2009).
[57] Zbigniew Brzezinski and John J. Mearsheimer, "Clash of the Titans," *Foreign Policy*, Jan/Feb 2005, 146.

21st century."[58] Secretary of State Hillary Clinton's *Foreign Policy* Op-Ed "America's Pacific Century" also illustrates the perception of the emerging Chinese strategic challenge to the US.[59] "The future of politics will be decided in Asia...and the [US] will be right at the center of the action...a strategic turn to the region fits logically into our overall global effort to secure and sustain America's global leadership."

In its "pivot to Asia," the Department of Defense announced plans to move 60% of its naval forces to the Pacific, a tremendous military and strategic escalation. As Professor Mearsheimer observes, China is likely to seek Asian regional hegemony to ensure no power can threaten it, and to assert the terms of acceptable behavior in the region. His assessment: "It is clear from the historical record how American policy makers will react if China attempts to dominate Asia. The United States does not tolerate peer competitors. As it demonstrated in the 20th century, it is determined to remain the world's only regional hegemon. Therefore, the United States will seek to contain China and ultimately weaken it to the point where it is no longer capable of dominating Asia. In essence, the United States is likely to behave toward China much the way it behaved toward the Soviet Union during the Cold War."[60]

Despite a symbiotic trade relationship, the United States is losing to China on the economic front, increasing American anxieties. The US has maintained the position of the world's largest economy for decades, but China is poised to overtake America in this position. According to the International Monetary Fund (IMF), China's economy is poised overtake the United States by 2016.[61] Because

---

[58] Security Developments Involving the People's Republic of China 2011," US Department of Defense,
http://www.defense.gov/pubs/pdfs/2011_cmpr_final.pdf
[59] Hillary Clinton, "America's Pacific Century," *Foreign Policy*, November 2011,
http://www.foreignpolicy.com/articles/2011/10/11/americas_pacific_century
[60] Mearsheimer, *Titans*.
[61] Peter Shadbolt, "Will the 'Age of America' End in 2016 ?" CNN, April 26, 2011,

economic supremacy often translates into political power, the US's ability to project power is set to suffer as a consequence.

Additionally, as a multipolar world emerges, more countries are relying less on the US for economic aid and support. The lack of reliance on the US translates into increased political independence. The US and the West, acting through the Bretton Woods institutions, have long been criticized by the developing world as implementing policies of "neo-colonialism." Coined by Ghana's first prime minister following independence Kwame Nkrumah, [62] the term "neo-colonialism" refers to imperialism that still extracts wealth and prevents economic development, but operates through more indirect methods. Superficially, affected nation-states have sovereignty and independence, but in practice, both economically and politically their independence is limited. "The essence of neo-colonialism is that the State which is subject to it is, in theory, independent and has all the outward trappings of international sovereignty. In reality, its economic system and thus its political policy is directed from outside," Nkrumah wrote in *Neo-Colonialism, The Last Stage of Imperialism*.[63] Many countries have the illusion of independence, but in practice have limited sovereignty. As one theorist puts it, many have seen emancipation "from the direct colonial control of the Empire." Not many, however, "have managed to achieve genuine independence in the sense of being able also to control their economic destinies." These post-colonial nations are, in truth, "neo-colonies."[64] "We are ashamed to admit, but economically we are

---

http://edition.cnn.com/2011/BUSINESS/04/26/us.china.economy/index.html?iref=NS1 Indeed, one IMF report reckoned that the Chinese GCP edged out the US economy already in 2014, based on purchasing power parity, although the statistics are fuzzy. In any case, China retains a growth rate of around 7% vs. the 2% rate in the US. Ben Carter, "Is China's economy really the largest in the world?" Dec. 16, 2014, http://www.bbc.com/news/magazine-30483762

[62] Kwame Nkrumah, anti-imperialist and pan-African leader, accused the CIA of being behind numerous setbacks of the third world. He was overthrown in a CIA-backed military coup.

[63] Kwame Nkrumah, Neo-Colonialism, The Last Stage of Imperialism, http://politicalanthro.files.wordpress.com/2010/08/nkrumah.pdf

[64] Yosh Tandon, "Whose Dictator is Qaddafi? The Empire and its Neo-Colonies," Insight on Africa 3, 1 (2011): 1-21.

dependencies—semi-colonies at best—not sovereign states," Julius Nyerere, the first president of the Tanzanian Republic, once lamented.[65]

The US dominated IMF-World Bank complex has frequently been characterized as an instrument of this "neo-colonialism," especially in developing countries. In 1966, Thomas Blough, economic advisor to the British Cabinet wrote: "…neo-imperialism does not depend on open political domination. The economic relations of the U.S to South America are not essentially different from those of Britain to her African colonies. The International Monetary Fund fulfills the role of the colonial administration of enforcing the rules of the game."[66] Nyerere once called the IMF a "device by which powerful forces in some rich countries increase their power over poorer nations."[67] In 1984 a former labor minister of Peru charged that the "IMF is the ruler of the developing world."[68] In 1986 Peru accused the IMF being a tool of economic colonialism.

US influence is also reflected at the United Nations, where disagreeing with the US in the Security Council is punished. In their 2011 study "Buying Votes and International Organizations,"[69] Axel Dreher and James Vreeland of Georgetown and the University of Göttingen in Lower Saxony, Germany concluded that "voting with the United States is rewarded and voting against the United States is punished." Their study found: "The United States uses its influence at the IMF to buy votes on the UN Security Council. Governments serving on the Security Council who publicly disagree with the United States on matters of international security are less likely to receive IMF loans, and if they do receive them, the loans are significantly smaller."

---

[65] Ibid.

[66] Donald Gibson, *Battling Wall Street: The Kennedy Presidency*, (New York: Sheridan Square Press, 1994), 114.

[67] Ibid., 117.

[68] Ibid.

[69] Axel Dreher and James Raymond Vreeland, "Buying Votes and International Organizations," Mortara Center Working Paper, May 2011, http://www12.georgetown.edu/sfs/docs/mwp_2011_9.pdf

It has long been observed that IMF-World Bank policies, known as the "Washington consensus," have notoriously failed to facilitate economic development. They have often been characterized as instruments of draconian economic exploitation. In practice, this model for developing countries demands so-called "conditionalities" that limit sovereignty on economic matters, demand deregulation, massive privatization, devaluation of currency, liberalization of foreign exchange, elimination of special government subsidies, and a draconian program of austerity limiting government spending on social programs. These policies, according to researcher Michel Chossudovsky, professor emeritus of the University of Ottawa, have facilitated a "globalization of poverty." "[The] "macro-economic stabilization" and structural adjustment programs imposed by the IMF and the World Bank on developing countries (as a condition for the renegotiation of their external debt) have led to the impoverishment of hundreds of millions of people," he concludes in his study *The Globalization of Poverty*[70].

As the multipolar world emerges, the "neo-colonies" are relying less on the US dominated IMF-World Bank complex and its putative development policies. Increasingly, this "Washington Consensus" is being replaced by a "Beijing Consensus" which offers an alternative development model. In fact, the World Bank has lagged behind China in lending to developing countries. The World Bank loaned approximately $100 billion from mid-2008 to mid-2010, compared to $110 billion by the Chinese Development Bank and Export Import Bank during a parallel period of time.[71] Indeed, in an interview, Chinese president Hu Jintao styled the BRICS group as the "defenders of the developing world" ahead of the landmark fourth BRICS summit at New Delhi in March, 2012.[72] China offers developing countries an alternative to the overtly draconian economic "conditionalities" and "economic hit men" of the IMF-

[70] Michel Chossudovsky, *The Globalization of Poverty and the New World Order*, (Montreal: Center for Research on Globalization, 2003).
[71] "China Tops World Bank in Development Lending," *Voice of America*, January 17, 2011, http://www.voanews.com/content/china-tops-world-bank-in-development-lending-114111049/133699.html
[72] "BRICS is the Defender of the Developing World," The Hindu, March 28, 2012, http://www.thehindu.com/opinion/interview/article3251562.ece

World Bank complex. China also avoids overt interference in the internal affairs of states. It does not hector its partners with hypocritical notions of "human rights" to further its foreign policy objectives. At the fifth BRICS summit in South Africa in 2013, the members decided to found the New Development Bank. It is scheduled to start lending in 2016, with a capital of $100 billion, focusing on infrastructure projects.[73]

AMERICA'S VASSALS REBEL

A decline in the economic sphere is coupled with decline in the geopolitical sphere. Power is redistributing on the Eurasian supercontinent. Any realignment of power on the Eurasian landmass is of decisive importance for US primacy. Zbigniew Brzezinski, who along with David Rockefeller founded the elite Trilateral Commission, outlined the basics precepts of American hegemony in his treatise *The Grand Chessboard*.[74] For Brzezinski, "the prize is Eurasia." Including Europe, the Middle East, and Eastern Asia, the Eurasian supercontinent is the primary theatre where the US's global supremacy is decided. According to Brzezinski, "America's global primacy is directly dependent on how long and how effectively its preponderance on the Eurasian continent is sustained."[75] As for tactics, he notes: "In a terminology that harkens back to the more brutal age of ancient empires, the three grand imperatives of imperial geo-strategy are to prevent collusion and to maintain security dependence among the vassals, to keep tributaries pliant and protected, and to keep the barbarians from coming together."[76]

As US power declines, the "vassals" of the unipolar order have begun to rebel and look towards rival centers of power such as Moscow and Beijing. Simultaneously, they have begun exerting a more independent foreign policy. This is an emerging tendency throughout the Middle East and Central Asia. With the "vassals" colluding and becoming noncompliant, it becomes more appealing to

---

[73] http://en.wikipedia.org/wiki/New_Development_Bank
[74] Zbigniew Brzezinski, *The Grand Chessboard: American Primacy and its Geostrategic Imperatives*, (New York: Basic Books, 1997).
[75] Ibid., 30.
[76] Ibid., 40.

shore up supremacy through imperialist wars, destabilizations, and secret intelligence operations.

An examination of vassal recalcitrance and emerging foreign policy independence is instructive. Yash Tandon, executive director of the South Centre, an Intergovernmental Organization (IGO) based in Geneva, posited the existence of two "proto-type" dictators in the empire's "neo-colonies." First, there are *Radical Nationalist Dictators* (RNDs): "those with 'nationalist' ambitions, those who wish to break from the empire and try and seek their nations' own destinies."[77] Examples offered by Tandon are "Kwame Nkrumah in Ghana, Gamal Abdel Nasser in Egypt, Patrice Lumumba in the Congo, Thomas Sankara in Burkina Faso, and of course Mugabe and Qaddafi." Hugo Chavez in Venezuela, Jean-Bertrand Aristide in Haiti, and Dr. Mahathir Mohamed in Malaysia are also considered "RNDs." The common goal of these leaders is to exercise national sovereignty and generate economic development. Egypt's Nasser built the Aswan High Dam and nationalized the Suez Canal; Colonel Muammar Qaddafi built the Great Man Made River (GMMR), the most ambitious irrigation project in the world; and Dr. Mahathir Mohamed defended Malaysia against attacks by international financial speculators by using currency and exchange controls. "They are problematic dictators," writes Yosh, "from the perspective of the Empire."[78] Indeed, as Brzezinski observes, the vassals must remain "pliant" and dependent.

The opposite type to "RNDs" are Tandon's *Mimicmen Puppet Dictators* (MPDs): "More pliant dictators, submissive to the empire but brutal when it comes to dealing with their own populations." Uganda's Yoweri Museveni can be considered a MPD, as well as Georgia's Mikhail Saakashvili. In selecting who is demonized and targeted for being a "dictator," the issue is not "democracy" or "dictatorship;" instead, it is whether or not the vassals are compliant: "The likes of Mugabe and Qaddafi, for example, are simply not performing as expected by the Empire. The issue at stake is not whether Mugabe and Qaddafi are 'dictators.' The issue is whether

---

[77] Tandon, "Whose Dictator?"
[78] Ibid.

they are the Empire's dictators, and can deliver what is expected of them by the Empire."[79]

The tendencies of RNDs and MPDs do not exist in a fixed mode: an MPD today can become a RND tomorrow or vice versa.[80] Within the context of the "Arab Spring," some dictators who can be considered *Mimicmen Puppet Dictators* began displaying tendencies characteristic of *Radical Nationalist Dictators*. This is because of the inherent tendency of the nation state to compel leaders and statesmen to act in the interests of their own nation. Simultaneously, with the existence of RNDs such as Muammar Qaddafi, already regarded as unpredictable and troublesome, the strategic situation of the hegemon is compounded. This continues as longtime allies began seeking to diversify geopolitical alliances.

The crisis of the American empire was evident in Afghanistan, where Hamid Karzai was a handpicked vassal. With the US greatly deindustrialized and dependent on the vicissitudes of the US dollar, it is significantly less capable of delivering progress on the economic front, which the imperatives of the national state require. This drives vassals such as Karzai into the orbit of rising powers such as China, who are better able to foster development. Despite the US arrangement, the relationship with Karzai became frayed, with indications he wanted to diversify alliances and seek a more independent foreign policy.

Reporting for *Foreign Policy* in "How Obama Lost Karzai," [81] Ahmed Rashid met with Karzai, someone he had known for 20 years. Karzai had become disillusioned: "The United States, he believed, was failing to answer his demands for help in building electricity infrastructure and roads and rehabilitating some 3 million returning refugees."[82] When one of Karzai's close advisors Mohammed Zia

---

[79] Ibid.
[80] Ibid., 7.
[81] Ahmed Rashed, "How Obama Lost Karzai," *Foreign Policy*, February 2, 2011,
http://www.foreignpolicy.com/articles/2011/02/22/how_obama_lost_kar zai?page=1
[82] Ibid.

Salehi was arrested by a US-led Afghan anti-corruption force on charges of corruption, he was determined to spite the Americans and freed him. "By October 2010, relations were so fraught that Karzai stormed out of a meeting with Eikenberry and Petraeus over private security firm contracts, which Karzai abruptly announced he was canceling again, telling his shocked interlocutors that he'd be better off joining the Taliban." By this time Karzai was also "now threatening to turn to Iran and Pakistan for help."

By March of 2010 Karzai had finished four meetings with China. During a three-day visit to the Middle Kingdom, Karzai pledged to increase bilateral relations, and hoped to further expand cooperation with China in the areas of politics, trade, defense, education, and on regional and global issues. He also noted that Sino-Afghan relations were at their best in history.[83] One of the most notable results of their confab, though, was a $4.39 billion project that the Metallurgical Corporation of China (MCC) set up with the Jiangxi Copper Company to tap one of the biggest copper mines in Afghanistan. This was the largest pledge of foreign direct investment in Afghanistan.[84] China's Xinhua news agency reported that Karzai's visit had "drawn wide attention at a time when major powers are speculating whether China would engage deeper in efforts to rebuild — and possibly offer military assistance to — the war-torn country."[85]

These Chinese overtures alarmed Washington. Immediately after this meeting, President Obama made an unannounced rush visit to Karzai to keep him in the Anglo-American orbit. The *New York Times* commented that "Mr. Obama's visit to Afghanistan came against a backdrop of tension between Mr. Karzai and the Americans. It

---

[83] "China, Afghanistan Pan Closer Partnership as Karzai Concludes State Visit," *Xinhua News*, March 25, 2011,
http://news.xinhuanet.com/english2010/china/2010-03/25/c_13224814.htm
[84] "Afghan copper deal helps build nation's future," *China Daily*, September 21, 2011, http://www.chinamining.org/News/2011-09-21/1316569605d49744.html
[85] "Closer Partnership," *Xinhua News*.

quoted a European diplomat in Kabul as saying, 'He's [Karzai] slipping away from the West.' "[86]

During this time Karzai's rhetoric and public posture became more strident and critical of the US. He acted publically in contradiction to the US vis-à-vis Iran, when America's public posture was isolation for the Islamic Republic. Karzai received his Iranian counterpart Mahmoud Ahmadinejad "with manifest warmth" in Kabul at the same time US Defense Secretary Robert Gates was on a visit in Afghanistan. Karzai also flew in to Tehran to celebrate the Persian Nowruz festival, which included a meeting with the Islamic Republic's Supreme Leader Grand Ayatollah Khamenei. Obama subsequently flew into Kabul for an unannounced "on-the-ground update." The *Times* reported from Kabul that Obama "personally delivered pointed criticism" to Karzai reflected "growing vexation" with him. Karzai became more vocal, asking NATO to leave Afghanistan. He also declared that in the event of a US-Pakistan war, he would support the Pakistani side. Pakistan, a key Chinese ally, also urged Karzai to dump the US in favor of China.[87] Additionally, Karzai made a notable visit to Moscow expressing interest in energy deals, infrastructure, helicopters, and training for Afghan forces. Thus, despite being a handpicked US vassal, Karzai began showing signs of recalcitrance. Over time his pointedly anti-American rhetoric became shriller.

Muammar Qaddafi was very much a RND leader, yet still a recalcitrant vassal in the world's existing power framework. Long at odds with Washington, Qaddafi began to signal an increased relationship with China and Russia. In Libya there were an estimated 35,000 Chinese workers, and China invested billions in Libya before the outbreak of the (artificially instigated) civil war. Qaddafi also commissioned Russian Railways to build a 554 km rail line between

---

[86] M K Bhadrakumar, "Karzai's China-Iran dalliance riles Obama," *Asia Times*, http://www.atimes.com/atimes/South_Asia/LC30Df01.html
[87] "Karzai Told to Dump U.S. Pakistan Urges Afghanistan to Ally With Islamabad, Beijing," *Wall Street Journal*, April 27 2011, http://online.wsj.com/article/SB100014240527487047293045762870410940 35816.html?mod=wsj_share_twitter

Benghazi east of the country and Sirte, at a total cost of 6.5 billion rubles or $222 million.

Perhaps the most significant development vis-à-vis multipolarity in the MENA region is the fraying Saudi-American partnership—a longtime hallmark of the regional political landscape. As a harbinger of this shift, in the summer of 2001, just prior to the September 11th attacks, Saudi crown prince Abdullah bin Abdul-Aziz signaled the time had come for the US-Saudi alliance to end. According to the *Wall Street Journal*, he wrote President Bush, pointedly declaring:

> A time comes when peoples and nations part. We are at a crossroads. It is time for the United States and Saudi Arabia to look at their separate interests.[88]

Following the urgency of the September 11th attacks, however, this public parting of the ways was averted. Nevertheless, the Kingdom of Saudi Arabia began diversifying its alignment on the "geopolitical marketplace," specifically by shifting eastward. After ascending to the throne in 2005 as King, Abdullah adopted a pro-Asian, "look east" trade policy.

From a slow start, beginning only in 1990, relations between the People's Republic of China—Asia's meteoric rising power—and the Saudi Kingdom have become the centerpiece of the Saudis' Asia pivot. In addition to China's commitment to non-interference, the backbone of this emerging partnership is economic interests and energy. With the vast abundance of Saudi oil reserves, and China's growing appetite for oil (it is today the world's largest crude oil importer), the Sino-Saudi partnership is economically a natural fit. In 2009, Saudi exports to China exceeded those to the US for the first time, and Saudi Arabia is now the biggest supplier of crude oil to China. Saudi Arabia's exports to Europe and North America together are outstripped more than three times by its exports to five Far Eastern countries (China, Japan, South Korea, India and Singapore).[89]

---

[88] "Saudi Arabia: A Chronology of US Saudi Relation," *PBS: Frontline*, http://www.pbs.org/wgbh/pages/frontline/shows/saudi/etc/cron.html
[89] Daniel Wagner and Giorgio Cafiero, "Is the U.S. Losing Saudi Arabia to China?" October 30, 2013, HuffingtonPost.com, http://www.huffingtonpost.com/daniel-wagner/is-the-us-losing-saudi-ar_b_4176729.html

The CEO of the Saudi state oil company Aramco stated, "the writing is on the wall" that China is the future growth market for Saudi petroleum.[90]

Illustrating this growing partnership, in the period preceding the "Arab Spring," the Riyadh-Beijing relationship was marked by routine high-level visits coupled with deal making. Foreign Minister Qian Qichen traveled to Saudi Arabia twice in 1990; in 1991 Chinese Premier Li Peng paid an official goodwill visit to Saudi Arabia; Defense Minister Chi Haotian visited in 1996, and Chinese President Jiang Zemin in 1999.[91] Crown Prince Abdullah bin Abdul-Aziz (today King) paid an official visit to China in 1998, holding talks with President Jiang Zemin and Premier Zhu Rongji, and the two governments signed a memorandum of understanding creating a joint economic and trade cooperation committee; Saudi Defense Minister Prince Sultan and Saudi Oil Minister Ali al-Naimi became frequent visitors to China, with the latter making at least six trips to China in just two years.[92] In 2006, Saudi King Abdullah paid a historic state visit to China, signing a protocol on bilateral cooperation concerning petroleum, natural gas, and minerals, in addition to several documents regarding investment, economic and trade cooperation, and technical support.[93] This was reciprocated twice by Chinese President Hu Jintao first in 2006 and then in 2009, where agreements on energy, health, transportation, and quarantine were signed.[94]

---

[90] Ibid.

[91] "Saudi Arabia and China Extend Ties Beyond Oil," Jamestown Foundation,
http://www.jamestown.org/programs/chinabrief/single/?tx_ttnews%5Btt_news%5D=3895&no_cache=1#.VD897PldWHQ

[92] Ibid.

[93] "President Hu arrives in Saudi Arabia for state visit, ChinaDaily.com, April 22, 2006, http://www.chinadaily.com.cn/china/2006-04/22/content_574220.htm

[94] Jasper Wong, "Saudi-China relations: Emblematic of China's new foreign policy challenges," The Interpreter, July 18, 2014,
http://www.lowyinterpreter.org/post/2014/07/18/Saudi-China-relations-Chinas-new-foreign-policy-challenges.aspx?COLLCC=1562972933&COLLCC=2475747365&

Via state energy and commodity companies, progress in cross-investment and development projects between the two powers has continued to develop as well. The Chinese oil and gas company Sinopec collaborated with Saudi Aramco on downstream projects in China, building a refinery in Qingdao in eastern Shandong province, and expanding a petrochemical facility in Quanzhou in the province of Fujian, with the Saudis investing approximately $1 billion. In 2006, Aluminum of China (Chalco), the largest aluminum producer in China, partnered with Saudi companies to build a $3 billion aluminum facility in Saudi Arabia.[95] That year, China invested $1.1 billion in the Saudi Kingdom overall. In 2009, China Railway Company won a $1.8 billion bid to build a monorail for the transportation of pilgrims to holy sites in and around Mecca.[96] In 2012 Saudi Basic Industry Corporation (SABIC) initiated an investment plan of US$100 million to set up a technology center in the Kangqiao area of Shanghai.[97]

Saudi Arabia's appetite for military hardware is also being diversified via China, causing concern for America, the West, and Israel. This opens doors to hardware and technology the US and the West are at times unwilling to sell to the Kingdom of Saudi Arabia (KSA). The first demonstration of this tendency was in 1980. "In response to the US refusal to sell Saudi Arabia long-range fuel tanks for F-15 fighters, Saudi Arabia brokered a deal with China to acquire between fifty and sixty nuclear-payload capable CSS-2 intermediate range ballistic missiles." This was met with US dismay, and the Reagan administration reprimanded the Saudis, demanding the weapons be inspected.[98]

---

[95] Jon B. Alterman, China's Soft Power: in the Middle East," https://csis.org/files/media/csis/pubs/090310_chinesesoftpower__chap5.pdf

[96] Geoffrey Kemp, _The East moves West : India, China, and Asia's growing presence in the Middle East._, (Washington, D.C : Brookings Institution Press, 2010), 82.

[97] "Saudi Arabia boosts investment in China," WantChinaTimes.com, April 11, 2012 http://www.wantchinatimes.com/news-subclass-cnt.aspx?id=20120411000118&cid=1103

[98] Kemp, _East Moves West_, 83.

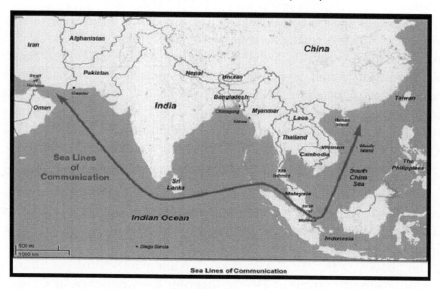

The path of China's so-called "String of Pearls" economic lifeline.

In March of 2011 Chinese president Hu Jintao met with Prince Bandar bin Sultan, acting as envoy of the Saudi King. They settled terms for new ballistic missiles capable of delivering nuclear warheads, to replace the CSS-2s. Intelligence and military sources revealed the sale covered two models. First, the DF-21 (NATO-designated CSS-5) a two-stage, solid-propellant, single-warhead medium-range ballistic (MRBM) system. It can deliver a 500kT nuclear warhead over a distance of 1,800 km. The second missile is a solid-fuel short-range ballistic missile (SRBM), the DongFeng 15 (export name M-9; NATO-designation CSS-6). [99] This was later followed in January 2012 by another Saudi-Chinese deal for "development and use of atomic energy for peaceful purposes."[100]

---

[99] David Dafinoiu, "Saudis Buy Advanced Nuclear-Capable Missiles from China," The Wall Street Shuffle, April 15, 2011, http://www.thewallstreetshuffle.com/saudis-buy-advanced-nuclear-capable-missiles-in-china/ See also Jeffrey Lewis, "Why did Saudi Arabia Buy Chinese Missiles?" *Foreign Policy*, January 30, 2014, http://foreignpolicy.com/2014/01/30/why-did-saudi-arabia-buy-chinese-missiles/

[100] "Saudi Arabia, China Sign Nuclear Cooperation Pact," *Wall Street Journal*, January 16, 2012,

Again, as in 1980, these deals were met by US consternation. American officials rushed to meet with Saudi leaders to keep them in the American orbit. US Defense Secretary Robert Gates and Saudi King Abdullah had a stormy interview that failed to bridge the widening gap in the US-Saudi alliance. More recently, the overt inclusion of long-range Chinese-made CSS-2 missiles in the KSA's military parade was interpreted as a diplomatic signal to Iran and the US.[101] The parade marked the first time they were seen in public.

Sino-Saudi interdependence also has implications for America's *geostrategy* to contain China. Anglo-American foreign policy circles recognized a strategic vulnerability in resource-poor China's increasing dependence on its critical oil and natural resource lifeline from the Arabian Gulf through the Indian Ocean. This line has come to be known as the "String of Pearls," from a 2006 Strategic Studies Institute report "String of Pearls: Meeting the Challenge of China's Rising Power across the Asian Littoral."[102] The paper explores this key Chinese strategic vulnerability, and the potential to contain China by suffocating its voracious energy needs, should it seek displace America's preeminence, or refuse to participate in the "international system." Because Saudi Arabia is China's primary supplier of oil, controlling Riyadh is critical to containing America's emerging rival China.

Around the period of the 2007-08 banking crisis, Riyadh's inclination towards *multipolarity* manifested in an unprecedented attempt to balance its exclusive alliance with the US by improving relations with an increasingly assertive Russian Federation. In February 2007 Russian President Vladimir Putin visited the Saudi King in Riyadh, where he was given the King Abdul-aziz Medal, the Saudi Kingdom's highest and most prestigious award for world

---

http://online.wsj.com/article/SB1000142405297020446800457716474202528 5500.html

[101] Simon Henderson,"Saudi Arabia's Missile Messaging," Washington Institute, April 29, 2014, http://www.washingtoninstitute.org/policy-analysis/view/saudi-arabias-missile-messaging

[102] Lieutenant Colonel Christopher J Pehrson, String of Pearls: Meeting the Challenge of China's Rising Power Across the Asian Littoral, http://www.strategicstudiesinstitute.army.mil/pubs/display.cfm?pubid=7 21

leaders and commanders. This was the first such mission to the KSA by a top Russian leader. At the meeting they discussed ways to enhance cooperation between the two countries in all areas.[103] A series of high-level meetings followed. Prince Bandar, Secretary General of the National Security Council, began meetings in Moscow with Russian President Vladimir Putin in 2007. Foreign Minister Prince Saud Al Faisal also visited Moscow in 2008. Russian Finance Minister Alexei Kudrin visited Riyadh in June 2008, followed by two more visits by Prince Bandar. In July 2008 Saudi Arabia signed an agreement on military-technical cooperation with Russia. The Saudis would receive armament supply sources, and "various Saudi and Russian agencies" would "work together for the benefit of bilateral relations."[104]

In August 2009, *Novaya Gazeta*, the anti-Kremlin Russian newspaper founded by Gorbachev, reported contracts for the delivery of combat equipment and weapons to Saudi Arabia to the tune of around $2 billion. Russian news agency Interfax reported that Saudi Arabia could soon become one of the biggest customers for Russian weapons and combat equipment. Subhash Kapila, expert from the South Asia Analysis Group, noted that if the deal to deliver a large consignment of Russian arms to Saudi Arabia went ahead, Moscow's influence on the military political situation in the Near East would grow.[105]

The Saudis also signaled diversification through Pakistan, which as a key Chinese ally could lead to forming a Riyadh-Islamabad-Beijing axis. The March, 2011 summit with China was preceded by meetings of Prince Bandar with Pakistani President Zardawi and later Chief of the Army Staff Gen. Ashfaq Parvez Kayani. The nominal topic of discussion for this meeting was the desecration of the Holy Quran, but inside sources stated the visit by Prince Bandar was concerned with the backdrop of domestic political tumult in

---

[103] Katz, Mark N, "Saudi-Russian Relations Since the Abdullah-Putin Summit," Middle East Policy; Spring 2009;113.
[104] Russia-Saudis "Russia, Saudi Arabia Sign Military Cooperation Agreement." BBC Monitoring Former Soviet Union (Jul 14, 2008).
[105] "Russian Commentator Analyzes Weapons Contracts with Saudi Arabia." BBC Monitoring Former Soviet Union (Sep 04, 2009).

Bahrain, a Gulf oil mini-state and Saudi junior partner. The Saudis attempted to quell the Bahraini uprising by sending in 1,000 troops to "assist the local security forces" battling protestors. The possibility of the prince asking Pakistan for "meaningful help to meet challenges in its neighborhood cannot be ruled out," sources stated. According to data obtained by the *Express Tribune*, there were already 60,000 Pakistanis, mainly ex-servicemen, serving in the defense and other security establishments of the KSA.[106]

This was followed by a meeting between Pakistani Prime Minister Yousaf Raza Gilani and King Abdullah bin Abdul-aziz at the Royal Palace in Saudi Arabia. Here the king proclaimed: "Pakistan and Saudi Arabia are one country; they are more than friends and more than brothers." Prime Minister Gilani reciprocated by assuring that "Pakistan's security was Saudi Arabia's security and Saudi Arabia's security was Pakistan's security." The Pakistani side followed Gilani's declaration by promising two army divisions into Saudi Arabia to protect the kingdom in the event of an uprising similar to those of Bahrain, Yemen, Egypt, Libya and other MENA nations.[107] The recruitment of ex-Pakistani military personnel for Bahrain's National Guard would continue as well.

The Saudi Kingdom would experience unrest itself in the midst of the "Arab Spring," but made a number of concessions and subventions for protestors. Menacingly, Martin Indyk, American foreign policy apparatchik and Vice President and Director at the influential Brookings Institute, declared pointedly, "the Saudi system is fragile."[108] Consequently, with the onset of the "Arab Spring," the Kingdom began viewing President Obama as a threat to its own internal security, for his actions during the course of the MENA uprisings, instead of a safeguard. This was a historical departure. For

---

[106] Irfan Ghauri, "Desecration of Holy Quran: Saudi Arabia urges restraint," *The Express Tribune*, March 26, 2011,
http://tribune.com.pk/story/137963/desecration-of-holy-quran-saudi-arabia-urges-restraint/
[107] http://www.wnd.com/2011/04/284429/
[108] Martin S. Indyk, "Amid the Arab Spring, Obama's Dilemma Over Saudi Arabia," *Brookings*, April 7, 2011,
http://www.brookings.edu/research/opinions/2011/04/07-middle-east-indyk

this reason, the Saudis leaned more on its ally Pakistan to ensure its immediate security.

Another source of tensions in the US-Saudi relationship is Riyadh's well-founded view of US regional hegemony and its partnership with Israel as a destabilizing force in the Arab world. For example, the US precipitously smashed the regime of Saddam Hussein in Iraq against Riyadh's advice, thereby bolstering the position of the Saudi's chief regional adversary Iran. The US refused to pressure or impose concessions on Israel (a recipient of billions in US aid) for the Palestinians. The centrality of the Palestinians' plight is imperative for the Saudi's regional posture, with the Kingdom among the largest donors of aid to Palestine. Reportedly, Riyadh also maintains a policy of surreptitious support for militant Palestinian resistance against Israeli occupation. According to one report, it has facilitated over $4 billion in funds to militant Palestinian resistance groups from 1998-2003. [109] Indeed, in the forthcoming decision towards Palestinian statehood at the UN, Prince Turki al-Faisal once again enunciated the fragility of the Saudi-US relationship over this issue. In a *New York Times* Op-Ed, "Veto a State, Lose an Ally," he pointedly cautioned: "Saudi Arabia would no longer be able to cooperate with America in the same way it historically has... Saudi leaders would be forced by domestic and regional pressures to adopt a far more independent and assertive foreign policy."[110]

Coupled with regional geopolitical considerations, another reason for undermining the Saudi Kingdom is base covetousness: the dream of reversing the nationalization of Saudi Aramco, the largest private company in the world worth an estimated $7 trillion.[111] The Saudis gradually increased their ownership in Aramco (originally Arabian-

---

[109] Jon Dougherty, "Saudi Royals Funding Palestinian Jihad - Riyadh reportedly has spent more than $4 billion on intifada," July 09, 2003 http://www.wnd.com/2003/07/19689/#LYtbR02S3FQIKJWk.99
[110] Turki al-Faisal, "Op-Ed: Veto a State, Lose An Ally," *New York Times*, September 11, 2011, http://www.nytimes.com/2011/09/12/opinion/veto-a-state-lose-an-ally.html
[111] "Bigger Oil, bigger oil," *Financial Times*, http://www.ft.com/cms/s/3/c5b32636-116f-11df-9195-00144feab49a,_i_email=y.html

American Oil Company) from half ownership together with America's Standard Oil in 1950, to complete ownership by 1980. Resuming control of Aramco would be a tremendously lucrative proposition for the US, with deeper geopolitical ramifications thanks to its monopoly on the KSA's vast oil resources.

In the period of the MENA uprisings the emerging multipolar framework saw the Saudis, traditional US ally, shift eastward, begin a dalliance with Russia, lean on their ally Pakistan for security, and voice discontent at overall US MENA policy — all to US consternation. With solidifying Sino-Saudi mutual dependence, the West could not only gain a tremendous pecuniary boon from the control of Saudi oil, but the potential to exploit China's strategic vulnerability. Simultaneously, undermining the KSA is a step towards nullifying a key wellspring of Arab independence, especially regarding Palestine, removing a threat to continued Western-Israeli MENA hegemony.

Within this framework, Egypt also holds geopolitical significance. Militarily strong, it is the Arab world's largest country with a population of 80 million. This is in addition to its dynamic history and geographic location. This includes proximity to the Suez Canal, a world strategic and lucrative chokepoint, and the fact that it spans North Africa and the Middle East while sharing a border with Israel. That Egypt is a close Saudi partner makes it a target for undermining the Saudi regional posture. Meanwhile, Egypt's diverse confessional makeup — with a Muslim majority and a sizable Christian Coptic minority — is a catalyst for the objective of unleashing regional "Lebanonization."

Here again, Egyptian President Hosni Mubarak, an American vassal who received billions annually in aid, at times refused US demands. Mubarak opposed Hillary Clinton's strategic gambit to create a protective nuclear umbrella for Washington's Gulf Arab allies together with Israel against Iran as a boogeyman. Israeli news outlet *Ynet* reported based on the Egyptian *Al-Gumhoria*:

> Al-Gumhoria newspaper says Egyptian president strongly objects to American proposal to Israel, Arab states to create nuclear umbrella against Iranian attack. The United States has offered Israel, Egypt and Persian Gulf countries to be part of a nuclear umbrella against an Iranian attack, Egyptian newspaper al-Gumhoria reported Thursday.

According to the idea, Israeli and American aircraft would be deployed in those Arab countries in preparation of a response against any expected Iranian strike. Everyone knows, the editor wrote, that those bases would be used to launch a war on Iran if the American diplomatic dialogue with Tehran were to fail... The deceptive thought was that Israel would in actual fact defend the Gulf states against the danger they are saying is approaching. We cannot rule out a possibility that they would even present the Gulf rulers with satellite images showing that an Iranian attack against the region is imminent. And this will lead to a war Israel has been planning for some time, with Israel turning later on into the only nuclear regional force in the Middle East, which will be a huge gain as far as they are concerned... The American defense umbrella which Israel will be part of is aimed at allowing Israel to enjoy the Gulf countries' trust and be part of the defense lineup over the economic wealth of oil-producing countries. This is indirect normalization and a concealed bribe to Israel.[112]

It highlighted that Mubarak was the only one who exposed this "satanic" plan: "The only one to reveal this satanic plan was President Hosni Mubarak, who was very firm in his response. He stressed that Egypt does not support free normalization with Israel, regardless of its reasons." With Iran as the ostensible enemy, this proposed "nuclear umbrella" would have entailed an increased American military presence and Arab dependence on the US. Mubarak rejected plans for US military bases in Egypt and a call for Egyptian troops for the Afghan war. Surely, Washington was not pleased with Mubarak's rejections.

The MENA uprisings took place at a time when the American Empire was in a weakened position, both economically and *geostrategically*. The unipolar world order of the last 20 years was rapidly waning. This trajectory continued even in 2013, after many of

---

[112] Roee Nahmias, "Report: Mubarak opposes US defense umbrella, *Al-Gumhoria* newspaper says Egyptian president strongly objects to American proposal to Israel, Arab states to create nuclear umbrella against Iranian attack," August 08, 2009, http://www.ynetnews.com/articles/0,7340,L-3765075,00.html

the events of the MENA uprisings. The *New York Times* lamented, "It is not every day that America finds itself facing open rebellion from its allies, yet that is what is happening with Saudi Arabia, Turkey and Israel."[113] As power redistributed into a multipolar framework, the vassals of the American empire rebelled. They began to formulate more independent foreign policies. In many cases, the strategic gambits of the empire were opposed by its vassals. The imperialist offensive in the midst of the "Arab Spring" was, *inter alia*, a reaction to this tendency.

MAINTAINING ISRAEL'S SECURITY

Also of paramount importance for the American offensive in the "Arab Spring" was bolstering the state of Israel's security. Stephen Walt of Harvard and John Mearsheimer of the University of Chicago expounded the far-reaching impact of the Israel lobby nexus for the US Middle East posture—with its most palpable manifestation the second Iraq War.[114] Although the Obama team represented a new cadre of foreign policy apparatchiks, with different tactics from the Bush II neocon team, Obama continued the policy of solidifying Israel's regional position, and even delivered unprecedented military aid to Israel.[115] Additionally, individuals with a neocon background

---

[113] "Allies in Revolt," *New York Times*, October 29, 2013,
http://www.nytimes.com/2013/10/30/opinion/allies-in-revolt.html?_r=0
[114] John Mearsheimer and Stephen Walt, *The Israel Lobby and U.S. Foreign Policy*, (New York: Farrar, Straus, and Giroux).
[115] See "Obama Requests Largest Amount of Military Aid to Israel Ever," National Jewish Democratic Council, February 12, 2012,
http://www.njdc.org/blog/post/israelaid021412
"No president in history has done more for Israel's security than Obama. The case for Obama's Israel policy begins with record-high levels of Foreign Military Financing. The Obama administration has increased security assistance to Israel every single year since the president took office, providing nearly $10 billion in aid--covering roughly a fifth of Israel's defense budget--over the past three years. To put this in perspective, this is about 20 percent higher than the remaining six dozen recipients of U.S. FMF combined. Historic aid levels have been complemented by other steps to ensure Israel's unrivaled military advantage in the region, including high-level consultation with Israeli officials on U.S. arms sales to the region, operational cooperation to improve Israel's conventional military and counterterrorism capabilities, and providing Israel with advanced

retained positions within the Obama administration. For the neocons, Israel is the centerpiece of foreign policy.[116] Obama's "Arab Spring" policies were contiguous with neocon stratagems and priorities. By weakening the Arab position through massive destabilization, unleashing regional "Lebanonization," and subverting recalcitrant vassals with more dependent proxies under the veil of "democracy," Israel emerges stronger in the face of these resultant fractured Arab states. Indeed, 3 years after the onset of the "Arab Spring," George Friedman of Stratfor noted, "Currently, Israel is as secure as it is ever likely to be." "Apart from Gaza, which is a relatively minor threat, Israel's position is difficult to improve," he added. [117]

---

technology, such as the fifth-generation stealth Joint Strike Fighter, to which no other state in the Middle East has access." Colin H. Kahl, *Obama Has Been Great for Israel Anyone who tells you otherwise is distorting reality. Foreign Policy,* August 16, 2012,
http://www.foreignpolicy.com/articles/2012/08/16/obama_has_been_go od_for_israel
[116] George H.W. Bush's response on defining a neocon, as described by Journalist Andrew Cockburn, is instructive: Amy Goodman: In 2006, you write that George W. Bush said to his father, "What's a neocon?" Andrew Cockburn: That's right. One of the rare moments of sort of communication between the two... Bush Jr. says, "Can I ask you a question? What's a neocon?" And the father says, "Do you want names or a description?" The President says, "I'll take a description." He says, "I'll give it to you in one word: Israel," which is interesting on all sorts of levels, including the confirmation that our president doesn't really read the newspapers."
Journalist and Author Andrew Cockburn on Donald Rumsfeld: His Rise, Fall, and Catastrophic Legacy, Democracy Now!, March 7, 2007,
http://www.democracynow.org/2007/3/7/journalist_and_author_andrew _cockburn_on
[117] George Friedman, "Gaming Israel and Palestine," Stratfor, July 29, 2015, https://www.stratfor.com/weekly/gaming-israel-and-palestine

PART THREE:

THE NEW "COLOR REVOLUTIONS."

THE MYTH OF THE "ARAB SPRING"

Many, disliking the status quo, are susceptible to being mobilized against those whom they perceive as self-interestedly preserving it. The Third World youth are particularly volatile. The rapid expanding demographic bulge in the twenty-five and under age-bracket represents a huge mass of impatience. This group's revolutionary spearhead is likely to emerge from among the millions of students concentrated in the often intellectually dubious tertiary-level educational institutions of developing countries. Semi-mobilized in large congregations and connected by the internet, they are positioned to replay, on a far vaster scale, what occurred years earlier in Mexico City and Tiananmen Square. Revolutionaries-in-waiting, they represent the equivalent of the militant proletariat of the nineteenth and twentieth century.[118]
— Zbigniew Brzezinski

Before the uprisings in the MENA region began, the American empire was in a weakened position geopolitically. It also faced an exhausted and overstretched military following the Afghanistan war and the second Iraq war. Meanwhile, the world was in the throes of economic depression. At this time the Arab world was due for a dramatic change. The ensuing events in the MENA region would come to the forefront of the international political agenda. Starting in December 2010, after years of autocratic rule by monarchies and dictatorships, a universal awakening began in the Arab world. Mass demonstrations on a grassroots level by idealistic youth, who clamored for dignity and democracy, began to topple governments in the region. Democratic protests spread infectiously. By the beginning of mid-January, Tunisia's Ben Ali had fallen, followed closely by Egypt's Hosni Mubarak. Other autocracies were not far behind.

---

[118] Zbigniew Brzezinski, *Second Chance: Three Presidents and the Crisis of American Superpower* (New York: Basic Books), 202.

Youth had triumphed over dictatorship's violent repression. The future was auspicious.

This was the so-called "Arab spring." This simplistic tale, although not completely devoid of truth, is a myth. While youth-led movements were a component in the fall of Arab governments of the region, they were not the decisive factor, nor were they purely homegrown. The massive protests were not the result of merely internal political dissension. In truth, there was another unstated crucial element. The youth-led movements that swept the Arab world were facilitated by a collection of NGOs (Non-Governmental Organizations) funded by the US and closely tied to the intelligence community with backing from the State Department. These NGOs played a role the CIA once did to covertly topple governments. And while the massive protests from the Arab youth did destabilize the existing regimes, there was not one case where this was sufficient to bring down a government. While in the foreground the youthful protestors took to the streets—absorbing all mainstream Western and Arab media coverage—in the background the classic coups d'état took place, which were needed to actually supplant existing regimes and power structures .

The desired results of the US-led wave of uprisings varied between "regime change," destabilization, and the smashing of existing state structures. The US radically shifted its strategy from the hard-line approach of the Bush II regime. Instead of direct and bellicose confrontation to overthrow undesirable governments, Washington used "soft power," or "people power coups." Where that was insufficient, in Libya and Syria, irregular warfare was instigated. To offset the waning of US influence, the overarching goal was to prevent increased *multipolarity* in the MENA region, smash undesired regimes, and to unleash large-scale "Lebanonization."

For decades, the clandestine subversion of sovereign states has been the specialty of the CIA and intelligence community. William "Wild Bill" Donavon, founder of the Office of Strategic services (OSS), precursor to the CIA, saw the business of the agency was subversion rather than intelligence-gathering. "[A]n internal CIA history of Donovan's imprint on the agency," revealed that "he saw intelligence analysis as a convenient cover for subversive operations abroad. This subterfuge proved useful down the years."[119]

Since the Cold War, through such subversive activities, US intelligence has engaged in attempts—both successful and unsuccessful—at "regime change" on almost every continent. The various methods used included everything from manipulating elections, and classic coups d'état, to the use of "death squads" that ruthlessly targeted military and civilian opposition in countries like El Salvador and Guatemala. Since 1945, the US has engaged in known attempts to overthrow over 50 governments. The list of targets includes Iraq, Nicaragua, El Salvador, Albania, China, Libya, Costa Rica, Indonesia, Ghana, Syria, Chile, Cuba, Iran, Greece, British Guyana, Dominican Republic, Democratic Republic of the Congo, Brazil, Venezuela, Ukraine, Yugoslavia, Serbia, and continues *ad nauseam*.[120]

In the MENA region, the West has traditionally relied on client states, and opposed any independent regimes.[121] Facing the threat of *multipolarity*, subversion against noncompliant "vassals" and enemy states would become even more vital to US foreign policy—especially after the US had enjoyed 20 years of unchallenged hegemony. Some Washington-aligned dictators had become recalcitrant, with emerging RND tendencies. Reflecting on Bush's war on Saddam Hussein, the late Muammar Qaddafi, leader of the Libyan Arab Republic, presciently asserted that many Arab leaders would be next. "In the future it's going to be your turn too," he quipped.[122] His words were prophetic, but ironically, he would be among those slated for execution.

---

[119] Johnson, *The Sorrows of Empire*, 10.
[120] See William Blum, *Killing Hope: U.S. Military and CIA Intervention Since World War II*, (Common Courage Press: 1995). General Wesley Clark, retired 4-star general, Supreme Allied Commander of NATO during the 1999 War on Yugoslavia has remarked: "We're going to take out seven countries in 5 years, starting with Iraq, and then Syria, Lebanon, Libya, Somalia, Sudan and, finishing off, Iran."
[121] Aburish, *Brutal Friendship*, 33.
[122] Muammar Qaddafi speech to the Arab League "Gaddafi foretold end of Arab dictators (English subtitles)," YouTube video, 3:11, posted by "gahgeer,"

AEI AND "CIVILIAN-BASED POWER"

American policy in the MENA uprisings was a departure from the predominantly "hard power" approach of the George W. Bush regime, in favor of "soft power" (the power of attraction, rather than force) and the sponsorship of civilian-based mass movements or "people power" in foreign policy. The two forms of power projection complement each other. This thinking in Washington sometimes ran counter to schools of thought in favor of direct warfare, which "soft power" and "civilian-based power" advocates believe is not the only way of toppling dictatorial "rogue" [123] regimes. This outlook is championed by the Albert Einstein Institute (AIE), a US think tank specializing in, and a wellspring of, the realm of "civilian-based power." In the words of Dr. Peter Ackerman[124] — offering a revision to Bush's "Axis of Evil" speech — "It is not true that the only way to 'take out' such ["rogue"] regimes is through U.S military action."[125] Ackerman and his school of thought argue that youth-led mass movements, such as US-backed "Otpor!" in Serbia against Slobodan Milosevic, could also be used against "rogue" regimes such as the DPRK (North Korea). Thus, "people power movements" trump direct warfare in removing dictators clinging to power.

In fact, Ackerman finds fault in NATO's bombing of Serbia, censuring the action as prolonging the survival of Milosevic. "A

March 5, 2011,
http://www.youtube.com/watch?v=SGwHOWUPKuo&feature=related
[123] That is, those "regimes" or states which do not conform to the dictates of Washington and its allies.
[124] Dr. Ackerman is a theoretician tied to Wall Street and the US corporate establishment. He is the former Chairman of US government-funded Freedom House; current Chairman of the D.C. based International Center on Nonviolent Conflict, which he founded along with Jack Duvall, former US Air Force officer; he is also Director of the Arlington Institute with James Woolsey, former director of the CIA; Managing Director of the private investment firm Rockport Capital Incorporated; a former investment banker of the now defunct junk bond firm Drexel Burnham Lambert, and a member of the elite corporate sponsored Council on Foreign Relations.
[125] Peter Ackerman, "How Serbian students brought dictator down without a shot fired," National Catholic Reporter, April 26, 2002,
http://natcath.org/NCR_Online/archives/042602/042602y.htm

dictator can survive external attack, because his military and his people rally around the only available symbol of national survival," he reasons. This is the so-called "rally 'round the flag effect." Ackerman argues that instead of the US funding costly conventional wars — which are bloody, financially burdensome, and a hindrance to soft-power projection — it should "quietly" utilize and fund civilian-based power, as it did in Serbia: "[M]assive civilian opposition can be roused with the shrewd use of strikes, boycotts, civil disobedience and other forms of nonviolent resistance — all of which can be quietly assisted, even funded from abroad, as happened in Serbia."[126] With these calculations, costly military means can be avoided. In a speech titled "Between Hard and Soft Power: The Rise of Civilian-Based Struggle and Democratic Change," Ackerman advocated the effectiveness of "civilian-based power" to the US State Department.[127] He emphasized its strategic value to policy makers, while offering a forum to potential dissidents in attendance.

Dr. Ackerman's "civilian-based power" school of thought stems from the concepts of "strategic nonviolent conflict" first developed by Dr. Gene Sharp, founder of the AEI, and renowned as the "Clausewitz[128] of nonviolence." Sharp authored the seminal work *From Dictatorship to Democracy*, a book touted as the manual for overturning dictatorships[129] throughout the world, as well as the influential study *The Politics of Nonviolent Action*. Curiously, the name "civilian-based defense" was suggested to Sharp by Major General Edward Atkeson, former deputy chief of intelligence for the US army in Europe, who would also serve on the board of the AEI.[130] Another influential figure is Colonel Robert Helvey, who served as AEI president. Helvey typifies the attraction of military types to this

---

[126] Ibid.
[127] Peter Ackerman, Chair, International Center for Nonviolent Conflict, Remarks to the Secretary's Open Forum Washington, DC June 29, 2004, "Between Hard and Soft Power: The Rise of Civilian-Based Struggle and Democratic Change," http://2001-2009.state.gov/s/p/of/proc/34285.htm
[128] Carl von Clausewitz, Prussian general, military theorist, and author of the influential work *On War*.
[129] Louise Gray, *Gene Sharp: How to Start a Revolution, Telegraph*, Oct 2011; See "Gene Sharp - How to Start a Revolution - Greek," https://www.youtube.com/watch?v=P3dN4ln9lzI
[130] Ibid.

novel approach. He was drawn to the AEI concept of "strategic nonviolence" when he was stationed in Myanmar, after witnessing the ineffectiveness of military solutions in toppling dictators. [131] According to India's RAW (Research and Analysis Wing intelligence agency), he was stationed in Yangoon, Myanmar, clandestinely organizing opposition groups. Helvey later imparted his ideas to the "Otpor!" movement that helped to supplant Milosevic in Serbia.

For Washington, these AEI strategies of "people power" were vital to its actions during the MENA uprisings. But their successful application had an important precursor: the "color revolutions" in the former Soviet sphere. Here the US showed it could craft "regime change" via successfully applying AEI concepts, and thus obviate costly and overt means.

WASHINGTON'S "COLOR REVOLUTIONS"

The MENA uprisings—with US sponsorship—incorporated "civilian-based power" techniques developed by organizations such as the AEI. During the Arab uprisings, these methods were put to the test. The ensuing subversions of increasingly independent Arab leaders relied on updated versions of what is called the "post-modern coup" or "color revolution."[132] "Color revolutions" were a series of "revolutions" that attempted, successfully or unsuccessfully, to overthrow governments in the former Soviet sphere. They are termed "color revolutions" because of the use of a specific color to identify and rally followers, a clever marketing and organizing technique, as in the "Rose Revolution" in Georgia or the "Orange Revolution" in Ukraine. These "post-modern coups" swept through the former Yugoslavia, Georgia, Ukraine, Kyrgyzstan and more.

Along with ideas from the AEI, "color revolutions" were reflective of ideas dating back to Britain's Tavistock Institute, where the

---

[131] See Jonathan Mowat, "Coup d'etat in Disguise: Washington's New World Order "Democratization" Template, February 9, 2005, http://www.globalresearch.ca/articles/MOW502A.html , a thorough and original analysis of Washington's "Color Revolutions."
[132] Ibid. See also F. William Engdahl, "Chapter Two: Controlling Russia: Color Revolutions and Swarming Coups," in *Full Spectrum Dominance: Totalitarian Democracy in the New World Order* (2009).

concepts of "rebellious hysteria" and "swarming adolescents" were developed after studying crowd behavior at rock concerts. [133] Tavistock also analyzed the behavior of the young people who, under the stewardship of the Situationist International, destabilized France and attempted to topple its nationalist President Charles De Gaulle. The RAND Corporation also later presented research on the phenomenon of "swarming" for military application. RAND compared the techniques of youth "swarming" to the behavior bees, which move as a group in a decentralized but connected manner.[134] This phenomenon played out in the "color revolutions."

The "civilian-based power" approach of mobilizing "swarming adolescents" against authoritarian governments made effective use of the Information Revolution. There was pervasive use of internet and mass communications technologies, which were burgeoning when the "color revolutions" began. As Laura Rosen in *Salon* emphasized, "the information age is shifting the advantage from authoritarian leaders to civic groups."[135]

Jonathan Mowat, writing for the Center of Research on Globalization, analyzes this phenomenon in his study "Coup d'état in Disguise: Washington's New World Order 'Democratization' Template."[136] His paper demonstrates how the "color revolutions" were sponsored from Washington to reorder the post-Cold War former Soviet sphere. This was done under the usual veil of promoting "democracy." According to Mowat the model was first employed in Serbia against Slobodan Milosevic with the "Otpor!" revolution. A first-hand account of the methods of "Otpor!" — the movement lauded by the AEI's Dr. Ackerman as an exemplary model for "regime change" — is provided by Michael Dobbs in the *Washington Post*. Its origins traced back to a private meeting in

---

[133] See Engdahl, "Swarming Coups," *Dominance*, 39-40.

[134] See John Arquilla and David Ronfeldt, "Swarming & the Future of Conflict," RAND: National Defense Research Institute, http://www.rand.org/content/dam/rand/pubs/documented_briefings/2005/RAND_DB311.pdf Also see Mowat, " 'Democratization' Template."

[135] Laura Rozen, "Dictator Downturn: It just isn't as easy being a tyrant as it used to be," *Salon*, February 3, 2001, http://www.salon.com/2001/02/03/dictators/

[136] Mowat, "'Democratization' Template."

October 1999 between the "Otpor!" revolutionaries and Doug Schoen, an American pollster, a year before the revolution began:

> [Schoen's] message, delivered to leaders of Serbia's traditionally fractious opposition, was simple and powerful. Slobodan Milosevic — survivor of four lost wars, two major street uprisings, 78 days of NATO bombing and a decade of international sanctions--was "completely vulnerable" to a well-organized electoral challenge. The key, the poll results showed, was opposition unity.

> Held in a luxury hotel in Budapest, the Hungarian capital, in October 1999, the closed-door briefing by Schoen, a Democrat, turned out to be a seminal event, pointing the way to the electoral revolution that brought down Milosevic a year later. It also marked the start of an extraordinary U.S. effort to unseat a foreign head of state, not through covert action of the kind the CIA once employed in such places as Iran and Guatemala, but by modern election campaign techniques.

> While the broad outlines of the $41 million U.S. democracy-building campaign in Serbia are public knowledge, interviews with dozens of key players, both here and in the United States, suggest it was much more extensive and sophisticated than previously reported.

> In the 12 months following the strategy session, U.S.-funded consultants played a crucial role behind the scenes in virtually every facet of the anti-Milosevic drive, running tracking polls, training thousands of opposition activists and helping to organize a vitally important parallel vote count. U.S. taxpayers paid for 5,000 cans of spray paint used by student activists to scrawl anti-Milosevic graffiti on walls across Serbia, and 2.5 million stickers with the slogan "He's Finished," which became the revolution's catchphrase.

> Regarded by many as Eastern Europe's last great democratic upheaval, Milosevic's overthrow may also go down in history as the first poll-driven, focus group-tested revolution. Behind the seeming spontaneity of the street uprising that forced Milosevic to respect the results of a hotly contested presidential election on Sept. 24, was a carefully researched

strategy put together by Serbian democracy activists with the active assistance of Western advisers and pollsters.

Dobbs further reported:

The U.S. democracy-building effort in Serbia was a curious mixture of secrecy and openness. In principle, it was an overt operation, funded by congressional appropriations of around $10 million for fiscal 1999 and $31 million for 2000.

Some Americans involved in the anti-Milosevic effort said they were aware of CIA activity at the fringes of the campaign, but had trouble finding out what the agency was up to. Whatever it was, they concluded it was not particularly effective. The lead role was taken by the State Department and the U.S. Agency for International Development, the government's foreign assistance agency, which channeled the funds through commercial contractors and nonprofit groups such as NDI and its Republican counterpart, the International Republican Institute (IRI). [137]

In the wake of the "Orange Revolution" of Ukraine, another US-sponsored "color revolution, the methods of the "post-modern coup" were also outlined by the London *Guardian's* Ian Traynor in a November 26, 2004 article, "US Campaign Behind the Turmoil in Kiev." Traynor reported:

[T]he campaign is an American creation, a sophisticated and brilliantly conceived exercise in western branding and mass marketing that, in four countries in four years, has been used to try to salvage rigged elections and topple unsavory regimes.

Funded and organized by the US government, deploying US consultancies, pollsters, diplomats, the two big American parties and US non-government organizations, the campaign

---

[137] Michael Dobbs, "US Advice Guided Milosevic Opposition Political Consultants Helped Yugoslav Opposition Topple Authoritarian Leader," *Washington Post*, December 11, 2000. *New York Times* also detailed US sponsorship; see "Who Really Brought Down Milosevic?" *New York Times* Magazine, November 26, 2000, http://www.nytimes.com/library/magazine/home/20001126mag-serbia.html

was first used in Europe in Belgrade in 2000 to beat Slobodan Milosevic at the ballot box.

Richard Miles, the US ambassador in Belgrade, played a key role. And by last year, as US ambassador in Tbilisi, he repeated the trick in Georgia, coaching Mikhail Saakashvili in how to bring down Eduard Shevardnadze. Ten months after the success in Belgrade, the US ambassador in Minsk, Michael Kozak, a veteran of similar operations in central America, notably in Nicaragua, organized a near identical campaign to try to defeat the Belarus hardman, Alexander Lukashenko.

Traynor further noted how the method of "engineering democracy through the ballot box and civil disobedience is now so slick that the methods have matured into a template for winning other people's elections."[138]

With this succession of "color revolutions," the application and effectiveness of "civilian-based power" for "regime change" was demonstrated. Additionally, as Traynor reported, the main agencies involved in this template were US-sponsored "NGOs": "The Democratic party's National Democratic Institute, the Republican party's International Republican Institute, the US State department and USAID are the main agencies involved in these so-called 'grassroots' campaigns, as well as the Freedom House NGO and billionaire George Soros's Open Society Institute." As we shall see, these groups were subdivisions of the principal US organization for funding foreign civilian organizations: the NED (National Endowment for Democracy). These same organizations and methods would be applied to the MENA uprisings, albeit in a more ambitious — and destructive — wave, destabilizing the entire region simultaneously and sparking regional conflagration.

CIA FRONT NED (National Endowment for Democracy)

The key institution in both the US sponsored "color revolutions" and MENA uprisings was the National Endowment for Democracy (NED). This institution was at the center of all the "color revolutions"

---

[138] Ian Traynor, "US Campaign Behind Turmoil in Ukraine," *Guardian*, November 25, 2004.

that swept Europe, and would be crucial to the wave of Arab uprisings. This institution is ostensibly an NGO, which implies it is "non-governmental." In reality, it was created by the US government. In fact, since its inception it receives an annual appropriation approved by the US Congress as part of the US Information Agency budget.[139]

On its website the NED makes the lofty claim of being "a private, non-profit foundation dedicated to the growth and strengthening of democratic institutions around the world."[140] Its functions are deeper than this. As is typical, the veil of "promoting" democracy is not contiguous with reality. On the NED in 1985 the *New York Times* wrote: "The National Endowment for Democracy is a quasi-governmental foundation created by the Reagan Administration in 1983 to channel millions of Federal dollars into anti-Communist 'private diplomacy.' "[141] According to this *Times* article, in one of its operations the NED channeled money to two center-right groups in France that opposed the policies of President Francois Mitterrand's Socialist Party.[142]

This was not an aberration. The NED was intended from its inception to be an instrument of US foreign policy. In practice, it is an example of Washington's use of "soft" and "civilian-based" power to influence world affairs. Like the CIA, it claims what it does is support "democracy." The countries where it operates however consider this destabilization—and with good reason. The NED manipulates the political process of target countries by financing political parties, co-opting labor unions, dissident movements, civic organizations, student groups, book publishers, newspapers and more, who are sympathetic to US foreign policy objectives.[143] It meddles in the internal affairs of targeted countries by supplying

[139] C.F.R. Part 67—Organization of the National Endowment for Democracy, Title 22: Foreign Relations, http://law.justia.com/cfr/title22/22-1.0.1.7.42.html
[140] See Ned.org, http://www.ned.org/about
[141] Ben A. Franklin, "Democracy Project Facing New Criticisms," *New York Times*, December 5, 1985, http://www.nytimes.com/1985/12/04/us/democracy-project-facing-new-criticisms.html?scp=4&sq=+Irving+Brown++France&st=nyt
[142] Ibid.
[143] Blum, *Killing Hope*, 303, 315.

funds, technical know-how, training, computers, fax machines, copiers, automobiles and more, to select political groups. The NED has also delivered money to the AEI (discussed above). It claims to be an NGO, but in reality it is a political action group. Most importantly, support from the NED entails alignment to US foreign policy objectives.[144]

The NED originated during the Reagan administration to privatize a portion of the intelligence community and usher in what was termed "project democracy." This was Washington's attempt at restructuring its by then discredited "regime change" operations against enemy states—many democratically elected. Nicolas Thompson, writing for *Washington Monthly*, describes Reagan's creation of the NED and other NGOs as his attempt to continue subversion, the undermining of communism, and to "do what the CIA used to do" through institution building:

> Ronald Reagan loved subversion, and he empowered CIA director William Casey to covertly organize a war in Nicaragua. But Reagan's more lasting legacy comes from his recognition that the weakness of communism could be exploited by international institution building. Reagan proclaimed in 1982 that "The march of freedom and democracy will leave Marxism-Leninism on the ash heap of history," and set in motion a major movement that led to the creation of a number of QUANGOs (quasi-nongovernmental organizations) like the National Endowment for Democracy (NED) that worked to build democratic opposition abroad. In a way, NED was chartered to do what the CIA used to do, only working bottom up and helping activists instead of working top down and lopping off heads.[145]

A key objective of this new institution was to allow more latitude in CIA operations. Washington needed to maintain the CIA's covert

---

[144] Ibid.

[145] William Thompson, "This Ain't Your Mama's CIA," *Washington Monthly*, March 2001,
http://www.washingtonmonthly.com/features/2001/0103.thompson.html
See also Engdahl, *Dominance*, 50.

activities in the area of the subversion of unsavory regimes—*without* public scrutiny. This is because in the 1960s and 70s the CIA received negative exposure during a series of revelations. The CIA was caught in the destabilization of foreign governments and attempted assassinations of heads of state in Latin America and abroad. Because of the resulting stigma of the agency, the NED was to serve as a replacement front to perpetuate funding for covert coups and destabilizations against sovereign states.

Some Washington insiders have described the NED as a "privatization of intelligence." In 1981, Ronald Reagan's Executive Order 12333 allowed for the intelligence community to enter into contracts with private companies. [146] This opened the door to a massive privatization of the US intelligence community, which already had historic ties with Wall Street. [147] By 2007 70% of the intelligence community was in the private sector. [148]

Allen Weinstein, the NED's intellectual architect, once candidly remarked to the *Washington Post*, "A lot of what we do today was done covertly 25 years ago by the CIA." [149] Indeed, as its current director Carl Gershman [150] explained, the NED is a perpetuation of CIA activities:

---

[146] See http://www.archives.gov/federal-register/codification/executive-order/12333.html#2.7 "2.7 Contracting. Agencies within the Intelligence Community are authorized to enter into contracts or   arrangements for the provision of goods or services with private companies or institutions in the United States and need not reveal the sponsorship of such contracts or arrangements for authorized intelligence   purposes. Contracts or arrangements with academic institutions may be undertaken only with the consent of appropriate officials of the institution."

[147] See Burton Hersh, *The Old Boys: The American Elite and the Origins of the CIA*, (Florida: Tree Farm Books, 1992).

[148] Tim Shorrock, "The corporate takeover of U.S. intelligence," *Salon*, June 1, 2007, http://www.salon.com/2007/06/01/intel_contractors/

[149] Hernandez Calvo Ospina, "US Overt and Overt Destabilization," *Le Monde Diplomatique*, August 4, 2007, https://mondediplo.com/2007/08/04ned

[150] Alongside Gershman, the Board of Directors or Administrative Council of the NED have included a variety of figures involved in clandestine foreign policy actions or those with hawkish foreign policy views such as Otto Reich, Bush's Assistant Secretary of State for Western Hemisphere and

We should not have to do this kind of work covertly. It would be terrible for democratic groups around the world to be seen as subsidized by the CIA. We saw that in the "60s, and that's why it has been discontinued. We have not had the capability of doing this, and that's why the endowment was created.[151]

Researcher William Blum notes in *Rogue State: A Guide to the World's Only Superpower*:

How many Americans could identify the National Endowment for Democracy? It is an organization which often does exactly the opposite of what its name implies. The NED was set up in the early 1980s under President Reagan in the wake of all the negative revelations about the CIA in the second half of the 1970s. The latter was a remarkable period. Spurred by Watergate, the Church Committee of the Senate, the Pike Committee of the House and the Rockefeller Commission, created by the president, were all busy investigating the CIA. Seemingly every other day there was a new headline about the discovery of some awful thing, even criminal conduct, the CIA had been mixed up in for years. The Agency was getting an exceedingly bad name, and it was causing the powers-that-be much embarrassment. Something had to be done. What was done was not to stop doing these awful things. Of course not. What was done was to shift many of these awful things to a new organization, with a nice sounding name—the National Endowment for Democracy. The idea was that the NED would do somewhat overtly what the CIA had been doing covertly for decades, and thus,

---

also a board member of the controversial School of the Americas; John "Death Squads" Negroponte, an ambassador to Latin America and Iraq, notorious for the presence of death squads following his presence; pro-war Project for a New American Century signatory neocons such as Elliot Abrams, a PNAC signatory and an official from the Reagan administration, Francis Fukayama, Zalmay Khalilzad, and Will Marshall. Wall Street corporate interests such as Citigroup, Ford, Goldman Sachs, CFR, Brookings, Exxon Mobil, Boeing, Conoco Phillips are represented on the board of the NED as well.

[151] Blum, *Rogue State*, 239.

hopefully, eliminate the stigma associated with CIA covert activities. It was a masterpiece. Of politics, of public relations and of cynicism.[152]

Dr. William Robinson, expert on Washington's democracy promotion initiatives, and author of *Promoting Polyarchy* explained: "In Latin America, in Eastern Europe with the Velvet Revolutions, in Africa, in the Middle East, really all over the world, the U.S. set up these different mechanisms now for penetrating these civil societies in the political systems of countries that are going to be intervened in, and to assure the outcome is going to be pleasing to Washington's foreign policy objectives."[153] On the NED's activities in Nicaragua during the 1990s, Noam Chomsky remarked: "It's about what you would expect from a bipartisan democracy campaign — it's an attempt to impose what is called democracy, meaning rule by the rich and the powerful, without interference by the mob but within the framework of formal electoral procedures. "[154]

Lawrence Wilkerson, Chief of Staff to former Secretary of State Colin Powell, explained the use of the NED as well as USAID to promote Washington's foreign policy:

> As I saw happen for example in Ukraine, as I saw happen in Georgia, as I see happening in other places too, they don't just propagandize or attempt to help with words and rhetoric [the] opposition; they actually do things that give that opposition more power... We do this through surrogates and non-governmental organizations and through people who are less suspecting of the evil that may lurk behind their actions than perhaps they were before. Have we learned some lessons in that regard? You bet! Do we do it better? You bet. Is it still just as heinous as it has always been? You bet![155]

---

152 Ibid., 238.
153 "Democracy promotion: America's new regime change formula," RT.com. http://rt.com/usa/democracy-promotion-usa-regime/
154 Tony Cartalucci, *Flashback: 1993 Noam Chomsky Exposes 'Democracy Promotion,'* Activist Post, December 24, 2011, http://www.activistpost.com/2011/12/flashback-1993-noam-chomsky-exposes.html
155 "Democracy Promotion." RT

Phillip Agee, former CIA case officer, and author of the *Inside the Company: CIA Diary*, an exposé on CIA activities, also explained in a revelatory interview how the NED was established and its functions.[156] Agee characterizes it similarly to Blum and Robinson; the NED is the CIA's "sidekick." "The NED emerged in the wake of a series of scandalous revelations—the worst ones at that point to hit the CIA," he remarked. It had been revealed that the CIA financed the NSA (National Students Association) overseas. This in turn sparked other revelations on CIA operations. Recalling the climate at the time as a CIA case officer, he stated "the gloom was something you could touch almost." Vice President Hubert Humphrey told a Stanford University audience the revelations on CIA activities represented "one of the saddest times, in reference to public policy, our government has had."[157]

In the wake of the revelations, Dante Fascell, congressman from Florida, began to discuss an *open* system for financing organizations overseas, but his suggestions went nowhere because of tensions over the Vietnam War. It was not until the early 1980s, with President Reagan's speech to the House of Representatives about a "democracy project," that it received new impetus. After Reagan established the NED, according to Agee, Blum and others, the CIA began to use it to conduit money into numerous operations. In one instance, it financed political parties in the Nicaraguan elections in the 1990s to the tune of about $12.5 million. In another, the CIA used the NED to overturn the government of Bulgaria.[158] Agee relates how the NED infiltrated and fomented student strikes and demonstrations.

More recently, the NED faced scrutiny by Congressman Ron Paul of Texas. Paul called into question US policy regarding Belarus—a

---

[156] "Modus Operandi CIA ~NED Takluk Negara - Phil Agee," YouTube, 6:48, posted by "Anwardotcom Aidc," February 25, 2010,
http://www.youtube.com/watch?v=Yjtj9h4mrOg
http://www.youtube.com/watch?v=4UEBlVFu-zc
[157] Ibid.
[158] In Bulgaria the NED poured in $ 2 million to influence the outcome of the election. Blum comments that this "was equivalent to a foreign power injecting more than $50 Million into an American electoral campaign." See Blum, *Killing Hope*, 314-320.

state integral to Russia's security—as set forth in "H.R. 515, the Belarus Democracy Reauthorization Act of 2011."[159] Paul noted the "title of this bill would have amused George Orwell," because "it is in fact a US regime-change bill," framing it with regard to the great law of international relations—reciprocity:

> Where does the United States Congress derive the moral or legal authority to determine which political parties or organizations in Belarus—or anywhere else—are to be US-funded and which are to be destabilized? How can anyone argue that US support for regime-change in Belarus is somehow "promoting democracy"? We pick the parties who are to be supported and funded and somehow this is supposed to reflect the will of the Belarusian people? How would Americans feel if the tables were turned and a powerful foreign country demanded that only a political party it selected and funded could legitimately reflect the will of the American people?

> It is particularly Orwellian to call US manipulation of foreign elections "promoting democracy." How would we Americans feel if for example the Chinese arrived with millions of dollars to support certain candidates deemed friendly to China?

The CIA may have been exposed, but continued unhindered with methods to impose "regime change" against unfriendly or noncompliant governments through its new instrument, the NED. The CIA's sponsorship of political organizations for "regime change" was reinvigorated—thanks to a cosmetic facelift under the NED. In the MENA uprisings it would again be a cornerstone of power projection.

1960s SPONSORSHIP OF YOUTH MOVEMENTS

The sponsorship of impressionable mass youth movements, as in the "color revolutions" and MENA uprisings, and the use of public institutions as a conduit for covert activities, were not novel ideas.

[159] Ron Paul, "Statement on H.R. 515, the Belarus Democracy Reauthorization Act of 2011,"
http://paul.house.gov/index.php?option=com_content&task=view&id=1885&Itemid=60

The CIA engaged in practices during the 1960s; as we have seen, Blum and Agee revealed that the National Students Association or NSA (no pun intended on the National Security Agency) was among the groups on the payroll of the CIA. In 1967, CBS aired a special report: "In the Pay of the CIA: An American Dilemma."[160] It explored how many individuals—both wittingly and unwittingly—were on the CIA payroll via front organizations. CBS reported that the key funding channels were tax free foundations, which represent the vast institutionalized wealth of the American establishment.

CBS interviewed NSA president Philip Sherburne, who helped to spark the scandal. Sherburne related that he became aware of CIA involvement in the National Students Association after he was set to ascend from vice president to president of the association. After signing a security agreement, he was shocked to learn about the CIA funding—as much as $400,000 a year to the NSA, and $1,800,000 to the International Student Conference for activities in places such as Vienna, Austria. CBS also reported the CIA had funded groups in British Guiana to overthrow that government. These revelations are what NED director Gershman referred to when he lamented: "It would be terrible for democratic groups around the world to be seen as subsidized by the CIA. We saw that in the "60s, and that's why it has been discontinued." In the MENA uprisings, as we shall see, this "sidekick" of the CIA—the NED—sponsored much of the region's turmoil. The scrutiny received in the 1960s would not be repeated.

US "SOFT POWER" SHIFT UNDER OBAMA

Before the coming of the Obama administration, the American empire appeared to be in crisis. US theoreticians surmised that soft and civilian-based power was needed to salvage the empire. The

---

[160] This approximately hour-long 1967 CBS special report by Mike Wallace, including Roger Mudd is accessible via YouTube. See "CIA: Charity, NGO, Think Tank, Media, NWO Funding 1of5," YouTube, 9:35, posted by "phoneyid," October 7, 2009,
http://www.youtube.com/watch?v=ZYKhXefObKQ See also "A Friend of the Devil" in *The New Yorker* online, March 23, 2015, with references to *Patriotic Betrayal: The Inside Story of the CIA's Secret Campaign to Enroll American Students in the Crusade Against Communism*, Karen Paget, Yale University Press, March 2015.

policies of the George W. Bush regime — unilateralism, disregard for the norms of international law — diminished American standing in the world. Discontent over the second Iraq war was widespread, in Europe and especially the Muslim world,[161] spurring worldwide protests. An international study released in March 2004 by the Pew Research Center found "discontent with America and its policies...intensified rather than diminished." [162] "Perceptions of American unilateralism remain widespread in European and Muslim nations, and the war in Iraq has undermined American credibility abroad." Madeline Bunting, editor of the London *Guardian*, wrote "American imperialism used to be a fiction of the far-left imagination, now it is an uncomfortable fact of life."[163] The aggressive policies of the Bush administration antagonized allies such as France and Germany. International relations theorist Immanuel Wallerstein presciently remarked, "When George Bush leaves office, he will have left the United States significantly weaker."[164]

American public support for more wars in the spirit of the "clash of civilizations" was also greatly reduced. Writing in the *Atlantic Monthly* in support of the Obama presidential campaign, journalist Andrew Sullivan commented that in the case of another 9/11-style attack, Bush would be unable to count on a similar unity in the American people. Some would even argue Bush himself was complicit:

> Perhaps the underlying risk is best illustrated by our asking what the popular response would be to another 9/11–style attack. It is hard to imagine a reprise of the sudden unity and solidarity in the days after 9/11, or an outpouring of support

[161] "A Year After Iraq War: Mistrust of America in Europe Ever Higher, Muslim Anger Persists" PewResearch, March 16, 2004, http://www.people-press.org/2004/03/16/a-year-after-iraq-war/
[162] Ibid.
[163] Madeline Bunting, "Beginning of the end: The US is ignoring an important lesson from history - that an empire cannot survive on brute force alone," *Guardian*, February 2, 2003,
http://www.guardian.co.uk/world/2003/feb/03/usa.comment
[164] Quoted in Chalmers Johnson, *The Sorrows of Empire: Militarism Secrecy and the End of the Republic*
(New York: Henry Holt, 2004), 287.

from allies and neighbors. It is far easier to imagine an even more bitter fight over who was responsible (apart from the perpetrators) and a profound suspicion of a government forced to impose more restrictions on travel, communications, and civil liberties. The current president would be unable to command the trust, let alone the support, of half the country in such a time. He could even be blamed for provoking any attack that came.[165]

The American empire needed a new direction in its global leadership. It needed a shift to "soft power" under Obama if it were to continue with viability.

Notably, Joseph Nye, Jr., of the elite Trilateral Commission, former Assistant Secretary of Defense for International Security Affairs and the theoretician credited with formulating the concept of "soft power," was an Obama backer. "A President Obama," he argued, "would do more for America's soft power around the world than anything else we could do."[166] Nye concluded, "The coming decades are not likely to see a post-American world, but the United States will need a smart strategy that combines hard- and soft-power resources — and that emphasizes alliances and networks that are responsive to the new context of a global information age." This strategy accurately reflected the eventual foreign policy of the Obama presidency: a combined use of hard and soft power resources founded in the information age, drawing in allies such as the UK and France, as well as ambitious regional actors such as Qatar and Turkey to project power.

---

[165] Andrew Sullivan, "Goodbye to All That: Why Obama Matters," *The Atlantic*, December 2007,
http://www.theatlantic.com/magazine/archive/2007/12/goodbye-to-all-that-why-obama- matters/6445/2/

[166] James Truab, "Is (His) Biography (Our) Destiny?" *New York Times*, November 4, 2007,
http://www.nytimes.com/2007/11/04/magazine/04obama-t.html?_r=2&pagewanted=1&hp

ADVISORS: A WINDOW TO FOREIGN POLICY

In terms of foreign policy, a sound analysis of how a candidate will act if elected is provided by looking at their advisors. During his 2000 election campaign, Bush called himself a "compassionate conservative" who would act with humility in foreign policy. His subsequent policies of preventive war and unilateralism did not at all correspond to this rhetoric. A better indicator was his advisors — the neocons. Bush picked many key aides from those who executed and planned the first Gulf War. In policy papers and plans they discussed what should be done if they were to retake power. Organizing as the PNAC (Project for the New American Century), they began lobbying for aggressive measures against Iraq and to fundamentally restructure the Middle East.[167] PNAC released a policy paper in September 2000 *Rebuilding America's Defenses*. It explicitly stated the US should aim to continue its unipolar world order:

> The United States is the world's only superpower... At present the United States faces no global rival... America's grand strategy should aim to preserve and extend this advantageous position as far into the future as possible. There are, however, potentially powerful states dissatisfied with the current situation and eager to change it, if they can...[168]

> The United States has for decades sought to play a more permanent role in Gulf regional security. While the unresolved conflict with Iraq provides the immediate justification, the need for a substantial American force presence in the Gulf transcends the issue of the regime of Saddam Hussein.[169]

Had PNAC and its endorsers been looked at rather than Bush's superficial rhetoric on humility and "compassionate conservatism," his later policies would have been unsurprising.

Likewise, Obama's advisors and endorsers provide a window into what policies he would follow. When pressed on his inexperience in the arena of foreign policy, Obama contended he would have the best

---

[167] Johnson, *Sorrows*, 228.
[168] Engdahl, *Oil Politics*, 251-52.
[169] Ibid.

advisors. Chief among them, and most experienced, was Zbigniew Brzezinski, who served as President Jimmy Carter's National Security advisor. Indeed, in *Barack H. Obama: The Unauthorized Biography* Dr. Webster G. Tarpley argues Obama was part of Brzezinski's circle since his years at Columbia University.[170] Obama transferred in 1981 to Columbia, where Brzezinski headed the "Institute for Communist Affairs." Obama wrote his senior thesis on Soviet nuclear disarmament—a Brzezinski specialty. Obama's years at Columbia are incredibly murky and he has never been willing to reveal much.[171] In 2007, during his very first speech on foreign policy in Iowa, Obama lavished praise on Brzezinski, whom he requested to introduce him. Calling Brzezinski his "amazing friend," Obama remarked he is "someone I have learned an immense amount from," and "one of our most outstanding scholars and thinkers." [172] Brzezinski in turn trumpeted his endorsement of Obama. In an

---

[170] Webster G. Tarpley, *Barack H. Obama: The Unauthorized Biography* (Progressive Press: CA, 2008), 69.

[171] The *New York Times* underscored Obama's secrecy on his Columbia years. See Janny Scott, "Obama's account of New York Years Often Differ from What Others Say," *New York Times*, October 30, 2007. Obama attempted to cloak details of his stay in NYC with charges of racism, claiming "no matter how many times the administration tried to paint them over, the walls remained scratched with blunt correspondence about "niggers." "A classmate, Joe Zwicker, said that this 'surprises me. Columbia was a pretty tolerant place. There were African-American students in my classes and I never saw any evidence of racism at all.' " Many Columbia alumni cannot recall anyone named "Obama." In a September 5, 2008 interview Wayne Allyn Root, Libertarian Party candidate for vice president, states he never heard of anyone named Obama nor could he find any classmates who could recall of him, despite being class of 1983 and having the same major. Root was asked "were you in the same exact class [as Obama]?" Root responds: "Class of '83, political science, pre-law Columbia University. You don't get more exact than that. Never met him in my life, don't know anyone who ever met him. At the class reunion, our 20th reunion five years ago, 20th reunion, who was asked to be the speaker of the class? Me. No one ever heard of Barrack! Who was he, and five years ago, nobody even knew who he was." Quoted in Tarpley, *Unauthorized Biography*, 71.

[172] YouTube, 1:10, posted by "ysmal2," March 13, 2008, http://www.youtube.com/watch?v=ASIETEx0T-I

interview with Bloomberg Television's "Political Capital with Al Hunt," he remarked that Obama

> recognizes that the challenge is a new face, a new sense of direction, a new definition of America's role in the world... He has a sense of what is historically relevant, and what is needed from the United States in relationship to the world... There is a need for a fundamental rethinking of how we conduct world affairs... Obama seems to me to have both the guts and intelligence to address that issue and to change the nature of America's relationship with the world.[173]

When pressed on his relationship to Brzezinski, the Obama team and its advocates attempted obfuscation. The Jewish community was concerned because of criticisms Brzezinski leveled against the pro-Israel lobby AIPAC, charging it with an inordinate influence on American foreign policy. On National Public Radio, *Jerusalem Post* correspondent Caroline Glick charged that Obama "surrounds himself with people who are anti-Semitic... anti-white like Rev. Wright... or simply anti-Israel like Zbigniew Brzezinski, and Robert Mallay, and Samantha Power his former advisor." Obama's Middle East advisor Mark Levine responded: "...ah, um, I'm speechless after what I've heard from Mrs. Glick... Zbigniew Brzezinski is NOT one of his foreign policy advisors, nor one of his advisors at all. This really points out the nature of the type of distortions that have been leveled to Senator Obama for quite some time."[174]

Columnist Colbert I. King of the *Washington Post* leveled similar criticisms against Hillary Clinton's campaign, which attacked Brzezinski to attack Obama: "it mattered not to Clinton's clan that Brzezinski is not a key Obama advisor, that Obama has said he has had lunch with Brzezinski once or that they have exchanged e-mails perhaps three times. Linking Obama to someone who is anathema to the Jewish community was the point to be scored — even if it meant committing a foul."[175] Yet *The Observer* also headlined a story citing

---

[173] See Tarpley, *Unauthorized Biography*, 372-3. Quoted from Bloomberg. "Zbigniew Brzezinski endorses Barack Obama," Friday, August 24, 2007
[174] Ibid, 374-5.
[175] Quoted in Tarpley, *Unauthorized Biography*, 373, from *Washington Post*, March 1, 2008.

"Obama Adviser Brzezinski" defending Samantha Power. [176] Tellingly, as noted, it was Brzezinski who introduced Obama during his first foreign policy speech as well.

Curiously, Obama decided to keep Robert Gates—a protégé of Brzezinski—as Secretary of Defense as a holdover from the Bush administration. During the Carter years, Gates served as Brzezinski's office aide. Brzezinski writes of him: "He then became my special assistant when I was in charge of the NSC under President Jimmy Carter." He noted Gates "was the first person I would see every morning and usually the last one in the evening."[177]

Gates was placed as Secretary of Defense during a period when the momentum was building against many in the PNAC/neocon faction. His predecessor Donald Rumsfeld resigned; Larry Franklin, a Department of Defense analyst, was convicted and given 12 years for passing information to AIPAC, the pro-Israel lobby, as well as an Israeli diplomat;[178] Vice President Dick Cheney's chief of staff Lewis "Scooter" Libby was sentenced to prison for perjury and obstructing a probe; Lord Conrad Black of the neocon think-tank the American Enterprise Institute was convicted of fraud, while former Deputy Secretary of Defense Paul Wolfowitz was forced to resign from his position as head of the World Bank amid scandals. Gates also fired the Secretary of the Air Force and its chief of staff for lax security over nuclear weapons, and appointed James Rodney Schlesinger, formerly of Brzezinski's Trilateral Commission and the Carter administration, to oversee nuclear security. All around, neocons faced expulsion.

Despite the Obama team's denials, many observers recognized Brzezinski's role as Obama's *éminence grise*, especially with his status

---

[176] Ibid, p. 375, http://observer.com/2008/03/obama-adviser-brzezinski-power-shouldnt-have-resigned/

[177] Zbigniew Brzezinski, "Leaders & Revolutionaries: Robert Gates," *Time*, May 12, 2008,
http://www.time.com/time/specials/2007/article/0,28804,1733748_1733757_1735600,00.html

[178] David Johnston, "Pentagon Analyst Gets 12 Years for Disclosing Data," *New York Times*, January 20, 2006,
http://www.nytimes.com/2006/01/20/politics/20cnd-franklin.html

as one of the primary theoreticians within the Anglo-American foreign policy elite. In particular, the Russian press has regarded Brzezinski as one of America's leading Russophobes.[179] *Moscow News* on April 3, 2008 noted "Brzezinski...is trying to conceal his involvement with Barack Obama's team."[180] Meanwhile, the London *Economist* commented that there was "A NEW brain for Barack Obama! It's 78 years old and it still works perfectly. It belongs to Zbigniew Brzezinski, the peppery ex-national security adviser to Jimmy Carter."[181]

Some mainstream analysts also recognized that Brzezinski's ideas would provide a framework for an eventual Obama foreign policy. Writing in the *Washington Post*, D.C national security state insider David Ignatius, often a mouthpiece for these elements, noted: "Zbigniew Brzezinski has written a new book that might be a foreign policy manifesto for Barack Obama. Its message is that America can recover from what Brzezinski calls the 'catastrophic' mistakes of the Bush administration, but only if the next president makes a clean break from those policies and aligns the country with a world in transformation... Stressing the need for a foreign policy makeover, [Brzezinski's] prescriptions seem tailor-made for a certain junior senator from Illinois."

Ignatius noted that Obama brings "a fresh face, unencumbered by the past" — a boost in soft power, in other words. Recognizing the folly of the Bush II regime, Ignatius pays homage Brzezinski, a critic of discredited Bush II era stratagems:

---

[179] Russian policy makers have long talked of the "Brzezinski plan" which according to them aims at destabilizing and Balkanizing Russia into multiple parts. See Douglas Birch, "Kremlin Powers May Be Split After Putin." 26 June, 2007, Web Apr 1. 2012.
http://www.washingtonpost.com/wp-dyn/content/article/2007/06/26/AR2007062600979_2.html See also Webster G. Tarpley, *Obama The Postmodern Coup: the Making of a Manchurian Candidate*, (Joshua Tree, CA: Progressive Press), 2008.
[180] Tarpley, *Unauthorized Biography*, 375.
[181] "A new brain for Barack Obama," *Economist*, Mar 14th 2007,
http://www.economist.com/blogs/democracyinamerica/2007/03/a_new_brai n_for_barack_obama

First, an encomium to Brzezinski: If there's any foreign policy analyst who has earned the right to be taken seriously today, it's this 78-year-old veteran of the Carter administration. Brzezinski was right about Iraq, warning early and emphatically of the dangers of an American invasion at a time when most foreign policy pundits (including this one) were, with whatever quibbles, supporting President Bush's decision to go to war.

In his book, *Second Chance*, Ignatius notes that "Brzezinski's real focus is the 'catastrophic leadership' of the current president," George W. Bush. Brzezinski concludes that the war in Iraq "has caused calamitous damage to America's global standing," meaning its soft power. It "has been a geopolitical disaster." Most importantly with regards to the MENA uprisings that took place under the Obama regime, Ignatius finds that "The most intriguing part of Brzezinski's book is what I would describe as the Obama manifesto....Brzezinski argues that the world is undergoing a "global political awakening."[182]

In his foreign policy assessment *Second Chance*,[183] Brzezinski describes how this "global political awakening" has taken shape as "socially massive, politically radicalizing, and geographically universal."[184] In an analysis, conforming to the "civilian-based power" approach and emphasizing its explosive potential with the Information Revolution, he argues that the world's youth bulge—particularly robust in the MENA region—can be easily mobilized for anti-establishment revolution:

> Many, disliking the status quo, are susceptible to being mobilized against those whom they perceive as self-interestedly preserving it. The Third World youth are particularly volatile. The rapid expanding demographic bulge

---

[182] David Ignatius, "A Manifesto For the Next President," *Washington Post*, March 14, 2007, http://www.washingtonpost.com/wp-dyn/content/article/2007/03/13/AR2007031301504.html
[183] Zbigniew Brzezinski, *Second Chance: Three Presidents and the Crisis of American Superpower* (New York: Basic Books.
[184] Ibid., 202.

in the twenty-five and under age-bracket represents a huge mass of impatience. This group's revolutionary spearhead is likely to emerge from among the millions of students concentrated in the often intellectually dubious tertiary-level educational institutions of developing countries. Semi-mobilized in large congregations and connected by the internet, they are positioned to replay, on a far vaster scale, what occurred years earlier in Mexico City and Tiananmen Square. Revolutionaries-in-waiting, they represent the equivalent of the militant proletariat of the nineteenth and twentieth century. [185]

Their only unifying doctrine, says Brzezinski, is not economic development for the Third World — nations which have endured decades of a "globalization of poverty" — but "dignity." Only by identifying with this "universal human dignity" can the US "overcome the risk that the global political awakening will turn against it," he suggests. [186] This "Obama manifesto" and its description of the "global political awakening" uncannily foreshadow the MENA uprisings. In a later *Newsweek* interview, Brzezinski explained the destabilization taking place in Egypt's Tahrir Square in terms of this "global political awakening":

> Today we have somewhere between 80 million and 130 million young people around the world who come from the socially insecure lower middle class and constitute a community of mutual infection with angers, passions, frustrations, and hatreds. These students are revolutionaries-in-waiting. When they erupt at volatile moments, they become very contagious. And whereas Marx's industrial proletariat more than a century ago was fragmented in local groups, today these young people are interacting via the Internet.[187]

---

[185] Ibid., 203-4.
[186] Ibid.
[187] "Egypt Is Seething, " *The Daily Beast*, Jan 30, 2011,
http://www.thedailybeast.com/newsweek/2011/01/30/egypt-is-seething.html

This was precisely the scenario foretold and outlined in *Second Chance*:

> To sum up, the ongoing political awakening is now global in its geographic scope... with only very remote peasant communities still immune to political stimuli; it is strikingly youthful in its demographic profile and thus more receptive to rapid political mobilization; and much of its inspiration is transnational in origin because of the cumulative impact of literacy and mass communications. As a result, modern populist political passions can be aroused even against a distant target despite the absence of a unifying doctrine such as Marxism... The majority of states existing today no longer rule relatively pliant populations, and many are vulnerable to being swamped by populist demands that transcend their capacity to respond effectively.[188]

EXPLOITING THE EGYPTIAN YOUTH BULGE AND WALL STREET'S FOOD PRICE INFLATION

When mass protests emerged in Egypt, political repression, corruption, poverty, food-price inflation, and unemployment were all ascribed as key underlying factors, but the most critical was massive youth unemployment—including among many who were highly educated—coupled with steep increases in global food prices. As one of the world's largest grain importers, Egypt was particularly susceptible to the latter.

Corruption was cited as a factor, but when measured against other states, Egypt's level of corruption is unremarkable. According to Transparency International, Egypt was ranked 80th in terms of corruption, a long way from the bottom. Its level of corruption was comparable to Italy, Greece, China, or India, while lower than Argentina, Indonesia, Vietnam, and most of the post-Soviet sphere.[189] No mass protests erupted in these countries.

---

[188] Ibid., p. 204, online at http://www.the-american-interest.com/2005/09/01/the-dilemma-of-the-last-sovereign/.

[189] Andrey V. Korotayev and Julia V. Zinkina, "Egyptian Revolution: A Demographic Structural Analysis,"

With the common notion that 40% of Egyptians lived below $2 a day income, poverty was also cited as a decisive factor in Egyptian discontent.[190] This omits that the level of extreme poverty—below a $1 a day income—was nearly completely eliminated. In this regard Egypt was one of the best performing states in the world with a figure of less than 2% below the extreme poverty line. Yet according to 2005–08 data, there were 13.4% living below the extreme poverty line in Georgia, 15.9% in China, 21.5% in Tajikistan and Vietnam, 22.6% in the Philippines, 26.2% in South Africa, 29.4% in Indonesia, 41.6% in India, 49.6% in Bangladesh, 54.9% in Haiti, 70.1% in Guinea, and 83.7% in Liberia.[191] Egypt's 20% of the population living on less than $2 a day on the eve of protests compared with 36.3% in China, 42.9% in South Africa, 43.4% in Armenia, 45% in the Philippines, and 48.4% in Vietnam. In fact, in many states more than half the population lived under the $2 poverty line: 50.8% in Tajikistan, 60.3% in Pakistan, 72.1% in Haiti, 75.6% in India, 81.3% in Bangladesh, 87.2% in Guinea, and 94.8% in Liberia.[192] No mass protests were seen in these countries.

At the heart of the mass protests was the MENA region's burgeoning youth bulge. Preceding the regional uprisings, the 28 and under demographic saw high growth. In fact, in the MENA region, two-thirds of the population was under 18.[193] The potential for creating "revolutionaries-in-waiting," in Brzezinski's parlance, was pronounced because of this sizeable demographic. The Carnegie Endowment for International Peace noted, "Recent political turmoil in the Arab world has put these youth at the forefront of the political

---

http://cliodynamics.ru/download/Korotayev_Zinkina_Egyptian_Revoluti on_Entelequia_New.pdf
[190]

https://web.archive.org/web/20110201013309/http://www.france24.com /en/20110125-egypt-braces-nationwide-protests
[191] Ibid.
[192] Ibid.
[193] "Arab Youth Unemployment: Roots, Risks, and Responses," Carnegie Endowment for International Peace, February 10, 2011, http://www.carnegieendowment.org/2011/02/10/arab-youth- unemployment-roots-risks-and-responses/4go See *The New Arab Revolts: What Happened, What it Means, and What Comes Next,* "Demographics of Arab Protests: An Interview With Ragui Assaad," February 14, 2011, (Council on Foreign Relations), 236.

and economic debate." Indeed, as sociologist Jack Goldstone noted, this conformed to historical trends:

> [The] rapid growth of youth can undermine existing political coalitions, creating instability. Large youth cohorts are often drawn to new ideas and heterodox religions, challenging older forms of authority. In addition, because most young people have fewer responsibilities for families and careers, they are relatively easily mobilized for social or political conflicts. Youth have played a prominent role in political violence throughout recorded history, and the existence of a "youth bulge" (an unusually high proportion of youths 15 to 24 relative to the total adult population) has historically been associated with times of political crisis. Most major revolutions … [including] most twentieth-century revolutions in developing countries—have occurred where exceptionally large youth bulges were present.[194]

In Egypt, unemployment was cited as a factor in overall discontent, but the Egyptian unemployment figure of approximately 9% was unremarkable according to global standards. Youth unemployment however was more pronounced. The Carnegie Endowment for International Peace noted, "the MENA region ranks among the worst in the world for youth unemployment, which approaches 30 percent."[195] In Egypt about half of the 2.5 million unemployed belonged to the 20–24 age group.[196] This produced a bloc of over one million youth unemployed with the time and the motive to topple the regime. Furthermore, on the eve of mass protests, the Egyptian Central Agency for Public Mobilization and Statistics found that more than 43% of Egyptian unemployed held university degrees.[197] Thus, the force spearheading protests was educated, receptive to new ideas, and able to utilize the unprecedented interconnectivity of internet and mass communication technology.

---

[194] Korotayev and Zinkina, "Egyptian Revolution."
[195] "Arab Unemployment," Carnegie Endowment.
[196] Korotayev and Zinkina, "Egyptian Revolution."
[197] Ibid.

The other crucial factor was steep increases in global food prices, due to Wall Street speculation in world markets. This allowed Egypt's unemployed highly-educated youth to draw in other sectors of Egyptian society to protests. The increase in global food prices pushed a large sector of the Egyptian population into poverty, creating a groundswell of discontent. From 2005 to 2008, the avarice of Wall Street speculators precipitated a worldwide food price increase of a staggering 80 percent.[198] From 2003 to 2008, the volume of index fund speculation increased by 1,900 percent. Morgan Stanley estimated the number of outstanding contracts in maize futures increased from 500,000 in 2003 to approximately 2.5 million in 2008. Holdings in commodity index funds ballooned from $13 billion in 2003 to $317 billion by 2008.[199]

For the roughly two billion people who spend more than half of their income on food, this steep price increase was devastating. 250 million people joined the ranks of the hungry in 2008, bringing the world's "food insecure" population to an unprecedented 1 billion.[200] According to the UN's Special Rapporteur on the Right to Food Olivier de Schutter, the price spike of 2007-08 had the effect of driving 130 to 150 million people into "extreme poverty," and added 40 million to the status of chronically hungry.[201] Wall Street's food price bubble only relented with the banking panic of 2008.

The effect of price increases was regionally pronounced, because half of the top 20 wheat importers in 2010 were in the MENA region.[202] With Egypt dependent on imported grain for about half its intake by 2010,[203] millions of its citizens fell into poverty. Along with

---

[198] Frederick Kaufman, "How Goldman Sachs Created the Food Crisis," *Foreign Policy*, April 27, 2011, http://www.foreignpolicy.com/articles/2011/04/27/how_goldman_sachs _created_the_food_crisis

[199] Tom Philpott, "How Wall Street Fuels Global Hunger" *Mother Jones*, September 16, 2011, http://www.motherjones.com/tom-philpott/2011/09/un-wall-street-speculation-fuels-global-hunger

[200] Kaufman, "Goldman Sachs."

[201] Philpott, "Global Hunger."

[202] *Arab Revolts*, 230.

[203] Ibid., 232.

Sub-Saharan Africa, the region was also the only one to see a rise in the numbers of the malnourished.

Historically, in the MENA region, cuts in critical food subsidies have led to mass protests. Thousands protested in 1977 when the pro-Western administration of Anwar Sadat attempted to cut subsidies for basic food stuffs at the behest of the IMF. In a prelude to the 2011 mass protests, in spring 2008 protests resulting from global food price growth surged in Egypt. The central event was a strike of spinning and weaving factory workers, where their dissent was aimed foremost at the decrease of living standards caused by Wall Street's food price spike. The response of the administration of Hosni Mubarak was to attempt to insulate the Egyptian people by expanding the scope of state subsidies for foodstuffs. However, this proved to be a only a slight mitigation because of the illicit use of lucrative subsidized grain on the black market, and the fact that state subsidies did not cover all food costs for a family. By 2010, when Wall Street and the City of London recovered via government bailouts, speculation in global food markets resumed with prices reaching the same critical levels as in 2008. By early 2011, World Bank President Robert Zoelick warned that global food prices had reached "dangerous levels." The stage was set for destabilization in Egypt and the MENA region. That Wall Street and the CIA have historic ties,[204] means the possibility of global market speculation being part of an intelligence community operation cannot be precluded. In any case, the US proceeded to exploit these conditions to foment regional tumult.

MENA ACTIVISTS: US TRAINED AND FUNDED

Under the veil of "democracy," the demographic and food price vulnerabilities of Egypt and the MENA region were exploited by the US for "regime change" and destabilization. The pro-democracy protestors that spearheaded the "Arab Spring" in Egypt and throughout the region were funded and trained under US auspices just as the "color revolution" movements in Serbia, Ukraine, and elsewhere before them. In a revelatory April 2011 article in the *New York Times*, "US Groups Helped Nurture Arab Spring," it was shown

---

[204] See Hersh, *The Old Boys.*

that the US played a larger role than previously known. The *Times* reported:

> Even as the United States poured billions of dollars into foreign military programs and anti-terrorism campaigns, a small core of American government-financed organizations were promoting democracy in authoritarian Arab states.
>
> The money spent on these programs was minute compared with efforts led by the Pentagon. But as American officials and others look back at the uprisings of the Arab Spring, they are seeing that the United States' democracy-building campaigns played a bigger role in fomenting protests than was previously known, with key leaders of the movements having been trained by the Americans in campaigning, organizing through new media tools and monitoring elections.[205]

According to interviews with activists, officials, and cables obtained by the *Times* MENA's pro-democracy groups received funding and training from CIA sidekick the NED, with its catalogue of subsidiary institutions: the International Republican Institute, its Republican Party branch, which has neocon Senator John McCain as its chairman; the National Democratic Institute, the NED's Democratic Party branch, chaired by former Secretary of State Madeleine Albright; Freedom House, which receives most of its funding from the State Department, chaired by former CIA director James Woolsey. These were organizations crucial to the original "color revolutions."

The *Washington Post* also revealed that federal agencies such as the US Department of Defense, Department of State, and Broadcasting Board of Governors funded a handful of technology firms to allow dissidents to go online without being tracked or to visit blocked news and social media sites.[206] This was to help them organize anti-regime

---

[205] Ron Nixon, "U.S. Groups Helped Nurture Arab Uprisings," *New York Times*, April 14, 2011, http://www.nytimes.com/2011/04/15/world/15aid.html?_r=3&pagewanted=1&emc=eta1

[206] Ian Shapira, "U.S. funding tech firms that help Mideast dissidents evade government censors," *Washington Post*, March 10, 2011,

activities and circumvent free-speech restrictions. AFP also revealed the US had trained around 5,000 activists. Michael Posner, the US assistant Secretary of State for Human Rights and Labor, stated the US government "budgeted $50 million in the last two years to develop new technologies to help activists protect themselves from arrest and prosecution by authoritarian governments." The article added that the US "has organized training sessions for 5,000 activists in different parts of the world. A session held in the Middle East about six weeks ago gathered activists from Tunisia, Egypt, Syria and Lebanon who returned to their countries with the aim of training their colleagues there."[207]

In preparation for the 2011 uprising, Egyptian dissidents traveled abroad. In 2008 militants of Egypt's April 6th movement—in the forefront spearheading the unrest[208]—attended a 2008 New York City meeting funded and co-hosted by the US State Department called the "Alliance for Youth Movements."[209] The meeting claimed to be a forum for grassroots activists and how they can help shape the world. Belying its anti-establishment and "revolutionary" cover, it included a wide array of representatives from the American corporate establishment.[210] The list included State Department staff, former National Security officials, advisors to the Department of Homeland Security, members of New York's elite corporate sponsored CFR, the NED funded Freedom House, and representatives from American corporations and mass media organizations such as AT&T, Google, Facebook, NBC, MSNBC, CBS, CNN, ABC, and MTV.

---

http://www.washingtonpost.com/wp-dyn/content/article/2011/03/09/AR2011030905716.html
[207] "US trains activists to evade security forces," AFP, April 8, 2011, http://www.activistpost.com/2011/04/us-trains-activists-to-evade-security.html
[208] "Egypt's opposition pushes demands as protests continue," BBC, February 1, 2011, http://www.bbc.co.uk/news/world-middle-east-12290167
[209] "Inaugural AYM Summit And Egypt's Shabab April 6 Movement," Movements.org, February 01, 2011, http://www.movements.org/blog/entry/first-aym-summit/
[210] "Alliance of Youth Movements Summit: Attendee Biographies," http://allyoumov.3cdn.net/f734ac45131b2bbcdb_w6m6idptn.pdf

Image: *Egypt's April 6th movement using the clenched fist symbol of US-sponsored Otpor! from Serbia. Otpor! reinvented itself to train similar US-backed "revolutions" including the dissidents in Egypt.*

The April 6th movement is supported by a crowdfunding website, movements.org, whose sponsors include corporations such as Google, Pepsi, and the Omnicon Group.[211] This myriad of corporate sponsors diminishes the anti-establishment credibility of these ostensibly grassroots "youth movements."

A report from Stratfor noted the Egyptian "April 6 Movement and Kifaya are the groups that have led the charge in actually getting protesters organized and onto the streets." These groups at the center of protests were first trained abroad in the methods of the Albert Einstein Institute. The US training and funding of MENA activists for the uprisings directly mirrored the same US strategy that ousted Milosevic of Serbia because the Egyptian April 6th movement was actually trained by the US sponsored "Otpor!" movement. In fact, Egypt's April 6th Movement used the same clenched fist symbol as Serbia's "Otpor!" which the US funded by the millions.

The "Otpor!" movement had reinvented itself as an organization to train other pseudo-revolutionaries under the name "CANVAS." *Foreign Policy* described CANVAS as "an organization run by young Serbs who had cut their teeth in the late 1990s student uprising against Slobodan Milosevic. After ousting him, they embarked on the ambitious project of figuring out how to translate their success to other countries." In 2009 April 6th visited CANVAS and learned the methods of Gene Sharp's AEI "non-violent revolution." In 2008 after the April 6th movement created a Facebook page garnering 60,000 followers, they staged a large protest, but it was ineffective due to police repression. *Foreign Policy* reports that in order to organize more effective protests in "the summer of 2009, Mohamed Adel, a 20-year-old blogger and April 6 activist, went to Belgrade, Serbia" to learn from CANVAS. The report adds: "In Belgrade, Adel took a week-long course in the strategies of nonviolent revolution. He learned how to organize people—not on a computer, but in the streets. And most importantly, he learned how to train others. He went back to Egypt and began to teach. The April 6 Youth Movement,

---

[211] Kevin Tucker, *Web of the Illuminati*, Lulu Press, 2013, p. 109. "Howcast, Google, MTV, Meetup, Pepsi, CBS, Youtube, Facebook, National Geographic, Omnicom Group, Gen Next, Columbia Law School, and most importantly the US State Department sponsor this organization."

along with a similar group called Kefaya, became the most important organizers of the 18-day peaceful uprising that culminated in President Hosni Mubarak's departure on Feb. 11." [212]

The AEI tactics used in the Egyptian protests were directly from the CANVAS curriculum. Copies of Gene Sharp's 198 "non-violent weapons" were translated into Arabic and distributed in Tahrir Square by pseudo-revolutionaries without attribution. A BBC reporter interviewed a protest organizer who was worried that revealing the American source of protest tactics would undermine its credibility. Off camera though he confirmed the work of the AEI was the basis for protest tactics. Many of those who participated in protests were unaware of the AEI's centrality to the protests. One delusional protestor was incredulous at the notion of an American institution as the source of tactics. When told of American involvement, he retorted: "This is an Egyptian revolution." "We are not being told what to do by the Americans. " In this way thousands of Egyptians were drawn into mass protests by the US sponsored revolutionaries, unbeknownst that it was a US sponsored destabilization.

LONDON TELEGRAPH CONFIRMS
EGYPT COUP PLANNED WITH WASHINGTON

In January 2011, the London *Telegraph* revealed aspects of the secret plan for "regime change" in Egypt which had been initiated approximately three years in advance. The *Telegraph* article headlined: "Egypt protests: America's secret backing for rebel leaders behind uprising: The American government secretly backed leading figures behind the Egyptian uprising who have been planning 'regime change' for the past three years, the *Daily Telegraph* has learned." [213] The *Telegraph* confirmed:

---

[212] Tina Rosenberg, "Revolution U," *Foreign Policy*, February 16, 2011, http://www.foreignpolicy.com/articles/2011/02/16/revolution_u
[213] "Egypt protests: America's secret backing for rebel leaders behind uprising," *Telegraph*, January 28, 2011, http://www.telegraph.co.uk/news/worldnews/africaandindianocean/egypt/8289686/Egypt-protests-Americas-secret-backing-for-rebel-leaders-behind-uprising.html

The American Embassy in Cairo helped a young dissident attend a US-sponsored summit for activists in New York, while working to keep his identity secret from Egyptian state police.

On his return to Cairo in December 2008, the activist told US diplomats that an alliance of opposition groups had drawn up a plan to overthrow President Hosni Mubarak and install a democratic government in 2011.

The *Telegraph* obtained documents showing US support for rebel leaders, also confirming the dissidents' attendance at the State Department sponsored "Alliance for Youth Movements." US Cairo embassy documents stated, "On December 23, April 6 activist xxxxxxxxxxxx expressed satisfaction with his participation in the December 3-5 \'Alliance of Youth Movements Summit \' and with his subsequent meetings with USG officials, on Capitol Hill, and with think tanks." In the document the unnamed Egyptian dissident expressed satisfaction with the support of other activists present at the State Department/corporate-sponsored "Alliance for Youth Movements." The document explained how the Egyptian "SSIS [internal intelligence] found and confiscated two documents in his luggage: notes for his presentation at the summit that described April 6's demands for democratic transition in Egypt, and a schedule of his Capitol Hill meetings." He met with Capitol Hill officials describing "his Washington appointments as positive, saying that on the Hill he met with xxxxxxxxxxxx, a variety of House staff members, including from the offices of xxxxxxxxxxxx and xxxxxxxxxxxx), and with two Senate staffers. xxxxxxxxxxxx also noted that he met with several think tank members. xxxxxxxxxxxx said that xxxxxxxxxxxx's office invited him to speak at a late January Congressional hearing on House Resolution 1303 regarding religious and political freedom in Egypt."

Although not providing more specific details for the regime change plan, it reveals the intimacy of April 6th and Washington officials. The unnamed dissident exhorts the US Senators and White House officials to oust Mubarak, comparing him to Robert Mugabe of Zimbabwe. When the decision for regional destabilization was made, Washington activated its close friends of the April 6th movement to create a climate of protests and tumult.

MUSLIM BROTHERHOOD AND POLITICAL ISLAM: STALWART WESTERN ALLY

Perhaps even more crucial to the Egyptian and MENA wide "Arab Spring" destabilization was the powerful Muslim Brotherhood. It is the world's foremost organization for political Islam. The group's breadth remains far-reaching with a cadre of influential Muslim clerics and scholars, and a cohesive structure of organization akin to a political party. The organization includes youth clubs, women's groups, electronic media, publications, and the sponsorship of paramilitary groups in flashpoints such as Algeria, Afghanistan, Libya, Syria, and Yemen. To actualize its Islamist ideology, it has a proclivity to seek the overthrow of existing regional governments. The group has routinely been involved in subversive and violent activities in the MENA region such as attempting to carry out and sanction assassinations against enemy political leaders. While the Western-trained and highly educated youth demonstrators could spearhead protests and encourage other discontented Egyptians to flood the streets, it was the Brotherhood that actually retained the requisite level of political organization and sophistication to seize power. Thus, the West would lean on the *Ikwhan* (Brotherhood) to govern in states where its sponsored coups were carried out.

This is no historical aberration. For many decades populist Islam has been used by Western governments as a bulwark against communism, an ideological counterpoise and battering ram against populist Pan-Arab nationalism, and a way to divert widespread anger at Western policies. Historically, the *Ikwhan* has been a partner of Western powers in these efforts, and even, at times, shockingly, with the state of Israel.[214] In fact, it was the West, the Eisenhower administration, the CIA, and British MI-6 who fostered its development and helped to build its international political profile to begin with.

Soon after it supplanted the Ottoman Empire as regional hegemon, the British Empire leveraged Islam for political purposes as an instrument to control Arabs. For example, it promoted and

---

[214] See Andrew Higgins, "How Israel Helped to Spawn Hamas," *Wall Street Journal*, January 24, 2009,
http://online.wsj.com/articles/SB111964664777469127

installed traditionalist Islamic religious figures as vassals to establish an aura of legitimacy for its rule. For the United States (who often seeks to emulate the British Empire) its first putative effective use of political Islam was at the onset of the Cold War, particularly during the Eisenhower administration. In their view, communism's often militant and virulent atheism was incompatible with Islam. In Eisenhower's calculus he could find an ally in political Islam. He readily embraced the Muslim Brotherhood. "We thought of Islam as a counterweight to communism," explained an American diplomat who met with Brotherhood officials at the time. Another veteran US diplomat stationed in Saudi Arabia in the late 1940s explained American officials in Cairo had "regular meetings" with the Muslim Brotherhood's founder Hassan al-Banna," and found him perfectly empathetic. "[215]

A mosque in Munich became a manifestation of the early American alliance with political Islam.[216] This Mosque in Germany had previously been the center of anti-Soviet propaganda during the apex of Nazi Germany's abortive attempt to conquer Eurasia. Recognizing a vulnerability of the USSR in its sizeable Muslim demographic, the Nazi regime used a cadre of Soviet Muslim defectors to disseminate anti-Soviet propaganda. After the war thousands of Soviet Muslims sought refuge in Munich, and established the Islamic Center of Munich. With the onset of the Cold War, they became a coveted prize for their language skills and contacts within the USSR. The CIA soon assumed the reins of the anti-Soviet program originally undertaken by the Nazis. Under the auspices of its organization "Amcomlib" (American Committee for the Liberation from Bolshevism)—one of the largest Cold War era propaganda operations—Robert H. Dreher of the CIA spearheaded the effort to use these former Nazi Munich Muslims for anti-Soviet purposes. Dreher also soon led the effort to use the Brotherhood ostensibly against Communism. With American backing, the Egyptian based Brotherhood established firm control over the

---

[215] Robert Dreyfuss, "Cold War, Holy Warrior," *Mother Jones*, http://www.motherjones.com/politics/2006/01/cold-war-holy-warrior
[216] "A Mosque in Munich," New America, https://www.youtube.com/watch?v=ZDuriZ68kuU

Munich Mosque (installing its members on the Center's board of directors) thereby creating a shelter and wellspring for political Islam.

Reportedly, the Brotherhood-American partnership was cemented in September 23, 1953 when Eisenhower met a delegation of Muslim dignitaries as part of a US government sponsored colloquium ostensibly on Islamic culture at Princeton University. In truth, power politics was at the heart of this American-Muslim confab. A now-declassified document reveals the true purpose of the meeting. "On the surface, the conference looks like an exercise in pure learning. This in effect is the impression desired, " it noted. The conference's true goal, was to "bring together persons exerting great influence in formulating Muslim opinion in fields such as education, science, law and philosophy and inevitably, therefore, on politics.... Among the various results expected from the colloquium are the impetus and direction that may be given to the Renaissance movement within Islam itself. "[217]

Among the delegates included the "honorable" Said Ramadan, the peripatetic de facto foreign minister and chief international organizer of the *Ikwhan*. In addition to his fervent opposition to communism because of its rejection of religion, Ramadan was fluent in English and also son-in-law to the Brotherhood's founder Hassan al-Banna. As an article in *Mother Jones* noted, "For an organization established as a secret society, with a paramilitary arm that was responsible for assassinations and violence, to be characterized as a harbinger of a rebirth of Islam may seem odd."[218] Indeed, by the CIA's own calculation Ramadan was described as a "Phalangist" and "fascist interested in the grouping of individuals for power." [219] Nevertheless, the CIA overtly began backing Ramadan[220] and the Brotherhood.

---

[217] Dreyfuss, "Cold War."
[218] Ibid.
[219] Ian Johnson, "Washington's Secret History with the Muslim Brotherhood," NY Review of Books, February 5, 2011,
http://www.nybooks.com/blogs/nyrblog/2011/feb/05/washingtons-secret-history-muslim-brotherhood/
[220] For further on the Ramadan-CIA connection see "Context of "1988: Al Taqwa Bank Co-Founder Is Long-time CIA Asset"
http://www.historycommons.org/context.jsp?item=a1988saidramadan

The CIA, MI-6, and Eisenhower administration soon found the *Ikwhan* and political Islam a useful tool against the revolutionary government and movement of Gamal Abdel Nasser in Egypt. The Eisenhower administration had initially enjoyed a brief period of cooperation with Nasser who came to power in 1952. With Nasser's nationalist orientation and fervent promotion of secular Pan-Arabism in the region though, he came to be viewed as unacceptable to US and British hegemony. The account of Miles Copeland, CIA operative based in Egypt, explains that opposition to Nasser was driven by the commercial community — the oil companies and the financial establishment.[221] Their ideological opposition to Nasser's secular Arab nationalist movement was also rooted in the direct threat posed to their anachronistic Western client regimes. Setting a precedent ominous for the imperialist powers, Nasser overthrew King Farouk, a monarch beholden to the moribund British Empire. Moreover, the secular nature and socialist component of Nasserism meant its cooperation with the USSR could not be precluded. For the neuralgically anti-communist Americans this was an eventuality they found anathema.

The broad regional appeal and promotion of Nasserism meant a counterpoise had to be developed. The US and British found this in the *Ikwhan*. British MI6 and the CIA jointly devised plans for Nasser's assassination and intensified its cooperation with the Brotherhood to destroy Nasser and undercut Nasserism. Quickly, the group was outlawed and denounced as a tool of the British by Nasser following an abortive attempt on his own life. The following years see a struggle pitting Nasser against the Muslim Brotherhood as a proxy of the US and British. The CIA noted that it funneled support to the group because of "the Brotherhood's commendable capability to overthrow Nasser."[222]

The West's cooperation with the Muslim Brotherhood and political Islam did not end with Nasser's death and the gradual

---

[221] "1954-1970: CIA and the Muslim Brotherhood Ally to Oppose Egyptian President Nasser," History Commons, http://www.historycommons.org/context.jsp?item=western_support_for_i slamic_militancy_202700#western_support_for_islamic_militancy_202700
[222] Ibid.

waning of Nasserism regionally. For the furtherance of its geopolitical imperatives, it continues a fruitful relationship with the Brotherhood and political Islam well after this period. After Nasser is succeeded in Egypt by Anwar Sadat, who eventually adopts a pro-American orientation, he promises *sharia* (Islamic law) will be implemented as the law of the land. Sadat purges the Egyptian government of Nasserites and frees Muslim Brotherhood prisoners. Political Islam begins to reemerge in Egypt, and an Islamic banking system is created, allowing for a wellspring of militant, radical Islamist movements. The Brotherhood issues an official statement ordering its members to support pro-market economic reforms encouraged by the International Monetary Fund. The draconian nature of these policies—which often include the precipitous breakup of the state sector economy and slashing of staple subsidies—produces a destabilizing effect on society (see Part II), and are to the benefit of Western multinational corporations.[223] These policies would also provide groundwork for the destabilization of 2011.

In the period preceding the Soviet invasion into Afghanistan, the CIA founded the Asia Foundation to fund leaders of the Afghan Islamist movement at Kabul University. Members of this organization soon clandestinely infiltrated the Afghan armed forces and later helped spearhead jihad forces with Osama bin Laden against the Soviet army. Because of his Soviet-friendly orientation, after Afghan prime minister Sardar Daoud overthrew the royal family becoming president, the US started to support and fund Afghan dissidents including the radical Islamic Party. The CIA, Iranian, and Pakistani intelligence, which was associated with Islamist fundamentalist groups, then carried out raids and an abortive coup against Daoud.[224]

The Brotherhood is later identified as leaders of the insurgency against President Daoud. Following the rebellion's failure, Brotherhood leaders such as Gulbuddin Hekmatyar and Rabani

[223] Melanie Colburn, "America's Devil's Game with Extremist Islam," *Mother Jones*, January/February 2006 Issue, http://www.motherjones.com/politics/2006/01/americas-devils-game-extremist-islam
[224] Ibid.

Sayyaf—members funded by the CIA's Asia Foundation—fled to Pakistan with support from Pakistani ISI. In backing these anti-communist fundamentalist groups, the United States was fully cognizant it was backing the Muslim Brotherhood. It was "recorded by many State Department and embassy memos, including one from CENTO that directly warned the Muslim Brotherhood was a rebellious threat to new regimes."[225] Following the secret directive of Carter regime NSC director Zbigniew Brezinski authorizing covert CIA aid to the Afghan muhjadeen, American officials visited Egypt to gain Arab support for the Afghan war: "Within weeks Egyptian President Anwar Sadat mobilizes arms and recruits fighters from the Muslim Brotherhood, and allows the US to station its air force base in Egypt. U.S. Special Forces train Islamist militants in bomb making, sabotage, arson and guerilla warfare. Many of the Islamist Arab recruits, including Osama bin Laden, who were trained as fighters by Green Berets and Navy Seals for the Afghan War, would go on to form the backbone of Al-Qaeda."[226]

The organization's ruthlessness was demonstrated in Algeria in 1989 when the Islamic Salvation Front (FIS) was established as a new political party. It originated from elements of American-sponsored Islamist movements of the period. Its members included many of the Muslim Brotherhood as well as Afghan war veterans. Algeria was subsequently plunged into civil war and entered a period known as the "black decade." In Afghanistan the US continued its cooperative relationship with the Taliban, and in 1997 and 1999 Taliban members visited Nebraska to see CIA-funded propagandist Thomas Gouttierre, "who produces children's textbooks stocked with Islamic fundamentalist and jihadist rhetoric for supposed State Department educational programs in Afghanistan and Pakistan."[227]

Following the September 11 attacks, the US initially adopted a posture of going after the Brotherhood, declaring some key members supporters of terrorism. By the second Bush second term however, it had reversed course. By 2005 "the State Department launched an

---

[225] Ibid.
[226] Ibid.
[227] Ibid.

effort to woo the Brotherhood."[228] The CIA also notably pushed for cooperation, with a CIA analysis from 2006 lauding the Brotherhood as exhibiting "impressive internal dynamism, organization, and media savvy."[229] With the coming of the Obama presidency, this policy was not altered, and his administration carried over some of the people from the Bush administration responsible for devising this strategy. The *Hindu* reported that Obama turned to the Brotherhood's most influential sheik Youssef Qaradawi as a mediator with the Afghan Taliban.[230] Reportedly, members of the Obama administration held ties to the Brotherhood itself. This included Imam Mohamed Magid, Department of Homeland Security Countering Violent Extremism Working Group Member, president of the Islamic Society of North America (ISNA) whose parent organization is the Muslim Students Association, a Muslim Brotherhood affiliate; as well as Huma Abedin, Secretary of State Hillary Clinton's deputy chief of staff, whose brother Hassan Abedin sits in on the board of the Oxford Centre of Islamic Studies along with influential Brotherhood sheikh Qaradawi. Huma's mother Saleha Abedin is board member of the International Islamic Council for Dawa and Relief affiliated with the Union for Good led by the Brotherhood's Qaradawi.[231] In Egypt she is regarded as a dangerous Muslim Brotherhood subversive. Thus, at the advent of the CIA/State Department sponsored "Arab Spring" offensive, the stage was set to once again lean on the *Ikwahn* to support American regional policy. The Brotherhood called for Mubarak's resignation and mobilized in the streets.

TAHRIR SQUARE PROTESTS IMPOTENT

In Egypt, after being schooled by Serbia's "Otpor!" in AEI tactics, the April 6th and Kifaya "revolutionaries-in-waiting," in Brzezinski's parlance, took to the streets in Egypt. Their efforts were supplemented by general malcontents and the Muslim Brotherhood.

---

[228] Johnson, "Secret History."
[229] Ibid.
[230] PRAVEEN SWAMI, "Mediator in Taliban-U.S. talks backed Kashmir jihad," *The Hindu*, December 29, 2011,
http://www.thehindu.com/news/article2755817.ece
[231] International Islamic Forum for Dialogue,
http://www.dialogueonline.org/brief.htm

Consistent with Brzezinski's analysis, the internet-oriented youth utilized the unprecedented potential for self-organization afforded by internet interconnectivity and mass communication technology. According government figures, internet users in Egypt were over a quarter of the population or 23.06 million by the end of October 2010. Meanwhile, the number of cell phone users reached 65.49 million during the same period. Opposition groups circulated SMS messages and posted appeals on social networking sites such as Facebook and Twitter to spread demonstrations.[232]

The protests in Egypt were generally thought to be peaceful in nature, but violence was widespread as a tactic to combat police. In fact, violent clashes between protestors and security forces resulted in at least 846 people killed and over 6,000 injured.[233] "Protestors" burned over 90 police stations and buildings associated with the ruling National Democratic Party. One protest participant described how after police responded with teargas, protestors threw stones at police.[234] Mohamed Gamal Bashir, a former member of a soccer group, describes how violence against police and the burning of police stations was central to the success of the "revolution." Bashir speaks of a group called "harafish," youth with no prospects that often skirt the edge of the law. He claimed they burnt police stations in their neighborhoods in response to decades of police oppression. "The power of this revolution came from these *harafish* burning police stations and from the collapse of the Interior Ministry. That was utilized by the political elites who centralized the struggle in Tahrir Square. Without this confrontation, the revolution wouldn't have been possible, and every police station was burnt to the ground because people have been dying inside them for years. There is a veneer of nonviolence but no one saw the battles in Suez and

[232] "Egypt protests a ticking time bomb: Analysts," January 27, 2011 http://www.thenewage.co.za/8894-1007-53-Egypt_protests_a_ticking_time_bomb_Analysts
[233] "Egypt: Cairo's Tahrir Square fills with protesters," BBC, July 8, 2011, http://www.bbc.co.uk/news/world-middle-east-14075493
[234] Abdel-Rahman Hussein," Was the Egyptian revolution really non-violent?" EgyptIndependent.com, January 24, 2012, http://www.egyptindependent.com/news/was-egyptian-revolution-really-non-violent

elsewhere—How is it peaceful when people are dying in the streets?" he added.[235]

Despite the mass protests and violence though, the regime of Mubarak remained firmly in power. The youth movements had no real mass political organization capable of seizing power. In a country of 80 million it could muster a few hundred thousand for protests at most. As Joshua Stacher reported for *Foreign Affairs* on February 7th, 2011, "Contrary to the dominant media narrative, over the last ten days the Egyptian state has not experienced a regime breakdown. The protests have certainly rocked the system and have put Mubarak on his heels, but at no time has the uprising seriously threatened Mubarak's regime."[236] The mass protests were incapable of shaking the regime. This was because as Eric Trager of *Foreign Affairs* noted, "The Army...is the backbone of the regime."[237] In fact, every Egyptian president since 1953 was an army officer. Throughout the ranks, Trager noted, "the message from the ruling military elite was clear, united, [and] fully supportive of Mubarak." Trager added "no acts of organizational fragmentation or dissent within the chain of command have occurred." Without the ability to break the power of the military that supported Mubarak, or co-opting them, the control of the regime could not be broken. It took pressure from the mighty US, the unipolar power and his erstwhile patron, to break the power of Mubarak.

MUBARAK OUSTED BY US-BACKED
MILITARY COUP AND PRESSURE

The impotent protestors in Tahrir Square were reduced to political props in the foreground. As they absorbed all corporate media attention, the real developments were happening in the background. Mubarak's eventual decision to step down was the result of pressure from a US-backed coup d'état driven by two figures within the Egyptian military: Chief of Staff Sami Hafez Enan and Defense Minister Field Marshal Muhammad Hussein Tantawi. This was also

---

[235] Ibid.
[236] Joshua Stacher, "Egypt's Democratic Mirage: How Cairo's Authoritarian Regime is Adapting to Preserve Itself," ForeignAffairs.com, February 7, 2011.
[237] Eric Trager, "Letter from Cairo: The People's Military in Egypt?" ForeignAffairs.com, January 30, 2011.

likely coupled with consideration of the vulnerabilities of the Suez Canal or the critical grain subsidy received from the US. These two figures—Enan and Tantawi—would later take the reins of governing in a US-backed military junta.

Geopolitical analyst Dr. Webster G. Tarpley observed, "There never was an 'Egyptian revolution,' but rather a behind-the-scenes military putsch by a junta of CIA puppet generals who evidently could not succeed in their goal of ousting Hosni Mubarak without the help of a heavy-duty ultimatum from Washington in the night between Thursday, February 10 and Friday, February 11, 2011."[238] On February 10th the Obama team exerted pressure on sectors of the Egyptian military urging Mubarak to step down. President Obama— head of state of the world's preeminent power—called for Mubarak to step down, abandoning America's longstanding support. On February 10th it was leaked that Egypt's Supreme Military Council had come together in the absence of Mubarak and issued a statement labeled "first" communiqué. It stated they would allow for a peaceful post-Mubarak transition. It appeared Mubarak capitulated. But this was the transition preferred by Mubarak himself, not the immediate ouster demanded by hardliners and the US. The Associated Press characterized it as a "soft coup."

Revealing the CIA's intimacy with the coup, CIA director Leon Panetta told a hearing of the House Intelligence Committee there was a "high likelihood" Mubarak would be ousted. President Obama prematurely declared, "history [is] taking place." "The people of Egypt have spoken, their voices have been heard." With these developments Mubarak was expected to issue a speech in which he would resign. He did not.[239]

---

[238] Webster G. Tarpley, "Mubarak Toppled By CIA," February 18, 2011, http://tarpley.net/2011/02/18/mubarak-toppled-by-cia-because-he-opposed-us-plans-for-war-with-iran/
[239] "Mubarak's defiance surprised US and threatened chaos'
CIA officials say they learned of army's plan to remove Mubarak, though Egyptian president decided last minute to change the ending," *Jerusalem Post* by *Associated Press*, February 12, 2011, http://www.jpost.com/Middle-East/Mubaraks-defiance-surprised-US-and-threatened-chaos

Instead, Mubarak issued a statement on Egyptian state television. His defiant message was that he would remain in office until a successor was elected in September. This produced surprise and consternation among the American establishment and in Tahrir Square. On CNN Fareed Zakaria lamented that the Egyptian military had now definitively chosen the side of Mubarak by granting him the long transition to September he wanted. Washington insider David Gergen indignantly bellowed that Mubarak's defiance should not be allowed to stand. President Obama was incensed at the initial failure of his putsch initiative. The *New York Times* reported that after news of Mubarak's decision to move towards a September transition, "Mr. Obama was furious." "Mr. Obama was demanding that change in Egypt begin right away." The president was "seething about coverage that made it look as if the administration were protecting a dictator and ignoring the pleas of the youths of Cairo."[240] Obama assembled his national security team in the Oval Office to discuss his public response, choosing language "that more clearly than ever" placed "the White House on the side of the demonstrators." The final version began: "The Egyptian people have been told that there was a transition of authority, but it is not yet clear that this transition is immediate, meaningful or sufficient." "It unmistakably aligned us with the aspirations of the people in Tahrir Square," a senior administration official involved in the White House meeting remarked.

Based on Egyptian accounts *Al-Arabiya* described the events that transpired to upset expectations. Mubarak was prepared to step down, but his son Gamal intervened:

> A heated argument broke out between Alaa and Gamal Mubarak, the two sons of the former Egyptian president, inside the presidential palace last Thursday during the recording of their father's last speech to the nation, Egypt's government-owned *al-Akhbar* newspaper reported on Sunday. Hosni Mubarak reportedly was supposed to announce his resignation in a speech that the military sent to

---

[240] Helene Cooper, Mark Landler, et al., "In U.S. Signals to Egypt, Obama Straddled a Rift," *New York Times*, February 12, 2011, http://www.nytimes.com/2011/02/13/world/middleeast/13diplomacy.ht ml?pagewanted=1&_r=2&hp

him on Thursday but his son Gamal and senior officials in his entourage pressed him to deliver a different speech in which he insisted on staying in power until September. The newspaper said Gamal lost his temper after he heard the recording of the speech that his father was supposed to deliver that night and in which he was going to declare stepping down. According to the report, American officials were aware of that recording but they did not know that Gamal had prompted his father to discard it and record a different speech, which was delivered that night. Earlier in that day U.S. President Barack Obama had told an audience in Michigan that "we are witnessing history unfold," a sign that Mubarak was stepping down. Hours later, President Obama heard something perplexing: Mubarak was not quitting. Obama apparently did not know that Mubarak's resignation speech was discarded by Mubarak's son in the last minute.[241]

Consequently, the US establishment was surprised and Mr. Obama apoplectic when Mubarak decided to remain in power as implored by of his son Gamal. This turn of events did not conform to the script. With its "first" communiqué the military establishment chose to maintain support for Mubarak. Following Gamal's intervention, they indicated they would not end support for Mubarak's own transition plan. Echoing these sentiments, their second military communiqué was issued on the same day Mubarak stepped down. In it they reiterated endorsement of Mubarak's plan for a gradual transition into September or October, supervised by Mubarak himself. The *Times of India* reported:

> Egyptian military today came out in support of a beleaguered President and asked protesters to go home, assuring them of free and fair elections in September and the lifting of a much-hated emergency law, in a stand that caused widespread disappointment among the people who pledged to take their campaign to its "final stage." As the powerful military

---

[241] "Gamal Mubarak convinced his father to change his last TV speech and to refuse to quit," AlArabiya.net, February 13, 2011, http://www.alarabiya.net/articles/2011/02/13/137490.html

unexpectedly threw its weight behind Hosni Mubarak, tens of thousands of angry people converged again on the streets and vowed to take the protest to the "doorsteps of political institutions." This dispatch continues: "As Mubarak dashed hopes of millions of his countrymen and global expectations by refusing to step down, the military Supreme Command Council met twice in less than 24 hours before announcing that it supported Mubarak's move to transfer some of his powers to Vice President Omar Suleiman. Egyptian state-television interrupted its programme to read out the Council's 'communiqué number 2' in which it vowed to lift the much-criticised emergency laws in the country, without specifying a date and said it would guarantee 'free and fair elections' in September, as outlined by Mubarak. But, in what appeared to be a warning to protesters, who for 18 days have been calling Mubarak to stand down after three decades in power, the military asked them to go home and get back to work.[242]

After Mubarak's initial defiance — with the military establishment behind him — he capitulated to US pressure and stepped down. The specific reason is murky, but two reasons *can* be ruled out: (1) that Mubarak departed as a result of mass protests. These were demonstrably impotent and ineffective, devoid of the ability to seize power or effectively alter the institutions that held power; (2) that the military establishment alone — whose support was indispensable for the regime's power — urged him to step down; this argument is vitiated by their "second" communiqué that established the military would continue to support Mubarak. Moreover, communiqué two was issued just before it was announced Mubarak would make an important speech, meaning their support was within the timeframe of his abdication. Dr. Webster G. Tarpley observes:

> The US theory of the indigenous coup will therefore have to explain why, if the Egyptian generals had turned against Mubarak in the night between Thursday and Friday, they still

gathered on Friday morning to proclaim and publish their continued support for the incumbent president. All indications are that the Egyptian generals, including the CIA puppets, were as surprised as the rest of the world when Mubarak announced that he was leaving. The military had proven itself incapable of forcing this decision. There must therefore have been some outside force which acted directly on Mubarak and induced him to tender his resignation on his own power. Given the nature of current world affairs, that power could only have been the United States, perhaps with some help from the British.

There was some other factor at play. Dr. Tarpley surmises it was a threat to the Suez Canal, Mubarak's family, or to the critical grain subsidy.[243]

In any case, the effort to oust Mubarak—from CIA/NED fostered street demonstrations to US-backed military generals—was a US-led effort for regime change. The two generals who led the drive to oust Mubarak regularly interfaced with the US side. In fact, Sami Hafez Enan, the Egyptian Army Chief of Staff, was present in Washington meeting with Pentagon officials when the US coup effort began. Voice of America reported, "When the demonstrations in Egypt began last week, the second-ranking Egyptian military officer was in Washington for a week of meetings with senior American officers. Lieutenant General Sami Anan cut his visit short and returned home on Friday."[244] While *Reuters* reported his counterpart Field Marshal Tantawi "has spoken with U.S. Defense Secretary Robert Gates by phone five times since the crisis began, including as late as on Thursday evening." [245] Defense Minister Tantawi, who would

[243] Tarpley, "Mubarak Toppled."
[244] Al Pessin ,"US-Egypt Military Relationship Might Impact Crisis," January 30, 2011 http://www.voanews.com/english/news/usa/US-Egypt-Military-Relationship-Might-Impact-Crisis-114979569.html
[245] "Egypt's Future After Revolution: Mohamed Hussein Tantawi, Interim Military Leader, Resistant To Change," Reuters, May 25, 2011, http://www.huffingtonpost.com/2011/02/11/egypt-military-resistant-change_n_822022.html

eventually lead the military junta interim government, early on developed a rift with Mubarak *Al-Arabiya* reported.[246]

That the Enan and Tantawi effort was US sponsored was confirmed in a *Washington Post* interview with a longtime Egyptian dissident. Lally Weymouth, senior editor at the *Post*, interviewed Saad Eddin Ibrahim, a longtime regime dissident who had once been tortured by the regime, in Cairo. Ibrahim told Weymouth:

> **The Egyptian chief of staff [Enan] on orders from the White House was escalating the pressure. President Obama's advisers, who are good friends—Samantha Power and Michael McFaul**—asked me to come [to Washington]. They relied on me as a source... After Mubarak's second speech, Obama became convinced [Mubarak had to step down].[247] [Emphasis added.]

Eddin revealed that his "good friends" Samantha Power and Michael McFaul—both of the National Security Council—were ordering chief of staff Enan, who was present in Washington when the crisis began, to pressure Mubarak. Mubarak's departure is thus revealed to be another Washington-backed coup, a far cry from the repeated media narrative of an idealistic youth-led revolution towards "democracy." In the aftermath, these military generals would continue to lead for an interim period before US ally the Muslim Brotherhood seized the reins of power. Despite mass media hype, the mass protestors sponsored by Washington were impotent, having achieved little. In truth, there was no Egyptian revolution, only a coup d'état directed from Washington by President Obama, Michael McFaul (who went on to become ambassador to Russia) and Samantha Power of the National Security Council. The Obama team successfully demonstrated the effectiveness of soft and civilian-based power for regime change.

---

[246] *New Arab Revolts*, 81.
[247] "In Egypt, a revolution with an asterisk," *Washington Post*, May 22, 2011, http://www.washingtonpost.com/opinions/in-egypt-a-revolution-with-an- asterisk/2011/05/20/AF0W3M9G_story.html

PART FOUR: THE NEW HUMANITARIAN IMPERIALISM.

THE OFFENSIVE AGAINST LIBYA

The only important intellectual difference between neoconservatives and liberal interventionists is that the former have disdain for international institutions (which they see as constraints on U.S. power), and the latter see them as a useful way to legitimate American dominance. Both groups extol the virtues of democracy, both groups believe that U.S. power—and especially its military power—can be a highly effective tool of statecraft.[248]
—Stephen Walt

There is no evidence.
—Dr. Slimon Bouchuiguir, Libyan League for Human Rights

Remaining recalcitrant Colonel Muammar Qaddafi ruled Libya for over four decades. Since his 1969 bloodless coup he presided over progressive changes in the country. In a conciliatory approach during his later years, he pragmatically granted concessions to the West in an attempt to adjust to the American-dominated unipolar world order. This *modus vivendi* was short-lived, and was soon met with Western duplicity. As they had demonized him as the "mad dog" since the Reagan years, and included Libya among its list of "rogue" states, it was no surprise when the US and the West sought his ouster in 2011. In fact, for nearly forty years the US actively worked towards this end.

In the current historical context—a period of pronounced restructuring of the international order with a diminishing of continued unilateral US dominance—the need to extirpate Qaddafi increased. With shifting dynamics on the African continent—the US

---

[248] Stephen Walt, "What intervention in Libya tells us about the Liberal neocon Alliance," *Foreign Policy*, March 21, 2011,
http://foreignpolicy.com/2011/03/21/what-intervention-in-libya-tells-us-about-the-neocon-liberal-alliance/

attempting to undercut an increased Chinese presence with US AFRICOM (Africa Command) — an unmanageable Pan-Africanist such as Qaddafi stewarding Africa was anathema. Qaddafi"s pan-African posture on the continent undercut US future designs for a strategic confrontation with increasing Chinese presence. His recent dealings with Russia for infrastructure and increased economic cooperation with China was also unacceptable. With Libya's economic and security cooperation with Egypt, it was also a critical link for the overall Arab position. Qaddafi also supported some of the most militant Palestinian groups against Israel, earning the ire of the neoconservative ilk. Economically, Libya was free from the dominion of Wall Street and the Western banking cartel while seeking to promote a similar condition for the multitude of economically exploited states on the African continent. Libya's abundant financial assets were ripe to be looted.[249] Furthermore, but not least of all considerations, Libya had some of the world's largest sources of untapped oil and natural gas which the neo-colonialists were covetous of. Because of these reasons, and historically recalcitrant tendencies, Qaddafi "had to go."

To smash the Libyan state, the next phase of the West's "Arab Spring" offensive represented a new direction. Whereas the earlier regime changes were, in effect, behind-the-scenes coups d'état supported by the "color revolution" template, when it reached Libya emphasis shifted to humanitarian imperialism coupled with the use of irregular armies. This was no Twitter revolution. In fact, Islamist extremists, including of the al-Qaeda grouping, were a crucial part of these Western-backed irregular armies.

Humanitarian imperialism is a brand of imperialism which uses an ostensible "humanitarian" concern or the "protection of civilians" as a pretext for imperialist assaults. Regardless of the new external trappings of this method, at its core, it is the same imperialism. With this tenuous "humanitarian" pretext, a direct, brutal, and ruthless military assault by NATO (North Atlantic Treaty Organization) and Qatar against Libya was carried out. This joint NATO-Qatari assault on a sovereign state was a textbook example of eminent historian

---

[249] See Manillo Danucci, "Financial Heist of the Century: Confiscating Libya's Sovereign Wealth Funds (SWF)," http://www.globalresearch.ca/financial-heist-of-the-century-confiscating-libya-s-sovereign- wealth-funds-swf/24479

Carroll Quigley's observation that in the "age of conflicts" "vested interests encourage the growth of imperialists wars" often with an "excuse" rather than a "cause."

With horrid human rights records of their own, the West and Qatar cynically cited concern for the safety of civilians. Economic sanctions and direct military intervention were enacted under this justification to smash the Libyan state. Quickly maneuvering at the UNSC (United Nations Security Council) — at a speed even outpacing the drive to smash the Iraqi state — Western powers pushed for the authorization of a military assault with their tenuous humanitarian pretext. Under the RtoP ("Responsibility to Protect") doctrine — and with the acquiescence of Russia and China — UNSC Resolution 1973 was passed authorizing military intervention under the mandate to "protect civilians" by "all means." In this way, the UN — whose role is ostensibly to promote international peace and security while respecting the sovereignty of nations — provided a legal legitimacy to the offensive. This was perfectly congruent with the new "soft power" emphasis of the Obama presidency.

In the aftermath of UNSC Resolution 1973, no such actions to protect civilians were carried out. The opposite occurred. NATO soon proceeded with a ruthless bombing campaign to topple the Qaddafi regime completely. Brushing aside the enumerated restrictions of the UN mandate, NATO and Qatar provided weapons; sent special forces on the ground to direct anti-Qaddafi rebels and jihadists; carried out targeted assassinations; facilitated acts of ethnic cleansing against black Libyans and pro-Qaddafi civilians; bombed civilian population centers and vital infrastructure with no military utility; cut off food and medical equipment for civilians; and allowed black Libyan civilians and migrant worker refugees to die at sea. These actions contravened both the spirit and letter of the UNSC resolution, itself of dubious legality.

Similar to the other Western-backed regime changes in the "Arab Spring," the groundwork was prepared by dubious Western financed and created NGOs in the orbit of the US intelligence community, albeit in a more novel approach. The Western offensive against Libya eschewed the "civilian-based power" approach because this template would be ineffective in Libya. Instead, it opted for a more militarily oriented operation from its onset. NGOs in the

Libyan offensive acted as propaganda outlets, censuring the Qaddafi regime for alleged human rights violations to justify the humanitarian imperialist attack. These groups made fraudulent or largely exaggerated claims against Qaddafi's government, presenting claims of widespread human rights violations. The dubious evidence of these NGOs was presented to the UNSC as evidence of a humanitarian catastrophe. In an act of malfeasance, the UN's High Commission for Human Rights unquestioningly accepted fatuous and hyperbolic claims of anti-Libyan Arab news networks such as al-Arabiya and Qatar's al-Jazeera as truthful. These media outlets, and NGOs, were regurgitating unfounded claims of the mendacious Libyan opposition.

This effort was accompanied by a massive Western and Arab media and diplomatic offensive which vilified Muammar Qaddafi, his Jamahiriya government, and ennobled the Libyan rebels as champions of "human rights" and "democracy." In reality, the uprising against Qaddafi was violent from the beginning and the Western-sponsored NGOs would later admit they had "no evidence" for their claims. Rebels slaughtered Libyan military and security forces at bases to seize their weapons. These deaths were then, paradoxically, explained as having been committed by the Libyan government itself, under the narrative that military personnel refused to attack civilians. In truth, rebels engaged in limitless brutality and were guilty of massive human rights violations themselves, being anything but democrats. In the ensuing Western facilitated civil war they were given carte blanche for wanton slaughter. This was most egregious in cities such as Sirte and Tawergha, which were ethnically cleansed.

Once direct Western military intervention was underway, the media's propaganda offensive also served to demoralize the Libyan people resisting the Western offensive. This made the media campaign an extension of the military offensive. In particular, Qatar's al-Jazeera, played a crucial role in demoralizing the Libyan national forces in the battle for Tripoli, capitol city and stronghold of the Libyan government.

Similar to other campaigns guided by the "Responsibility to Protect" (RtoP) doctrine, reality was presented in a simplistic Manichean good against evil dynamic in which the "bad guy" Muammar Qaddafi had to be defeated by the forces of good: the US,

NATO, and the champions of freedom and democracy, the Libyan rebels. This was a fatuous, partial, and self-serving understanding of the Libyan crisis. In this way, the situation was divorced from the complexities of political, geostrategic, social, and diplomatic realities. But by resisting—until his last breath—Qaddafi exposed the brutal reality of the West's so-called "Arab Spring," with unrelenting NATO aerial bombing, predator drones, tomahawk missiles, assassinations, neo-colonial Western special forces on the ground, and most troublingly solidarity and collaboration with Islamist extremists. It became clear there was nothing to romanticize.

DEMONIZING QADDAFI AS THE "MAD DOG"

In analyzing the Libyan uprising it is important to dispel commonly inculcated myths about Qaddafi and his rule over Libya. Muammar Qaddafi was, for the majority of his rule, in conflict with the West and in his later years initiated a shaky rapprochement. The West's duplicity ensured it continued to favor "regime change," creating a tendency to demonize the leader. During the uprising both Western and Arab media unquestioningly relayed self-serving Libyan opposition and US government propaganda. For those seeking understanding of unfolding events, these propaganda attacks from mainstream media ensured the Libyan crisis was more readily viewed from the lens of the West and its allies.

Continuing the trend of decades of entrenched anti-Qaddafi propaganda, throughout the uprising mainstream media, Western and Arab officials, coupled with Libyan opposition, continually demonized Qaddafi. With well-nigh unanimous consensus, he was characterized as a brutal thug devoid of the capability or legitimacy to lead Libya any longer. There was no shortage of invective against the embattled leader when the uprising began. The *New York Times* characterized him as a "thug and a murderer." [250] His Libyan government was called a "vicious regime," "murderous regime," and more. John Kerry, then of the Senate Foreign Relations Committee,

---

[250] Editorial, "At War in Libya," *New York Times*, March 21, 2011, http://www.nytimes.com/2011/03/22/opinion/22tue1.html?_r=0.

derided him as a "thug who is killing Muslims."[251] Congressman Steve Rothman referred to him a "brutish thug," while President Obama denounced him as "a tyrant." Although Qaddafi's rule was far from ideal, these purely negative and Manichean characterizations do not correspond to reality.

Before the 2011 crisis even, he was a common Western bête noire. Demonized as the "mad dog," Libya during his leadership was subject to bombing and economic warfare. For decades, the West carefully crafted a vilified image of Qaddafi. The conception of Qaddafi as a "murderer" in the Western consciousness largely relies on his alleged sponsorship of the 1988 Lockerbie bombing in which 270 Pan Am Flight 103 passengers and crew were killed. He is also blamed for the 1986 Labelle Discotheque bombing in Berlin, Germany where 3 people were killed and 270 injured.

On the basis of these claims, Qaddafi has long been categorized as an enemy of the US. President Ronald Reagan ordered an aerial bombing attack on Libya at the time with Qaddafi's alleged sponsorship of these attacks as justification. This attack killed his young daughter and resulted in the deaths of dozens of people, mostly civilians. For Libyan culpability in the bombing of the West Berlin nightclub, President Reagan dubbed Qaddafi the "mad dog of the Middle East." Furthermore, he announced with certitude, "our evidence is direct, it is precise, it is irrefutable."[252] In reality, evidence of Libya's direct involvement was dubious and never presented to the world.

In later years Qaddafi made a pragmatic move to normalize relations with the US and the West. Libya made a perfunctory gesture of accepting responsibility for the bombing. It agreed to pay $2.7 billion to families of victims of the Lockerbie bombing and in other attacks. Libya however "did not admit guilt" and "made it clear that they were simply taking a practical step toward restoring

---

[251] John F. Kerry, "A no-fly zone for Libya," *Washington Post*, March 11, 2011, http://www.washingtonpost.com/wp-dyn/content/article/2011/03/10/AR2011031004684.html
[252] "Address to the Nation on the United States Air Strike Against Libya April 14, 1986," http://www.reagan.utexas.edu/archives/speeches/1986/41486g.htm

ties with the West." [253] Qaddafi's son Saif explained in a CNN interview, representing the Libyan government's view, the alleged perpetrator was "innocent." Upon further examination, it is clear the case against Libya was tendentious and politically driven; the evidence of Qaddafi's complicity is flawed and fraudulent.

Reagan's assertion of "irrefutable evidence" vis-à-vis the Berlin attack is based on alleged interceptions of communications between Tripoli, Libyan capital, and the Libyan embassy in East Berlin. Reagan declared Qaddafi sent orders to the embassy "to conduct a terrorist attack against Americans, to cause maximum and indiscriminate casualties." [254] These cables referred to are, at most, interpretations and paraphrases and there were disputes as to their meaning. The complete, unedited, and literal texts of the communications were never released to the public. The cables were intercepted by the National Security Agency (NSA) and decoded through the assistance of German intelligence, the BND, which had earlier broken Libyan code. When the cables were decoded, Germany's *Der Spiegel* reported that the content of the cables were not clear and there were differing versions. The NSA and German BND also came to different conclusions about the meaning of the messages. Regardless, "these disagreements were quickly pushed aside for political reasons." [255] The German security officials cautioned against "premature accusations," and also insisted that Libya should not be the only focus of investigation. The German officials were also looking into rival disco competitors and drug dealers. A senior official in Bonn, the West German capital, explained to investigative journalist Seymour Hersh the German government remained "very critical and skeptical" of the American position linking Libya exclusively to the bombing. Moreover, Hersh reported, "Some White House officials had immediate doubts that the case

---

[253] "An Erratic Leader, Brutal and Defiant to the End," *New York Times*, October 20, 2011,
http://www.nytimes.com/2011/10/21/world/africa/qaddafi-killed-as-hometown-falls-to-libyan-rebels.html?pagewanted=all
[254] "Address to the Nation."
[255] Blum, *Killing Hope*, 281-289.

against Libya was clear-cut."[256] The discotheque was also a hangout place for black American soldiers and Libya is not likely to have targeted blacks and other minorities, given Qaddafi's pro-African posture.

Moreover, it was later uncovered that there was Western and Israeli intelligence involvement. The German prosecutor Detlev Mehlis relied on the testimony of Eter Mushad to indict the Libyans in question. It was subsequently discovered by the German television channel ZDF that Eter was a false witness and a CIA agent. Meanwhile, Mahammed Aamir, the individual who planted the bomb, was an agent of the Mossad.[257]

The evidence against Libya for the explosion of PanAm Flight 103 is equally shaky. Originally, five months after the tragedy, the State Department announced the CIA was "confident" the perpetrators were part of the Popular Front for the Liberation of Palestine-General Command (PFLP-GC) based in Syria. This remained a fixed judgment by the US. Then — after Syria was poised to join the coalition to go to war against Iraq in 1990 — US officials claimed they had new evidence of the culpability of Libyan intelligence. Two Libyan officials were subsequently indicted in absentia.

The only evidence presented was shaky: two small pieces of metal allegedly from electronic timing devices. In December 1993 a program aired by the BBC "Silence Over Lockerbie," presented new findings, casting doubt on Libyan culpability and suggesting the US and UK blamed Libya to shift blame away from Syrian based rogues or Iran.[258] The Swiss manufacturer of the electronic devices used recanted his earlier story that only Libya bought the electronic devices. Some, he remembered, were purchased by East Germany. There were strong connections between the Syrian-based PFLP-GC and the Communist East German secret police. An engineer with the Swiss company also stated he explained to East German connection with the PFLP-GC to investigators. A German prosecutor Volcker

[256] Ibid.
[257] Thierry Meyssan, "The lynching of Muammar Gaddafi," Voltairenet.org http://www.voltairenet.org/article171731.html#nh2
[258] Blum, *Killing Hope*, 281-89.

Rath, specializing in Lockerbie, declared, "No German judge could, with the present evidence, put the two suspects into jail."[259]

Later, in August 2005, the chief Scottish investigator declared that the bomb timer, the main piece of evidence was planted by a CIA agent. The expert who analyzed the timer for the court admitted the "CIA dropped it off" after he manufactured it. Additionally, a star witness, a Maltese shopkeeper who sold a pair of pants located on the booby-trapped suitcase, admitted to receiving $ 2 million to bear false witness. Scottish authorities later decided to review the case, however the health of Abdel Basset Ali Mohmed Ali Megrahi, one of the Libyans blamed, did not permit it.[260] In short, the case against Libya and Qaddafi was based on fraud.

Even before any of these incidents or alleged crimes by Qaddafi, the Reagan administration from its onset was decidedly partisan and against Qaddafi. Qaddafi led a largely progressive regime that ran counter to Reagan era dogma and geopolitical imperatives. Although Libya did not entirely achieve the socialist ideal, Qaddafi was a proponent of Arab Socialism. In 1977 he changed the official title of the country from the "Libyan Arab Republic" to the "Socialist People's Libyan Arab Jamahiriyah." He emerged on the scene of the Arab world as a Nasserist. In the Libyan Revolution he led, junior military officers seized the government and overthrew a monarchy obsequious to Western interests. This is the same scenario that took place in Egypt under Gamal Abdel Nasser.

Like Nasser, Qaddafi saw himself in opposition to existing imperialism, placing him at odds with the West. Libya from 1911 until the end of World War II was an Italian colony. After defeating Italy, the British and US established a nominally independent regime headed by a monarch, King Idris. Shortly after deposing Idris in a bloodless coup, the junior class of officers Qaddafi led notably closed existing US and British military bases. They expelled all foreign military personnel, numbering approximately 4600. To US consternation, most prominently was the Pentagon's Wheelus Air Base in Tripoli, one of America's largest, which allowed it to project

---

[259] Ibid.
[260] "Lynching of Gaddafi."

power in the Mediterranean basin. The US also lost the El Watia gunnery range. Additionally, Qaddafi nationalized the oil industry, as well as commercial interests such as banking where Western companies held a large stake. Libya also began to distinguish itself internationally for a strong anti-imperialist position and support for revolutionary struggles. This included the African National Congress in South Africa, the militant Palestine Liberation Organization, and the Irish Republican Army.

Colonel Qaddafi with Egypt's Gamal Abdel Nasser, the leader who mounted a regional campaign against Anglo-French and Israeli imperialism. Nasser's subsequent victory over the Anglo-French entente ushered in a paradigm shift for the region. Like Qaddafi, he came from the junior military officer class which overthrew a monarchy subservient to Western interests.

Libya thus joined the list of enemy states seeking autonomy and self-determination outside of the Western neo-colonial yoke. Shortly after entering office President Reagan created a special group for studying "the Libyan problem." "Nobody advocates being nice to him," was the mentality at the time. In 1981 the CIA drafted a plan exposed by *Newsweek* involving a "large-scale, multiphase and costly scheme to overthrow the Libyan regime," obtaining Qaddafi's "ultimate" removal from power. The plan called for the formation of a "counter-government" challenging his claim to govern as well as small-scale guerrilla operations.[261] This scenario is eerily reminiscent of the one that would play out in 2011 under the auspices of the Obama regime.

---

[261] Blum, *Killing Hope*, 281-89.

The Reagan administration used a vast disinformation campaign against Qaddafi. It declared the existence of a "Libyan hit squad" seeking to assassinate Reagan. The administration claimed there were a number of terrorists trained in Libya who had entered the US. In reality, these allegations were a complete fabrication. Jack Anderson, syndicated columnist, described how unreliable the group of informers was. Several of them had connections with Israeli intelligence, which would benefit from a US-Libyan rift. Many officials, including senior FBI, remained skeptical about the reports. The Deputy Secretary of State William Clark was charged with heading a task force on Libya in mid-1981. Seymour Hersh analyzed this task force years later:

> According to key sources, there was little doubt inside Clark's task force about who was responsible for the spate of anti-Qaddafi leaks—the CIA, with the support of the president, [Secretary of State] Haig, and Clark. "This item [the Libyan hit squad] stuck in my craw," one involved official recalls. "We came out with this big terrorist threat to the U.S. Government. The whole thing was a complete fabrication."...One task force officially eventually concluded that [CIA Director] Casey was in effect running an operation inside the American Government: "He was feeding the disinformation into the (intelligence) system so it would be seen as separate, independent reports" and taken seriously by other Government agencies.[262]

The alleged assassins were also Lebanese who aided Reagan in negotiating the release of US hostages in Beirut. They had an antipathy for Qaddafi, and would have been eager to discredit him. Thus, the pre-2011 regime change depiction of Qaddafi, a point of reference for many, was specious.

QADDAFI'S LIBYA:
AFRICA'S HIGHEST ECONOMIC DEVELOPMENT

Economically, Qaddafi's rule over Libya was often depicted as inept and exploitive. Preparing his military assault, President Obama

---

[262] Ibid.

baselessly charged that Qaddafi had "exploited [the Libyan people's] wealth." [263] Elliot Abrams in the *Wall Street Journal* contended Qaddafi's regime "has left Libya far worse than he found it on the day of his coup in 1969."[264] These broad characterizations are anti-historical, flat wrong, and ignore some of the significant achievements of his 40 year reign. Gerald Perreira (who at one point worked in Libya) of the *Black Agenda Report* commented when the US sponsored uprising broke out: "The media and their selected commentators have done their best to manufacture an opinion that Libya is essentially the same as Egypt and Tunisia and that Qaddafi is just another tyrant amassing large sums of money in Swiss bank accounts. But no matter how hard they try, they cannot make Qaddafi into Mubarak or Libya in to Egypt." Indeed, belying the appraisal of Abrams, even in 1981, *Newsweek* observed, "You don't see poverty or hunger here. Basic needs are met to a greater degree than in any other Arab country."

The reality of Libya under Qaddafi is starkly different than its portrayals in the corporate media. After Qaddafi's bloodless coup over Idris, he initiated many progressive changes. The conditions of the Libyan people was ameliorated. Rather than an "exploiter" of the nation's oil wealth, the Libya of Qaddafi attained the highest standard of living on the African continent. The Human Development Index (HDI) is a composite statistic used to rank countries by level of "human development" with a comparative measure of life expectancy, literacy, education, and standards of living by the UN. It is a measure of well-being and the impact of economic policies on quality of life. The primary criteria are the basic dimensions of human development: health, education, and income.[265]

[263] "Remarks by the President in Address to the Nation on Libya," Whitehouse.gov, http://www.whitehouse.gov/the-press-office/2011/03/28/remarks-president-address-nation-libya

[264] Elliot Abrams, "Our Bargain With the New Gadhafi," *Wall Street Journal*, February 25, 2011, http://online.wsj.com/news/articles/SB1000142405274870384200457616321 2492956024

[265] Alexandre Valiente, "Celebrating The Great Achievments Of Muammar Gaddafi," Libyadiary.wordpess.com, November 9, 2011, http://libyadiary.wordpress.com/2011/11/09/celebrating-the-great-acheivments-of-muammar-gaddafi/

Prior to the 2011 uprising, Libya was listed by the UN as having the highest HDI in Africa, even achieving a higher HDI than some countries in Eastern Europe such as Ukraine. It also enjoyed the lowest infant mortality rate in Africa. Its incarceration rate was relatively low as well, ranked 61st, with a rate lower than the Czech Republic. A 2007 article in African Executive Magazine commented, "[Libya has] utilized the revenue from its oil to develop its country. The standard of living of the people of the people of Libya is one of the highest in Africa, falling in the category of countries with a GNP per capita between USD 2,200 and 6,000."

Libya's Nasserist social policy also maintained robust social safety programs. Housing was a basic right. Every person was provided a decent house or apartment rent free. Homelessness, which was endemic in the pre-Gaddafi era, "where corrugated iron shacks dotted many urban [centers] around the country," was nearly eradicated. Subject to family constraints, women were free to work and to dress as they pleased. Electricity was free for all citizens. Free land was given to farmers. Mothers who gave birth to a child received $5,000. Newlyweds received funds to purchase an apartment. Life expectancy was in the seventies. There was also free health care. People had access to doctors, hospitals, clinics and medicines — all without charge, and with a 1: 673 doctor-patient ratio. According to the assessment of the World Health Organization (WHO): "Health status has improved: The Government provides free health care to all citizens. The country has achieved high coverage in most basic health areas. The mortality rate for children aged less than 5 years fell from 160 per 1000 live births in 1970 to 20 in 2000. In 1999, 97% of one-year-old children were vaccinated against tuberculosis and 92% against measles." The WHO stated:

> Health services: The General People's Committee (GPC) through the Central Health Body is responsible for direction and performance of health services and health status. The actual execution is the mandate of the shabiat [local administrative district]. Almost all levels of health services (promotive, preventive, curative and rehabilitative) are decentralized, except Tripoli Medical Centre and Tajoura Cardiac Hospital, which are centrally run. A growing private health sector is emerging. The Government encourages the

expansion of private clinics and hospitals. The family physician practices and health insurance are being introduced. The country enjoys a very high rate of primary health care.[266]

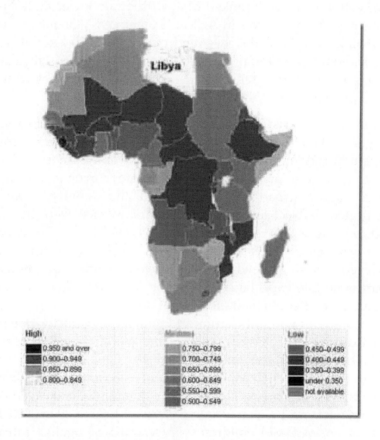

The UN's Human Development Index showed Libya was the only country in Africa to rank in the "high" group.

Additionally, illiteracy was almost wiped out under Qaddafi. "The literacy and educational enrolment rates are highest in North Africa," the WHO noted. Libya was hesitant to adopt neoliberal reforms on essential food staples, with many subsidies maintained until the NATO assault. In *Qaddafi and the Libyan Revolution*, written

---

[266] Ibid.

in 1987, British journalists Andrew Lycett and David Blundy remarked:

> The young people are well dressed, well fed and well educated. Libyans now earn more per capita than the British. The disparity in annual incomes... is smaller than in most countries. Libya's wealth has been fairly spread throughout society. Every Libyan gets free, and often excellent, education, medical and health services. New colleges and hospitals are impressive by any international standard. All Libyans have a house or a flat, a car and most have televisions, video recorders and telephones. Compared with most citizens of the Third World countries, and with many in the First World, Libyans have it very good indeed.[267]

Qaddafi also notably oversaw the creation of the Great Man-made River, the most ambitious irrigation project in history – an example of effective economic dirigisme. According to the Guinness Book of World Records it was the largest irrigation project in the world. "It is impossible not to be impressed with the scale of the project," wrote the BBC, before the 2011 revamping of the anti-Qaddafi demonization campaign began.[268]

Because it is largely a desert country, finding fresh water has always been a problem for Libya. The GMR water pipeline project brought millions of liters of water from beneath the Sahara Desert to various regions in Libya. The water flow supplemented supplies for domestic agricultural and industrial needs in the country, enhancing the potential of the entire region. In Libya, the new water sources allowed for a vast increase in irrigated farmland in thousands of hectares. In a country that is over 95% desert, the GMR was a much needed internal improvement. One account given to the BBC in 2006 by Adam Kuwairi, a senior figure in the Great Man-made River Authority (GMRA) explained the impact the fresh water on his

---

[267] Stephen Lendman, "Why Libya Was Attacked," *The Illegal War on Libya*, (Clarity Press), 2007.

[268] "Gaddafi's Death: Celebrating Murder While Ushering in Civil War," Globalresearch.ca, October 26, 2011, http://www.globalresearch.ca/gaddafi-s-death-celebrating-murder-while-ushering-in-civil-war/27308

family. "The water changed lives. For the first time in our history, there was water in the tap for washing, shaving and showering," he told the BBC. "The quality of life is better now, and it's impacting the whole country." "Libya is now a world leader in hydrological engineering," it also noted, "and it wants to export its expertise to other African and Middle-Eastern countries facing the same problems with their water."[269]

For the London and Wall Street ilk at the time of its inception however, this massive project was scandalous. The *Financial Times* of London bemoaned that it was Qaddafi's "pet project," and Qaddafi wanted to be "something other than the scourge of the West." In celebration of the project's inauguration, with many Arab and African leaders present, Qaddafi pointedly declared, "After this achievement, American threats against Libya will double." He stated the US "will make excuses," but "the real reason is to stop this achievement, to keep the people of Libya oppressed."[270] This would later actualize. In the later brutal NATO assault the project was wantonly attacked—an act of historical vandalism.

The achievements of Libya under Qaddafi are remarkable considering that Libya began as one of the poorest countries in the world before he assumed leadership. When Libya was granted independence in 1951, under King Idris the country was backwards, overwhelmingly illiterate, and poverty-stricken, with some of the lowest living standards:

> When Libya was granted its independence by the United Nations on December 24, 1951, it was described as one of the poorest and most backward nations of the world. The population at the time was not more than 1.5 million, was over 90% illiterate, and had no political experience or know-how. There were no universities, and only a limited number

---

[269] Ibid.
[270] Mathaba, "Libya's 'Water Wars' and Gaddafi`s Great Man-Made River Project," May 13, 2013, http://www.globalresearch.ca/libyas-water-wars-and-gaddafis-great-man-made-river-project/5334868

of high schools which had been established seven years before independence.[271]

Transformed from having an aggravated state of backwardness to the highest standard of living on Africa is surely an achievement by any objective measure, especially one that reflects the needs of a society. This was not expressed in corporate mainstream media outlets or Western officialdom.

Qaddafi's image in the West is the product of deliberate mythmaking to suit the necessities of the Western establishment. It in no way reflected the actualities, good or bad, of his 40 year reign. As Aburish explains in *A Brutal Friendship*, "We see the Middle East through indelible good and bad images which exaggerate, reduce, supersede, overlook, twist or replace simple facts." Middle East leaders are not judged by what is acceptable for their people but what is acceptable to the West.[272] Qaddafi's appraisal in the West exemplified this reality. Thus, the depiction of Qaddafi emphasized him as a madman or ruler lacking legitimacy because he "had to go."

THE JAMAHIRIYA SYSTEM

To be sure, the Libyan Jamahiriyah system created by Qaddafi had its shortcomings. But no state allows itself to be existentially challenged internally. Characteristic of the region, repressive tendencies of Qaddafi's leadership existed (something so overly emphasized in prevailing discourse to render discussion here superfluous). Nonetheless, his method of governance was not devoid of popular participation. Qaddafi, for his part was no democrat by conventional Western standards. In fact, the Libyan Jamahiriyah system established by Qaddafi emphatically rejected the Western version of "democracy" as facile and a "travesty." Instead, the Libyan Jamahiriya system — "Jamahiriya" roughly meaning "people's republic" — emphasized *direct* democracy. Before the 2011 vilification campaign, in 2006 Qaddafi participated in a forum at Columbia University on the subject of democracy. In the dialogue Qaddafi explained that the only place true democracy existed in the world

---

[271] Mahdi Darius Nazemroaya, "Qaddafi: Mad Dog or Brother Leader?" *The Illegal War on Libya*, (Clarity Press, 2007).
[272] Aburish, "Images and Reality," *A Brutal Friendship*.

was Libya. Whereas other states used "indirect democracy" in which "representatives" theoretically acted out the interests of the people, in Libya the people did so directly. The system of "indirect democracy" practiced and promoted by the West was a disguised form of dictatorship, he argued. In Libya the Jamahariyah system hinged on 30,000 small scale congresses, where people could voice their opinions. In Libya, no law could be enacted without the approval of the people voting in the people's congresses. According to Qaddafi, everything else is "false and fake."[273]

According to some accounts, a degree of conventional civic and political freedom existed. Even the NDI, Washington's instrument of "democracy promotion" in the world, (see Chapter II) offered a jarring contrast to the 2011 diplomatic and media demonization campaign against Libya:

> NDI met with several high profile lawyers who said that they were free to defend human rights cases in the courts without political intervention. It is well-known that many of Libya's high profile lawyers are also amongst the most vocal supporters of reform to the political system. At the current time universities are the only forum [though the NDI just mentioned the courts] where freedom of expression is tolerated. Prominent professors are generally free to teach as they wish, even in sensitive matters of political science...these professors who support change and are bold enough to speak or write about it are generally tolerated by the regime...even the Green Book Center, representing the heart of Libyan political orthodoxy, holds conferences and debates in which it is possible to hear people expressing views that are critical of the system.[274]

According to other accounts, in the centerpiece of Libyan democracy — the General People's Congress where all laws had to be approved — people could express themselves freely. Key leaders of the National Transitional Council (NTC), the Western-backed

[273] Joe Freindly, "Gadhafi streaming dialog at Columbia U. '06. ," October 27, 2011, https://www.youtube.com/watch?v=zg5TBi59Ghg
[274] Maximillian Forte, *Slouching Toward Sirte: NATO's War on Libya and Africa,"* (Montreal: Baraka Books), 65-66

organization that would eventually assume power, expressed in private to US officials views that were ambivalent rather than an outright denunciations of "despotism." NTC chair Mustafa Jalil, while serving as Minister of Justice before the 2011 offensive told US diplomats "Libyans could 'say anything they wanted' in the forum of the General People's Congress. He insisted journalists were free to write anything they chose, provided they did not make personal accusations against anyone (i.e. slander)." [275] This undercuts the prevalent Manichean portrayals of absolute tyranny by Western media and diplomats.

Some other features of the Libyan system and society would be considered backwards by modern standards. This included a tribalism continuing to prevail on the demographic landscape. The country's administrative system was highly decentralized and perpetuated this arrangement. The country was divided into 33 *shabiats* or districts, each having its own functional secretariats responsible for planning, implementing, monitoring, and evaluating development projects and services.

To maintain power Qaddafi sometimes emphasized and played the tribal game. This, as a result, perpetuated want of concrete and cohesive national institutions. When Qaddafi assumed power he allied himself with the Tripoli area Western and Southern tribes against the Eastern Cyrenaica tribes near Benghazi. These eastern Benghazi based tribes were the beneficiaries of the monarchy of King Idris Qaddafi supplanted. They were highly resentful of this, and would provide animus for the eventual rebel cadre that overthrew the Qaddafi regime.

In his rousing speech on February 22, 2011 Qaddafi praised Libya's tribes. He decried the "rats" paid by foreign intelligence agencies as a "shame to their children, their families, and their tribes, that is if they have children, families, and tribes." He declared "Libyan tribes are honorable...and they are rallying around me during this month... All the tribes...they are all shouting the same

---

[275] Ibid.

thing. They are all confronting. We have confronted America — with
its might and power."[276]

The railways systems in Libya planned to be built under Russian
and Chinese auspices might have been a way to curb prevailing
tribalism. These railway systems, running east to west, would have
connected areas of Libya hitherto unconnected, bringing disparate
regions and social groups together. The NATO-Qatar offensive
against Libya eradicated this possibility. With the NATO bloc more
effective as a wrecking ball against modern states, creating these
much needed works of infrastructure will not be forthcoming.

QADDAFI BENDS THE KNEE

The most notable defect of Qaddafi's rule is that, in his final years
leading Libya, he began acquiescing to Western dictates. His
rapprochement with the West altered the course he set the country
on in his 1969 revolution. Glen Ford of the *Black Agenda Report*, who
visited Libya, observed prior to the NATO-Qatar assault: "[Qaddafi]
strode onto the world stage when he and other young officers kicked
out a King named Idris, who had charged foreign corporations the
lowest prices in the world to suck out the nation's oil wealth. That
was back in 1969. By the time I had my encounter with Khadafi, 40
years later, in late October of 2009, he was still calling himself a
socialist and sworn enemy of capitalism, and pushing his Green Book
as a universal guide to social justice. But Khadafi had clearly reached
an accommodation with the United States and the rich men of
Europe."[277]

His most disastrous concession was to adopt Western
neoliberalism. By initiating significant privatization, his commitment
to the hitherto successful Arab socialism of Nasser was reversed. This
plunged many Libyans into poverty.

The context of these concessions is instructive though. Qaddafi's
short-lived *modus vivendi* was in the wake of the brutal and fear-

---

[276] "Excerpts From Libyan Leader Muammar Al-Qaddafi's Televised
Address." *The New Arab Revolts: What Happened, What It Means, and What
Happens Next*, (New York: Council on Foreign Relations, 2011), 414-420.
[277] Glen Ford, "Khadafi On the Outs," Black Agenda Report, February 22,
2011, http://blackagendareport.com/content/khadafi-outs

provoking 2003 Anglo-American "shock and awe" assault on Iraq. In this context, he became a survivalist. In an act of pragmatism, Qaddafi sought to cut a deal with duplicitous Western leaders just five days after Saddam Hussein was captured. Libya announced its rejection of terror, and it was ending unconventional weapons and ballistic missile programs. Thousands of nuclear reactor components were taken from a site in Tripoli and shipped to the Oak Ridge National Laboratory in Tennessee. Libya would assist the US in its so-called "war on terror," and open itself up for foreign oil investment. This was all in exchange for a lifting of economic sanctions. Additionally, Libya was compelled to accept responsibility for the Lockerbie bombing, despite the tenuous evidence for its culpability. It was forced to pay $2.7 billion in indemnities.[278] The example of Libya, in retrospect, shows the ramifications of the unjustifiable war against Iraq in 2003 went beyond tangible results in Iraq.

Western neoliberalism required Libya "open its markets" and "restructure" its economy. This entailed privatization and the typical litany of draconian neoliberal "reforms" imposed on debt-ridden countries by the IMF. In reality, Libya did not have foreign debt; it had a positive trade balance of $27 billion annually. One analyst commented, "The only reason the IMF demanded an end to subsidies of basic necessities was to undercut the social basis of support for the regime."[279]

The Western imposed "market liberalization," stewarded by Qaddafi's Western educated son Saif al-Islam, resulted in a $5 billion annual cut in existing subsidies. This was a crushing burden for the Libyan people. As is typical, the vast majority of people were adversely affected by these "structural adjustments." Since Qaddafi's 1969 Revolution the state subsidized 93 percent of the value of basic commodities, chiefly fuel. Subsequent to adopting the Western IMF program, fuel prices hiked 30 percent, and the price of electricity for consumers was doubled by the state. This precipitated price increases in a number of goods and services. The neoliberal plan also

---

[278] Sarah Flounders, "US/NATO War in Libya: A Continuation of Past Crime," *The Illegal War Against Libya*, (Clarity Press), 2012.
[279] Ibid.

called for Libya to privatize 360 state-owned companies and enterprises. This included steel mills, cement plants, engineering firms, food factories, truck and bus assembly lines and state farms. As a corollary, thousands of workers were left jobless. Libya was forced to sell a 60 percent ownership in the state oil company Tamoil Group, and to privatize the General National Company for Flour Mills and Fodder.

Libya was forced to revise its successful protectionist economic policy[280] precipitating dislocation and anger for Libyan factories and workers. The Carnegie Fund charted the impact soon after these policies were adopted in a 2005 report "Economic Reforms Anger Libyan Citizens." It observed: "Another aspect of structural reform was the end of restrictions on imports. Foreign companies were granted licenses to export to Libya through local agents. As a result, products from all over the world have flooded the previously isolated market." The Libyans were unable to offset the competition.

To make matters worse, tribalism continuing to prevail in Libya exacerbated the situation. The neoliberal restructuring posed the

---

[280] Contrary to today's prevailing discourse, most economically developed states—from the US and Britain to Germany, Japan, and South Korea—have used protectionism and economic nationalism to advance their economies and raise their standards of living. See Michael Lind, "Free Trade Fallacy," Prospect, January 1, 2003,http://web.archive.org/web/20060106154801/http://www.newameri ca.net/index.cfm?pg=article&DocID=1080 and Raveendra N. Batra, *The Myth of Free Trade: A Plan for America's Economic Revival.* (New York: C. Scribner's Sons, 1993). See also Ha-Joon-Chang, *Kicking Away the Ladder: Development Strategy In Historical Perspective,* (London: Anthem Press, 2003). Curiously, there is precedent for anti-protectionist "free-trade" policy as a stratagem of imperialist policy. Ironically, the US was once victim of such policy. The British Empire used it against the newly independent United States to strangle it in the cradle. President John Adams recalled in 1819: "I am old enough to remember the war of 1745, and its end; the war of 1755, and its close; the war of 1775, and its termination; the war of 1812, and its pacification...The British manufacturers, immediately after the peace, disgorged upon us all their stores of merchandise and manufactures, not only without profit, but at certain loss for a time, with the express purpose of annihilating all our manufacturers, and ruining all our manufactories." America learned well.

question of which individuals, and therefore tribes, would be permitted to privatize key lucrative domestic industries. In Russia and the former Soviet Union was the *nomenklatura*; in Libya there were the tribes. Old rivalries resurfaced.

Leaked US Embassy cables published by the London *Telegraph* showed the tumult this Western plan precipitated, and how the US closely monitored the fruits of its demands. In a cable titled "Inflation on the rise in Libya" the impact of the "radical program of privatization and government restructuring" was examined.

> Particular increases were seen in the prices for foodstuffs -- the price of previously subsidized goods such as sugar, rice, and flour increased 85 percent in the two years since subsidies were lifted. Construction materials also increased markedly: prices for cement, aggregate, and bricks have increased by 65 percent in the past year; the price of steel bars has increased by a factor of ten.

> The [state's] termination of subsidies and price controls as part of a broader program of economic reform and privatization has certainly contributed to inflationary pressures and prompted some grumbling...

> The combination of high inflation and diminishing subsidies and price controls is worrying a Libyan public accustomed to greater government cushioning from market forces.[281]

Thus, under Western auspices Libya was impoverished. Paradoxically, this was later cited as evidence Qaddafi misgoverned, yet he adopted polices demanded by the West itself. These economic "reforms" eroded internal stability and Qaddafi's social base of support, providing groundwork for the coming Western sponsored uprising.

Additionally, Qaddafi's rule in Libya never successfully diversified its economy from oil dependence. The majority of the Libyan budget was from oil revenues. Completely free from

---

[281] "INFLATION ON THE RISE IN LIBYA," *Telegraph*, January 31, 2011, http://www.telegraph.co.uk/news/wikileaks-files/libya-wikileaks/8294902/INFLATION-ON-THE-RISE-IN-LIBYA.html

economic sanctions and neoliberalism, it is difficult to say if this would have continued. Libya was making inroads towards establishing a foothold in agricultural products.

Meanwhile, Qaddafi's deference to Western demands amid threats also seemingly exposed a contradiction in his anti-imperialist posturing. His rapprochement with duplicitous Western leaders such as Nicolas Sarkozy[282] — French President who later spearheaded the destruction of the country — belied his erstwhile anti-Western rhetoric. This may warrant criticism, but Qaddafi was attempting to adjust to the "New World Order." He commented at the time that it was "the era of globalization, and there are many new factors which are mapping the world."[283] In hindsight, that the American empire's "New World Order" demands absolute servility is manifest. Nothing less than abject servitude is tolerated.

Recognizing some of the shortcomings of the existing Libyan system, Qaddafi began to be publicly critical of the government for "failing to address the needs of the people." In response, Qaddafi initiated a plan to begin a wealth redistribution scheme based on local democratic rule. He decried the "failure of the General People's Committees to effectively distribute Libya's oil wealth to its people." He added that contravening to the ideals of the 1969 revolution, "widespread corruption and failed implementation at all levels of government had engendered widespread dissatisfaction with public services, especially education, health, and infrastructure development."[284]

His plan, if adopted, would have given the people direct access to the nation's wealth and created more decentralization. Before the ruthless NATO campaign, he had begun discussing this wealth redistribution project. Concerning this plan a February 18, 2011 Congressional report stated:

---

[282] Qaddafi reportedly contributed 50 million euros to the campaign of Sarkozy. Kim Willsher,"Gaddafi 'contributed €50m to Sarkozy's 2007 presidential election fund,' " *Guardian,* March 12, 2012, http://www.theguardian.com/world/2012/mar/12/gaddafi-contributed-sarkozy-2007-election

[283] F. William Engdahl. *A Century of War: Anglo-American Oil Politics and the New World Order.* (London: Pluto Press, 2004), 266.

[284] Forte, *Sirte,* 66.

In March 2008, [Qaddafi] announced his intention to dissolve most government administrative bodies and institute a Wealth Distribution Program whereby state oil revenues would be distributed to citizens on a monthly basis for them to administer personally, in cooperation, and via local committees. Citing popular criticism of government performance in a long, wide ranging speech, [he] repeatedly stated that the traditional state would soon be "dead" in Libya and that direct rule by citizens would be accomplished through the distribution of oil revenues. [The military], foreign affairs, security, and oil production arrangements reportedly would remain national.[285]

In Libya laws had to be approved by the General People's Congress, and Qaddafi's proposal was shelved, the Deputy Chief of Mission at the US Embassy noted. As Maximilian Forte explains in *Slouching Towards Sirte,* "If there is one thing that all dictators depend upon is a commanding, if not absolute, control over revenues, and a strong state structure. Yet, here we have the US Embassy [in its diplomatic cables] telling us that Qaddafi was dispensing with both, and was being stopped from doing so. Asserting that Qaddafi was 'out of touch' with his own people would seem to be a remarkable statement of misunderstanding; [according to US diplomatic cables] not even the US Embassy believed that."[286]

SMASHING AFRICA'S LEADING STATE TO SHORE UP AFRICOM VS. CHINA

A significant aspect of Qaddafi's rule in Libya was his pan-African reorientation of Libya. Qaddafi supported—in the spirit of Ghana's Kwame Nkrumah—a unified and economically developed Africa, independent of Western economic and military hegemony. His clothing was adorned with African regalia and his billboards in Libya promoted an embrace of the African continent. Notably,

---

[285] Nazemroaya, "Brother Leader," *Illegal War,* 92.
[286] Forte, *Sirte,* 66.

Qaddafi was a proponent and founding father of the African Union,[287] and continued to support its institutions.[288]

Economically, this included the creation of an African central bank, and African Monetary Fund. The bank was prepared to lend for development projects at zero interest. This would have been a counterpoise to the draconian IMF and predatory Western banks, a critical sinew of Africa's continued external dependence and impoverishment.[289] Libya under Qaddafi allocated over two-thirds of the $42 billion designated for the launch of the African Monetary Fund and an African Investment Fund. This money was expropriated by the Obama administration. His African plan called for a gold-backed African currency, undermining the dollar's reserve currency status. Additionally, Libya funded Africa's only communications satellite, thereby saving users hundreds of millions of dollars with low-cost incoming and outgoing calls. [290] Africa was previously forced to use Western satellites at exorbitant rates.

Qaddafi maintained a tight partnership and close personal friendship with South Africa's Nelson Mandela, who referred to Qaddafi as "brother leader." Qaddafi supported Mandela and the anti-apartheid movement while others in the international community sided with the oppressive apartheid regime. Mandela offered acerbic rebukes to those who criticized his partnership with Libya, at one point telling his critics to "throw themselves in a pool." [291] Qaddafi was the last official guest to visit Mandela as president.

When the NATO-Qatar offensive in Libya eventually succeeded in smashing the Libyan state, Mandela's African National Congress Party lamented, "It is regrettable that the Libyan conflict ended with

---

[287] It might be objected that the AU is a corrupt institution subservient to Western interests, but the point is to emphasize a pan-African orientation of Libya via support for existing African institutions.
[288] Forte, *Sirte*.
[289] Dan Glazebrook, "NATO's War on Libya is an Attack on African Development," *Counterpunch*, September 06, 2011, http://www.counterpunch.org/2011/09/06/natos-war-on-libya-is-an-attack-on- african-development/print
[290] Lendman, "Why Libya was Attacked," *Illegal War*.
[291] Forte, Sirte, 142.

the gruesome killing of the Libyan Leader Muammar Qaddafi...We once again call on western countries under the command of NATO to stop the bombardment of Libya and its people." (ANC statement, Oct. 21)[292] The ANC's Youth League went further: "[It] Salutes Colonel Muammar Qaddafi, a brave soldier and fighter against the re-colonization of the African continent. Brother Leader was ruthlessly killed by rebels armed by NATO forces who invaded Libya because of its natural resources. Brother Leader resisted imperialist domination of the African continent and never agreed to the continued draining of natural resources from beneath Africa's soil. He understood and appreciated that Africa's natural resources should be economically used to benefit the people of Africa."[293]

Qaddafi promoting Pan-Africanism in murals and paintings.

The morally bankrupt and illegal war against Libya was not merely an attempt to extirpate a recalcitrant vassal state or a covetous oil grab (although these factors are not to be minimized). *Geostrategically*, looming large is US AFRICOM, (Africa Command) an instrument to militarize the African continent and Mediterranean basin under American military hegemony. Libya—today neutralized—would have inhibited this project.

---

[292] Abayomi Azikiwe, "Qaddafi Lynched By US-NATO," *The Illegal War Against Libya*, (Clarity Press, 2012), 123.
[293] Ibid.

Perhaps the most remarkable new dynamic to take hold on the African continent is its emerging partnership with China. Although "the prize is Eurasia," Africa's steady and increasing partnership with China gives it a particular importance on the "grand chessboard" of geopolitics. The new African Union headquarters that was funded by China is emblematic of the new Sino-African relationship. Until China began to take notice, Africa was given less consideration by the West. A resource-poor China is increasingly relying on a resource-rich Africa for critical raw material and mineral resources. Notably, China now receives approximately a third of its oil from Africa.[294] The Council on Foreign Relations places China's imports of African oil at 1.5 million barrels per day. Additionally, China invests an estimated $5.5 billion annually in Africa.[295]

Unsurprisingly, US apparatchik Secretary of State Hillary Clinton expressed dismay at the growing Sino-African relationship, trying to dissuade Africans from the emerging partnership. She insinuated China is guilty of a "new colonialism."[296] This was the same paradigm Ghana's Kwame Nkrumah warned Africans were victims of due to Western policies. Indeed, the Western dominated IMF-World bank complex has long been accused of "neo-colonialism" by many in the developing world. Regardless of its merits, for African leaders China's indifference to the internal affairs of sovereign states contrasts with the West's proclivity for constant interference and hectoring with hypocritical notions of "human rights." Chinese investment in Africa has offered a token building up

---

[294] Shelly Zhao, "The Geopolitics of China-African Oil," China Briefing, April 13, 2011, http://www.china-briefing.com/news/2011/04/13/the-geopolitics-of-china-african-oil.html

[295] Ali Jafrani, "China's Growing Role in Africa: Myths and Facts," Carnegie Endowment For International Peace, February 9, 2012, http://carnegieendowment.org/ieb/2012/02/09/china-s-growing-role-in-africa-myths-and-facts/9j5q

[296] Mathew Lee, "Hillary Clinton Warns Africa Of 'New Colonialism,'" HuffingtonPost.com, June 11, 2011, http://www.huffingtonpost.com/2011/06/11/hillary-clinton-africa-new-colonialism_n_875318.html

the continent's infrastructure as well. [297] The history of Western looting of the African continent, slavery, postwar colonial wars, assassinations, coups d'état, and regime change policies is not far from the African consciousness.

According to David Shinn, former US ambassador to Ethiopia and Burkina Faso, the expanding Chinese engagement in Africa's infrastructure, mineral sector and telecommunications is producing "deep nervousness" in the West. [298] Undercutting the Chinese presence in Africa is a step towards containing a meteorically rising China. American geostrategic imperatives are to starve a resource poor China of critical raw materials and oil—a key vulnerability—as part of the strategy of "containment." Pepe Escobar of the *Asia Times* comments, "The name of the game for the US and the Europeans is to pull no punches to undermine China's myriad commercial deals all across Africa."[299] A cursory glance at a map of this region illustrates how an increased US presence in the region would be a step in doing just that. This policy mirrors US Middle East policy, which dictates as David Harvey explains: "Whoever controls the Middle East controls the global oil spigot and whoever controls the global oil spigot can control the global economy, at least for the near future."[300]

US AFRICOM's strategic objective is "protecting access to hydrocarbons and other strategic resources which Africa has in abundance, a task which includes ensuring against the vulnerability of those natural riches and ensuring that no other interested third parties, such as China, India, Japan, or Russia, obtain monopolies or preferential treatment," according to testimony by Peter J. Pham, US

---

[297] Glazbrook, "Attack on African Development," *Counterpunch* http://www.counterpunch.org/2011/09/06/natos-war-on-libya-is-an-attack-on-african-development/print
[298] Teo Kermeliotis, "Is the West losing out to China in Africa?" CNN.com, September 9, 2011, http://edition.cnn.com/2011/BUSINESS/09/08/america.losing.influence.africa/
[299] Pepe Escobar, "Obama, the king of Africa," *Asia Times*, October 18, 2011, http://www.atimes.com/atimes/Global_Economy/MJ18Dj06.html
[300] Forte, Sirte, 192.

Fall of the Arab Spring

State Department advisor. [301] Vice Admiral Robert T. Moeller affirmed it is AFRICOM's goal to protect "the free flow of natural resources from Africa to the global market."[302] This includes Africa's strategic energy choke points and transit routes crucial to the world economy. Unable to compete economically with China, America has sought to leverage its remaining bulwark: its military and extensive regime change apparatus. The US must leverage these assets because, as noted by Jennifer Cooke, head of the Africa program at the Center for Strategic and International Studies in Washington D.C. the "US does not the kind of finances available to mount splashy new economic initiatives in Africa."[303]

The original plan for AFRICOM was for it to be headquartered in Africa itself. The Bush II administration stated, "We will work closely with our African partners to determine an appropriate location for the new command in Africa."[304] Qaddafi opted out of AFRICOM, and opposed attempts for it to gain a foothold on the African continent. No African country was willing to host US AFRICOM, thanks in no small part to Libya. States in Africa offered money by the US to host a base, were typically offered double by Qaddafi to refuse it. In 2008, "this ad-hoc opposition crystallized into a formal rejection by the African Union."[305]

Before the NATO-Qatar attack, the group that provided gestation for the concept of AFRICOM—a coterie of congress members, oil lobbyists, and military officers—recognized Libya would present a challenge to their involvement in Africa's emerging strategic significance. This group, calling itself the African Oil Policy Initiative Group (AOPIG) tied their economic and military objectives for the

---

[301] F. William Engdahl, "NATO's War on Libya is Directed against China: AFRICOM and the Threat to China's National Energy Security," Center for Research on Globalization, September 25, 2011, http://www.globalresearch.ca/nato-s-war-on-libya-is-directed-against-china-africom-and-the-threat-to-china-s-national-energy-security/26763?print=1
[302] Ibid.
[303] Forte, *Sirte*, 191
[304] Ibid., 198.
[305] *Glazebrook*, "Attack on African Development."

continent together. It recognized both China and Libya as adversaries the US must challenge.[306]

Seeking co-option, US ambassador to Libya Gene Cretz strategized on how AFRICOM might be made more amenable to Libya. He suggested to his superiors there might be ways for it to "quietly gain traction in Libya," showing the "appropriate deference" through symbolic gestures. Short of this, Qaddafi was "likely [to] continue his public opposition to an expanded role for the command, to include a physical presence, on the continent." A diplomatic cable from Ambassador Cretz to AFRICOM commander General William "Kip" Ward, who was scheduled to meet Qaddafi highlighted the US apprehension towards Libya vis-à-vis AFRICOM. Cretz explained: "Your meeting with Muammar al-Qadhafi will afford a key opportunity to engage at the strategic level, explain US Africa Command's mission and potentially mitigate possible Libyan obstruction of the Command's efforts on the continent." Cretz nevertheless estimated Qaddafi would be "unlikely to become a vocal supporter of US Africa Command." Still, the US might be able to attain "tacit acquiescence."[307]

Cretz also outlined to General Ward Qaddafi's anti-imperialist stance and the implications for AFRICOM. "Qaddafi excoriates European states for having colonized Africa and strongly argues against external interference in internal African affairs," he explained, adding further how he had a "neuralgic issue" with "the presence of non-African military elements in Libya or elsewhere on the continent." Libya was especially prideful of having expelled foreign military following the 1969 revolution. Concerning China, the Libyan government characterized its approach as "soft" while the US "hard." Qaddafi predicted China was going to "prevail because it does not interfere in internal affairs" of sovereign states.[308] US anxiety over Libya's posture towards AFRICOM is evident. Libya was not amenable to a militarized presence of US or non-African forces, especially without its leadership. Smashing Libya removed this potential barrier and neutralized it as a recalcitrant force seeking to

---

[306] Forte, *Slouching*, 197.
[307] Ibid., 199.
[308] Ibid., 202

bind African unity under its stewardship. With Libya's destruction, checking China on the continent could proceed apace without Libya as impediment.

WARMONGERING FROM THE LEFT: THE R-TO-P DOCTRINE

Central to the anti-Libyan operation was the doctrine of "Responsibility to Protect" or "RtoP." This Western pseudo-internationalist doctrine provided direct justification for the NATO bombing operation. It would provide the veneer of legitimacy and give carte blanche for regime change. RtoP holds that if a government is unable or unwilling to protect their own civilian population, the "international community" (itself a nebulous concept) may proceed to intervene, including UN Chapter 7 military intervention. This is in contravention to the UN Charter itself, which states Chapter 7 may be undertaken only in the case of a threat to international peace and security. In the case of an RtoP invocation, the UN Charter's central tenet of recognizing the sovereignty of independent nation-states is abrogated.

Notwithstanding this colonial-esque negation of national sovereignty, at first glance, the RtoP doctrine has the verisimilitude of cogency. Indeed, based on this doctrine, nominal left liberals, who once provided a critique of the bellicose right-wing administration of the second Bush, turned into eager warmongers for empire. Many of this ilk fervently supported NATO's destruction of Libya. This included left figures such Rachel Maddow of MSNBC, Cenk Uygur, Juan Cole, Amy Goodman of Democracy Now! and even the otherwise credible Chris Hedges at first.   After all, during the Rwandan Genocide, one of foremost tragedies of the post-Cold War period, the international community remained idle, thereby permitting wholesale genocide—at least according to the accepted narrative. However, upon further examination—and thoroughly confirmed by direct NATO intervention—the RtoP doctrine is reduced to the absurd by weight of its own ambiguities, contradictions, untruths, and application.

Tracing the origins of the concept is instructive in this light. There are a number of proponents of the RtoP concept, but the first to publicize the concept was Gareth Evans, former Foreign Minister of Australia and CEO of the corporate sponsored International Crisis Group (ICG) think-tank. Although this group claims to be "committed to preventing and resolving deadly conflict," many of its Wall Street and oil cartel moneyed interests that sponsor it economically benefit from conflict. The ICG is the creation of some of the leading Atlanticist foreign policy circles with many of its advisors being directly responsible for initiating conflicts to begin with. Key advisors include a number of notables such as Shimon Peres, President of Israel, a country renowned internationally for its deplorable human rights violations; Richard Armitage of the US Defense and State Departments, who reportedly threatened to bomb Pakistan "into the Stone-Age," according to that country's leader; General Wesley Clark, NATO commander who guided the destruction of the former Yugoslavia; Lord Robertson of Port Ellen, a former NATO Secretary-General; Zbigniew Brzezinski, who boasts of luring Russia into the Afghan War quagmire; meanwhile, the current ICG chair Thomas Pickering, former US Ambassador to El Salvador, is implicated in the creation of the US sponsored death squads in that country.

Moreover, for the Atlanticist elite that filled ICG's ranks, their world outlook is decidedly neocolonial. George Soros, international currency speculator and ICG board of trustees member, typified this outlook in a 2004 article in *Foreign Policy*, magazine of the elite corporate sponsored CFR. On the question of sovereignty, Soros argued:

> **Sovereignty is an anachronistic concept** originating in bygone times when society consisted of rulers and subjects, not citizens. It became the cornerstone of international relations with the Treaty of Westphalia in 1648...Today, though not all nation-states are democratically accountable to their citizens, the principle of sovereignty stands in the way of outside intervention in the internal affairs of nation-states. But true sovereignty belongs to the people, who in turn delegate it to their governments. If governments abuse the authority entrusted to them and citizens have no opportunity

to correct such abuses, outside interference is justified. [309]
[Emphasis added.]

Consistent with this colonialist precept, Evans published a seminal paper expounding the concept of RtoP in the CFR's foreign policy journal *Foreign Affairs*. On the question of external intervention into the internal affairs of an otherwise sovereign state, Evans argued, it should be "reframed not as an argument about the 'right to intervene' but about the 'responsibility to protect.' " As explained by geopolitical analyst F. William Engdahl, this newfangled doctrine and its restructuring of international law presented a number of pressing questions:

> [Evans's] clever linguistic "reframing" created a necessary blurring of lines of the original UN Charter Principle of sovereign equality of states, of Article 2, Section 1 of the Charter. There was a very sound reason that the founding nations signing the UN Charter in 1946 decided to exclude UN police intervention into internal disputes of a sovereign state.
>
> Who should now decide which side in a given conflict is right? Under "responsibility to protect" essentially the United States and a few select allies could potentially define China as in violation of the human rights of its Tibetan or other ethnic minority citizens and order NATO troops to intervene in a humanitarian action. Or NATO might decide to intervene into the internal unrest in Chechnya, an integral part of the Russian Federation, because Moscow troops are attempting to enforce order over insurgents being secretly armed by NATO via Al-Qaeda or Mujahideen networks in Central Asia. Or a similar "humanitarian" excuse might be used to call for a NATO no-fly zone over Belarus or Ukraine or Venezuela or Bolivia or perhaps at some point, Brazil.

---

[309] George Soros, "The Peoples' Sovereignty: How a new twist on an old idea can protect the world's most vulnerable populations," *Foreign Policy*, January 1, 2004, http://www.foreignpolicy.com/articles/2004/01/01/the_peoples_sovereignty

The so-called humanitarian "responsibility to protect" doctrine opens a Pandora's Box of possibilities for those powers controlling world opinion via CNN or BBC or key media such as the *New York Times,* to justify a de facto neo-colonial policy of military intervention. This is the real significance of what Gareth Evans blithely terms "reframing."[310]

Building upon the theory of Evans, one of the foremost proponents of the RtoP doctrine is Samantha Power, National Security Council advisor in the Obama regime. In fact, along with Secretary of State Hillary Clinton, US Ambassador to the UN Susan Rice, and Anne-Marie Slaughter, Director of Policy Planning at the State Department, Power was the key figure in driving Obama towards a military offensive in Libya. A self-described "genocide chick," Power's career is a longstanding boon to the weaponization of human rights. Power gained prominence in 2002 with her book *A Problem From Hell: America and the Age of Genocide.*[311] Power's *magnum opus* is highly instructive on the spurious reasoning of left-wing humanitarian imperialism.

In her tendentious work, Power's central premise is that when confronted with acts of genocide in the 20th Century, America remained idle. "Why does the US stand so idly by?" she posits. The US "has made modest progress in its responses to genocide," but it has not taken sufficiently bold action in this regard, she argues. The US should, says Power, be more willing to deploy its armed forces to prevent human-rights catastrophes—that is, engage in "humanitarian intervention," a euphemism for war.

Confirmed in her selective omissions of US government actions abroad, undergirding Power's thinking is the belief in American exceptionalism. As with many US apparatchiks, she accepts

---

[310] F. William Engdahl, "Humanitarian Neo-colonialism: Framing Libya and Reframing War," Center for Research on Globalization, May 04, 2011, http://www.globalresearch.ca/humanitarian-neo-colonialism-framing-libya-and-reframing-war/24617

[311] Samantha Power. *A Problem from Hell: America and the Age of Genocide.* (New York: Basic Books, 2002).

axiomatically the mythology of the US as the indispensable nation that has achieved the highest form of human organization. This is the bombastic thesis of Francis Fukiyama. Power holds that America, being *sui generis*, can only be a force of virtue abroad. Its actions are inherently benign. In addition to a proclivity for imperial intervention, this is a point of convergence between left and right-wing foreign policy circles in America.

Contrary to the tendentious appraisal of Power, the US government has been active in many 20th century genocides — often as a participant in facilitating slaughter. In her 600 page book, Power rarely mentions 20th century genocides the US took part in. For example, Indonesia's genocidal conquest of East Timor, which was explicitly approved by President Ford and Secretary of State Henry Kissinger. Both Ford and Kissinger met with Indonesian President Suharto — installed in one of many US backed coups d'état against sovereign states — prior to the invasion. Kissinger remarked to General Suharto, "It is important that whatever you do succeed quickly."[312] In addition to US imprimatur, the genocidal invasion against East Timor was launched and carried out with US supplied weapons. In the ensuing decades, the Indonesian army continued to receive US military training and aid as it kills 100-200,000 East Timorese, with these figures and designation of "genocide" from a UN sponsored investigative body.

The US backed Suharto regime demonstrated its penchant for wanton slaughter immediately after seizing power. It initiated a bloody reign of terror domestically, lasting several years (primarily 1965-66). The regime purged supporters of erstwhile president Sukarno, leftists, and communists, murdering hundreds of thousands of its own people. In fact, it was the US embassy in Indonesia that supplied the names of people to be executed for alleged communist sympathies.[313] Power showed scant interest in this dramatic 20th century genocide directly facilitated by the US; her book committed merely one sentence to this bloody tragedy.

Power is similarly disinterested in genocidal US economic sanctions against Iraq during the 1990s that are attributable to the

---

[312] Johnson, *Sorrows of Empire*, 76.
[313] Ibid., 68.

deaths of millions of Iraqis. Perhaps, Power accepted the logic of her fellow American apparatchik Madeline Albright, former US Secretary of State, who at the time callously remarked these genocidal sanctions were "worth it." [314] After all, America is the world's benign hegemon.

Power is equally unconcerned with the genocide of opposition and peasant groups in Latin America by American sponsored *escuadrones de la muerte* (death squads). The infamous School of the Americas (SOA) in Ft. Benning, Georgia taught state terrorism to over 60,000 Latin American military and police officials. Many of these individuals are implicated in cases of rape, torture, assassinations, and massacres.[315] In El Salvador the US sponsored a coup by Salvadorian military officers which led to a vicious war against largely unarmed civilians by death squads. In 1986 a Pentagon official boasted, "Every soldier in [the Salvadorian] army has been trained by us in one way or another." These American trained death squads were responsible for the December 1981 El Mozote massacre of 900 Salvadoran civilians. Overall, these death squads slaughtered 38,000 people before Reagan sent Vice President Bush to order them to relent.[316]

Similarly, in Guatemala the US aided in the decades-long genocide against Mayan peasants. This slaughter was carried out with American armaments, CIA backing, and military training at the SOA. Mayan peasants told harrowing stories of a scorched earth policy of village raids where homes were burned, people killed after torture, women raped, and crops destroyed. A joint UN and Catholic Church truth commission designated this systematic slaughter "genocide" with the death toll placed at 200,000. There are similar examples *ad nauseam* with the same modus operandi followed in

---

[314] ttj1776's channel, "Madeleine Albright says 500,000 dead Iraqi Children was "worth it" wins Medal of Freedom,"
https://www.youtube.com/watch?v=omnskeu-puE
[315] Chalmers, *Sorrows*, 136.
[316] Ibid., 125.

Africa and elsewhere.[317] For Power though, none of this amounts to a "problem from hell."[318]

Of all the 20th century genocides, perhaps the centerpiece to the narrative of American inaction is the genocide in Rwanda, which saw the wanton slaughter of between 500,000 to 1,000,000 people. Although the putative narrative faced scant scrutiny globally, upon further examination it is evident America was by no means inactive during this tragedy. It helped guide the country towards conflict, militarily and economically, so its proxies would emerge triumphant at the helm of a US client state.

The common understanding of the Rwandan Genocide views this tragedy from a decidedly Manichean lens in which the minority Tutsi socio-political group were victims at the hands of the majority Hutu socio-political group. According to Africa expert Keith Harmon Snow this prevailing narrative is wrong.[319] Both Tutsis and Hutus were slaughtered en masse, and violence was instigated by Anglophone Tutsi expatriates in neighboring Uganda to reassert dominance over the country.

Prior to Rwandan independence, the elitist Tutsi, who were 20 percent of the population, represented the ruling elite of the country. They were the compradors of first German and then Belgian colonialists. To keep the Hutu majority subjected, the ruling Tutsi class employed brutality, slavery, and terrorism at the behest of their colonial overlords. Following a wave of nominal independence movements, Hutus overthrew the Tutsi monarchy, transferring the

---

[317] South Korea, where the US supported authoritarian military regimes that continued to rule until the 1990s, is another example. South Korea's junta carried out numerous massacres against discontents with tacit American support. See Chalmers Johnson, "South Korea: Legacy of the Cold War," *Blowback: The Costs and Consequences of American Empire*, (New York: Henry Holt and Co).

[318] Chase Madar, "FLASHBACK: SAMANTHA POWER AND THE WEAPONIZATION OF HUMAN RIGHTS," WrongKindofGreen.org, http://wrongkindofgreen.org/2012/05/10/flashback-samantha-power-and-the-weaponization-of-human-rights/

[319] Keith Harmon Snow, "Real Rwandan genocide & brainwashing of the Western mind," RT, April 11, 2014, http://rt.com/op-edge/real-genocide-rwanda-hutu-extremist-848/

country to the rule of the majority Hutu with the Belgian colonialists accepting and fostering a new Hutu elite. This led to some Tutsi being killed, with some fleeing and others remaining in the country. From this point onward though, Rwanda would continually be subjected to attacks by elite Tutsi guerrillas, now supplanted from power. Funded, armed, and trained outside of Rwanda, these guerrillas attacked Rwanda spreading violence and terrorism. This included the bombing of cafes, nightclubs, restaurants, and buses. A pattern soon emerged which would inform the 1994 Rwandan Genocide: following attacks by expatriate Anglophone Tutsi guerrillas, domestic Francophone Tutsis in Rwanda would suffer brutal reprisals. As a byproduct this gave credence to the narrative of Tutsis as exclusively victims. For the elite Tutsi expatriates, the Francophone Tutsis suffering reprisals in Rwanda were collateral damage, even at times considering them Hutu collaborators.

According to Michel Chossudovsky, professor emeritus at the University of Ottawa, America was a hidden hand in the ensuing carnage. In his estimation, "Washington's hidden agenda consisted in establishing an American sphere of influence in a region historically dominated by France and Belgium. America's design was to displace France by supporting the [Tutsi] Rwandan Patriotic Front [RPF] and by arming and equipping its military arm, the Rwandan Patriotic Army (RPA)."[320] What emerged in Uganda was a brutal power struggle between the existing French supported Hutu-led government, and the Tutsi RPF tacitly backed by Washington. In a frank appraisal Bernard Debré, former Cooperation Minister in the government of French Prime Minister Henri Balladur, illustrated this: "What one forgets to say is that, if France was on one side, the Americans were on the other, arming the Tutsis who armed the Ugandans. I don't want to portray a showdown between the French and the Anglo-Saxons, but the truth must be told."[321]

---

[320] Prof. Michel Chossudovsky, "Twenty Years Ago, The US was Behind the Genocide: Rwanda, Installing a US Proxy State in Central Africa," Center for Researcch on Globalization, April 06, 2014,
http://www.globalresearch.ca/twenty-years-ago-rwanda-installing-a-us-proxy-state-in-central-africa-the- us-was-behind-the-genocide/5376742
[321] Ibid.

In this ensuing competition, the US strategy was carried out via Washington's local vassal Yoweri Musaveni of Uganda. As foremost ally of Washington in the Lake Victoria region, Museveni was the chief patron of the Anglophone Tutsi RPF. Uganda under the aegis of Museveni became the staging area for US sponsored guerrilla movements not only in Rwanda but in Sudan and Zaire (now Congo). In fact, the Tutsi RPA was a branch of the Ugandan army. All throughout the invasion of Rwanda by Tutsi guerrillas it was supplied by military bases inside Uganda. Museveni's chief of military intelligence in the Ugandan Armed Forces was RPF leader Major General Paul Kagame. He was trained in Leavenworth, Kansas at the US Army Command and Staff College (CGSC). After leaving Leavenworth he returned to lead the RPA following their 1990 invasion into Rwanda. This was presented publicly as a war of liberation by Tutsi guerrillas. Today Kagame is president of Rwanda.

Contrary to their mainstream depiction, the RPF and RPA were far from saintly. They engaged in egregious atrocities in Uganda including terrorism to seize power. In neighboring Congo RPA forces organized a campaign of genocide mostly against Hutus. This included the execution of hundreds of thousands of men, women, and children, the burning of villages. Rape and disappearance of Hutu people were common. In the 1994 carnage in Rwanda they employed similar tactics and often used machetes to save bullets. As a consequence, Snow argues, and following the earlier pattern of reprisals, during the 1994 genocide hundreds of thousands of Francophone Tutsis were brutalized, killed, and raped in acts of genocide by existentially fearful and waning Hutus.[322] Nevertheless,

---

[322] One Rwandan insider close to the RPF comments: "Kagame's ambition caused the extermination of all of our families: Tutsis, Hutus and Twas. We all lost. Kagame's take-over took away the lives of a large number of Tutsis and caused the unnecessary exodus of millions of Hutus, many of whom were innocent under the hands of the genocide ringleaders. Some naive Rwandans proclaimed Kagame as their savior, but time has demonstrated that it was he who caused our suffering and misfortunes... Can Kagame explain to the Rwandan people why he sent Claude Dusaidi and Charles Muligande to New York and Washington to stop the UN military intervention which was supposed to be sent and protect the Rwandan people from the genocide? The reason behind avoiding that military intervention was to allow the RPF leadership the takeover of the Kigali

hundreds of thousands of Hutus were also killed, and there were far more Hutu deaths than Tutsi.[323]

Far from being a "bystander," militarizing Uganda and its constituent RPF — with their proclivity for atrocities — was integral to US regional foreign policy. The military buildup of the Ugandan United People's Defense Force (UPDF) and RPA was supported by the US and UK, the former colonial power. The Anglo-American bloc provided military training with the support of their intelligence agencies for Tutsi incursions into Rwanda:

> From 1989 onwards, America supported joint RPF [Rwandan Patriotic Front]-Ugandan attacks upon Rwanda... There were at least 56 "situation reports" in [US] State Department files in 1991... As American and British relations with Uganda and the RPF strengthened, so hostilities between Uganda and Rwanda escalated... By August 1990 the RPF had begun preparing an invasion with the full knowledge and approval of British intelligence.[324]

The Ugandan military — many in their ranks Tutsi RPF — were trained by US Special Forces and American mercenaries under the Africa Crisis Reaction Initiative (ACRI). Military Professional Resources Inc., mercenary commandos responsible for training, were also on contract with the State Department.

Funds for the Ugandan military and its UPDF — active in Rwanda, the Congo, and elsewhere — were facilitated via the IMF as a conduit. While foreign loans were ostensibly designated for economic and social reconstruction, civilian programs were cut, and part of the

---

Government and to show the world that they – the RPF – were the ones who stopped the genocide. We will all remember that the genocide occurred during three months, even though Kagame has said that he was capable of stopping it the first week after the aircraft crash. Can Major-General Paul Kagame explain why he asked to MINUAR to leave Rwandan soil within hours while the UN was examining the possibility of increasing its troops in Rwanda in order to stop the genocide?" Quoted in Chossudovsky, "Behind the Genocide."

[323] Snow, "Rwandan Genocide."
[324] Chossudovsky, "Behind the Genocide."

loans were diverted into defense and the UPDF. The World Bank was responsible for scrutinizing the budget of Uganda during this process. Under the aegis of the "public expenditure review" (PER) the government of Uganda was under obligation to provide information on the precise allocation of its budget; specifically, its Ministry of Defense faced scrutiny. Nonetheless, despite following a policy of austerity on civilian expenditures, its creditors turned a blind eye to increasing military spending. A portion of this bolstered the invading RPA that would spark the Rwandan Genocide.[325]

What emerged from the carnage of the Rwandan civil war and ensuing Genocide was a US client state similar to, and allied with, Uganda. In the strategic framework, France was expelled. The new Rwandan state would be led by Tutsi RPF head Paul Kagame, trained in Leavenworth, Kansas. This led to further regional destabilization and wanton slaughter. With US trained forces, Uganda and Rwanda, both now twin pillars of US hegemony, proceeded to intervene militarily in Zaire, (now Congo) still under the French orbit at the time. Continuing surreptitious support for the RPF, US Special forces were active during this period in training. The *Washington Post* provided a detailed account:

> Washington pumped military aid into Kagame's army, and U.S. Army Special Forces and other military personnel trained hundreds of Rwandan troops. But Kagame and his colleagues had designs of their own. While the Green Berets trained the Rwandan Patriotic Army, that army was itself secretly training Zairian rebels.… [In] Rwanda, U.S. officials publicly portrayed their engagement with the army as almost entirely devoted to human rights training. But the Special Forces exercises also covered other areas, including combat skills… Hundreds of soldiers and officers were enrolled in U.S. training programs, both in Rwanda and in the United States…
>
> [C]onducted by U.S. Special Forces, Rwandans studied camouflage techniques, small-unit movement, troop-leading procedures, soldier-team development, [etc]… And while the training went on, U.S. officials were meeting regularly with

---

[325] Ibid.

Kagame and other senior Rwandan leaders to discuss the continuing military threat faced by the [former Rwandan] government [in exile] from inside Zaire... Clearly, the focus of Rwandan-U.S. military discussion had shifted from how to build human rights to how to combat an insurgency... With [Ugandan President] Museveni's support, Kagame conceived a plan to back a rebel movement in eastern Zaire [headed by Laurent Desire Kabila] ...

The operation was launched in October 1996, just a few weeks after Kagame's trip to Washington and the completion of the Special Forces training mission... Once the war [in the Congo] started, the United States provided "political assistance" to Rwanda,... An official of the U.S. Embassy in Kigali traveled to eastern Zaire numerous times to liaise with Kabila. Soon, the rebels had moved on.

Brushing off the Zairian army with the help of the Rwandan forces, they marched through Africa's third-largest nation in seven months, with only a few significant military engagements. Mobutu fled the capital, Kinshasa, in May 1997, and Kabila took power, changing the name of the country to Congo...U.S. officials deny that there were any U.S. military personnel with Rwandan troops in Zaire during the war, although unconfirmed reports of a U.S. advisory presence have circulated in the region since the war's earliest days.[326]

The loss of life and suffering as a result of this joint Rwanda and Uganda offensive—tacitly supported by the US—was immeasurable. It is estimated that the deaths in the ensuing First and Second Congolese Wars were well over 6 million people. None of this figures into the calculus of Samantha Power; she untenably regards the Clinton administration as mere "bystanders" during this period.

Overall, what emerges from the argument of Samantha Power and the RtoP coterie is an exculpatory history that cleanses a long history

---

[326] Lynne Duke, "U.S. Faces Surprise, Dilemma in Africa," *Washington Post*, July 14, 1998, http://www.washingtonpost.com/wp-srv/national/longterm/overseas/overseas3a.htm Quoted in Chossudovsky, "Behind the Genocide."

of wanton slaughter directly committed or facilitated by US action abroad. Although this position is shaky, it is also a necessary prerequisite to the fiction that the US has engaged in a "consistent policy of non-intervention in the face of genocide." It is also a byproduct of the American exceptionalist world outlook. America can but act virtuous because it has achieved the highest form of human organization. The imperial hubris is strong.

As the RtoP call to action, what emerges is a dangerous missionary militarism. It engenders alacrity for America to intervene with the full weight of its unmatched military might on behalf of the forces of "good." Power's ilk likes to frame this as "humanitarian intervention," but the use of bombing, troops, and other punitive measures makes this simply a euphemism for war. Accordingly, the notion that war is humanitarian is not only Orwellian, but quantitatively untenable. The June 2014 issue of the *American Journal of Public Health* notes approximately 90% of all deaths in war are civilian. "The proportion of civilian deaths and the methods for classifying deaths as civilian are debated, but civilian war deaths constitute 85% to 90% of casualties caused by war, with about 10 civilians dying for every combatant killed in battle."[327] The historical verdict is that "Since the end of World War II, there have been 248 armed conflicts in 153 locations around the world. The United States launched 201 overseas military operations between the end of World War II and 2001, and since then, others, including Afghanistan and Iraq ...."[328] Although we cannot cover the entirety of American atrocities since the 20th century, to be sure, it is evident America holds a tremendous share of the burden for these war related civilian deaths. In fact, that civilians are the primary victims of war is also confirmed by the very conduct of recent "humanitarian interventions" lauded by humanitarian imperialists in places such as the former Yugoslavia and Libya. In these interventions NATO created civilian casualties as collateral damage, and deliberately attacked civilian infrastructure and individuals. One analyst comments, "A top defense of war is that it must be used to prevent something worse,

---

[327] 90% of All Deaths In War Are Civilians, Washington's Blog, http://www.globalresearch.ca/90-of-all-deaths-in-war-are-civilians/5382520
[328] Ibid.

called genocide. Not only does militarism generate genocide rather than preventing it, but the distinction between war and genocide is a very fine one at best."[329]

THE NATO BLOC'S VAST DISINFORMATION CAMPAIGN

Truth is said to be the first casualty of war.[330] The war against Libya thoroughly confirms this dictum. In fact, in addition to being used to garner support and legitimacy for aggression under the RtoP doctrine, mendacious propaganda was used by the NATO bloc as a direct instrument of war. From beginning to end, the war against Libya depended on a vast disinformation campaign to attain its objectives. This deception operation is, perhaps, one of the most efficacious examples of propaganda as a weapon of war in the modern era. Central to this disinformation operation was the propagation of myths that Qaddafi employed black African mercenaries, rape against women, unleashed unmitigated lethal force, and used his air force against unarmed civilians.

The myth that Qaddafi used his Air Force to strafe civilians in the eastern stronghold of Benghazi was a linchpin for justification of NATO's "no-fly zone" and regime change. The Atlantic powers gave sharp rebukes to Libya on the basis of this specious claim. For example, British Prime Minister David Cameron, key NATO state leader, declared: "We must not tolerate this regime using military force [referring to the jet attacks] against its own people." "In that context I have asked the Ministry of Defence and the Chief of the Defence Staff to work with our allies on plans for a military no-fly zone." [331]

Despite providing justification for war, this bold claim has not been proven hitherto; the existing evidence stands against this claim. Mainstream news outlets such as BBC and al-Jazeera (both of their state patrons supporting the anti-Libya operation) regurgitated this claim emanating from the foreign backed Libyan opposition. [332]

---

[329] Ibid.

[330] Sun Tzu.

[331] Nazemroaya, "Mad Dog or Brother Leader."

[332] David Kirkpatrick, "Libyan aircraft strafe protests Battles batter besieged capital; regime splinters around Khadafy," *New York Times*, February 22, 2011,

France 24, sponsored by the French Foreign Affairs Ministry, broadcast its version of unfolding events in Libya on February 21, 2011 with this canard that Libyan army planes bombed civilians. Later this claim was debunked by the French ambassador to Tripoli in the French Parliament.[333] Monitoring the picture in Benghazi from space, Russian military officials asserted these strikes never took place.[334] Satellite imagery showed no damage by jets. Even the US Department of Defense had to concede at the time such attacks could not be confirmed. In response to the question, "Do you see any evidence that he [Qaddafi] actually has fired on his own people from the air?" Secretary of Defense Robert Gates responded, "We've seen the press reports, but we have no confirmation of that."[335] Chairman of the Joint Chiefs of Staff Admiral Mike Mullen added, "That's correct. We've seen no confirmation whatsoever." Indeed, in the era of the iPhone and mass access to video technology, no substantiating video evidence existed, despite a plethora of footage coming out of Libya at the time. Furthermore, for all the hype of the Libyan Air Force as a threat to civilians, it was inadequate militarily (hence eagerness to proceed with a military operation). In the estimation of Admiral Locklear, US Navy commander who led the attacks against Libya at the war's onset, "[Libya's] air force before coalition operations was "not in good repair," and [Libya's] tactical capability consisted of several dozen helicopters."

Concerning attacks and a general threat to civilians, the Federal German government drew a similar conclusion. German MP Sevim Dagdelen explained, "The reasons given to provide legitimacy for the war against Libya were lies. Something which has long been criticized by many in the peace movement has now been confirmed by the Federal Government in its answer to a Minor Interpellation (Bundestag printed paper 17/5409), under the heading 'Background

---

http://www.boston.com/news/world/africa/articles/2011/02/22/libyan_forces_bomb_protests/

[333] Julien Theil, "Was the Case for R2P Based on Fraud? The Universal Periodic Review of Libya," *The Illegal War on Libya*, (Clarity Press, 2012).

[334] " "Airstrikes in Libya did not take place" – Russian military," RT, March 01, 2011, http://rt.com/news/airstrikes-libya-russian-military/

[335] "DOD News Briefing with Secretary Gates and Adm. Mullen from the Pentagon," Defense.gov, http://www.defense.gov/transcripts/transcript.aspx?transcriptid=4777

to the armed attack on Libya.' " In response to the inquiry the Federal German government stated it "does not possess any detailed information about attacks on civilians by the Libyan Air Force." Dagdelen added, "The alleged widespread and systematic bomb attacks on civilians by the Libyan military never took place. The Federal Government was also unable to explain why protection of civilians and access to humanitarian aid would not have been possible without the use of force by the West."[336]This partly explains the German distancing from the NATO operation during the tumult. German foreign minister Guido Westerwelle emphasized its distance from the United Nations Security Council (UNSC) Resolution 1973 authorizing the use of force. Germany accepted sanctions, but refused to partake in military actions, subsequently withdrawing its ships in Libyan territorial waters.

The allegation Qaddafi's forces used rape as a weapon of war was another enumerated reason for the authorization of war against Libya. Secretary of State Hillary Clinton, chief proponent of Obama's Libya war, declared the US was "deeply concerned by reports of wide-scale rape" in Libya. Susan Rice, U.S. Ambassador to the UN, who was instrumental in the drive for war at the UN and in the Obama administration, "told a closed-door meeting of officials at the UN that the Libyan military is using rape as a weapon in the war with the rebels and some had been issued the anti-impotency drug [Viagra]. She reportedly offered no evidence to back up the claim."[337] In truth, this allegation was baseless and contrived. Both Doctors Without Borders and Amnesty International investigated and "found no first-hand evidence in Libya that rapes are systematic and being used as part of war strategy." The senior crisis responder for Amnesty International in Libya for three months following the foreign sponsored uprising stated, "we have not found any evidence

---

[336] Sevim Dagdelen, "No information available concerning attacks on civilians," May 16, 2011,
http://www.sevimdagdelen.de/de/article/2164.no_information_available_concerning_attacks_on_civilians.html
[337] "US Intel: NO Evidence of Viagra as Weapon in Libya," NBCNews.com,
http://www.nbcnews.com/id/42824884/ns/world_news-mideastn_africa/#.U-hcnPldX4U

or a single victim of rape or a doctor who knew about somebody being raped." Investigations in Eastern Libya "have not turned up significant hard evidence supporting allegations of rapes by Qaddafi's forces."[338]

This malicious canard was a Benghazi based Libyan opposition fabrication to generate hysteria and support for their cause. Human Rights Watch also reported, "We have not been able to find evidence." An Amnesty representative explained, "rebels dealing with the foreign media in Benghazi started showing journalists packets of Viagra, claiming they came from burned-out tanks, though it is unclear why the packets were not charred."[339]

At the UNSC's approval of military force against Libya, US ambassador to the UN Susan Rice issued a statement claiming a reason to authorize a "no-fly zone," was to prevent the influx of planes bringing in foreign African "mercenaries" in support of Qaddafi. This was the oft-repeated African mercenaries fiction. Western and Gulf state media drummed up anti-black hysteria by repeating this canard. In its article "Libyan Oil Buys Loyal African Allies for Qaddafi," the *New York Times* claimed Qaddafi recruited "about 200" young men from Mali, and repeated disinformation that he recruited 3,000 to 4,000 mercenaries on a $1,000 salary. The *Times*'s March 11 story however stated US intelligence officials were unable to confirm this. The London *Guardian* on March 16, had to offer a clarification to its previous report alluding to the use of mercenaries by Qaddafi from tribes in neighboring countries. There is "no evidence that members of the Zaghawa are involved in the present conflict," wrote the *Guardian*.[340] In truth, external black Africans had come to Libya, but these were volunteers who supported Qaddafi's pan-African vision and support for African economic

[338] Patrick Cockburn,"Amnesty questions claim that Gaddafi ordered rape as weapon of war," *Independent*, June 24, 2011,
http://www.independent.co.uk/news/world/africa/amnesty-questions-claim-that-gaddafi-ordered-rape-as-weapon-of-war-2302037.html
[339] Ibid.
[340] Wayne Madsen, "Gaddaffi's African 'Mercenary' Story is a Disinformation Ploy by the CIA," April 04, Strategic Culture Foundation, http://www.globalresearch.ca/gaddaffi-s-african-mercenary-story-is-a-disinformation-ploy-by-the-cia/24129

development.[341] While this hype of African mercenaries was being augmented, Genevieve Garrigos, who headed Amnesty International (AI) France gave it credence. AI later conceded though, "Today we have to admit there is no evidence Qaddafi employed Mercenary forces." In a later interview on July 2011 Garrigos admitted the African mercenaries canard "was just a rumor spread by the media."[342] At the UN it was claimed that civilians were "targeted by Colonel Muammar Al-Qadhafi, his allied forces and mercenaries." Thus, the mercenary myth worked to support the UNSC war resolution.

What emerged in the mainstream media as a popular "peaceful protest" in Libya had all the earmarks of a foreign supported armed uprising. As we shall see, it was not Qaddafi who initiated violence from the onset of the uprisings, but the opposition. Libya's February 17th, "Day of Rage" was announced not in Libya itself by dissidents in Tripoli or Benghazi, but externally via the London based National Conference of Libyan Opposition (NCLO).[343] The Congressional Research Service (CRS) report of published February 18, 2011:

> The National Conference for the Libyan Opposition (an umbrella organization of opposition groups headed by the National Libyan Salvation Front (NLSF) [...] and Internet-based organizers called for a "day of rage" to take place on February 17. Similar events had been organized by anti-government groups in many other countries in the Middle East and North Africa over the previous month. On February

---

[341] Ibid.

[342] Forestgamertube, "Lies behind the 'Humanitarian War' in Libya: There is no evidence! (Part 1), NATO Crimes In Libya." October 05, 2011, https://www.youtube.com/watch?v=j4evwAMIh4Y

[343] Doug Sounders, "Libya's major opposition forces united beneath tricolour rebel flag," *Globe and Mail*, February 27, 2011, http://www.theglobeandmail.com/news/world/africa-mideast/libyas-major-opposition-forces-united-beneath-tricolour-rebel-flag/article1922712/

17, [2011] hundreds of protestors took to the streets in Benghazi and in other cities in its vicinity.[344]

The NCLO was created in London in 2005 by Ibrahim Sahad as an updated iteration of the dissident National Front for the Salvation of Libya (NFSL). As the spearhead of Libyan opposition groups since the 1980s, the *Daily Globe and Mail* reported NFSL organized several attempted armed uprisings and assassination attempts against Qaddafi. According to US Library of Congress records, the NFSL was supported and trained by the CIA. While he helped direct the 2011 uprising in Libya from Washington D.C, Sahad gave interviews with corporate controlled media. He was presented as a credible and implicitly impartial source of information.

By all counts, these "peaceful protestors" were armed insurgents. The US government's own sources conceded it was not entirely an uprising of the oft-repeated "peaceful protestors." The CRS:

> On the evening of February 15, [2011] the [...] demonstrations began when several hundred people gathered in front of the Benghazi police headquarters to protest the arrest of attorney and human rights activist Fethi Tarbel. As the February 17 [2011] "day of rage" neared, protests escalated in Benghazi and other cities despite reported police attempts at dispersion with water cannons, tear gas, rubber bullets, and batons. There were multiple reports of protestors setting police and other government buildings on fire.[345]

However repressive a state apparatus Qaddafi had at his disposal, no state tolerates "setting police and other government buildings on fire" without responding with lethal force. That this uprising had a military dimension was evident from its onset. Videos soon emerged following the "Day of Rage" showing a Benghazi army base totally decimated and bombed out with manifest signs of an armed battleground. This included the destruction of large chunks of steel-

[344] Christopher Branchard and Jim Zanotti, "Libya: Background and U.S. Relations," Congressional Research Service, February 18, 2011, http://fpc.state.gov/documents/organization/157348.pdf
[345] Ibid.

reinforced concrete walls.[346] No "peaceful protestors" could do this. These Libyan rebels were not civilians, but an armed force. These "protestors" seized armored vehicles and heavy weapons at the base. The *New York Times* March 1, 2011 article "Libyan Rebels Said to Debate Seeking U.N. Airstrikes" featured images of Libyan insurgents receiving military training, "suggesting the unrest is the result of a yet another NFSL military operation rather than a 'spontaneous' protest turned violent," one analyst noted.[347]

One of the most fantastic features of the narrative emanating from Western and Gulf media was the canard that Libyan security forces were eliminated by their own side for refusing to fight or kill "protestors." According to independent journalist Mahdi Darius Nazemroyah, reporting from Libya, "Video evidence from within Libya actually proved video footage presented alongside these reports about Libya was spun. It was not the Libyan forces that killed these men, but elements within the Libyan opposition."[348] Qatar's al-Jazeera — under the control the ruling al-Thani family, a key sponsor of the uprising — rather clumsily attempted to give credence to this narrative. New America Media news agency explained:

> After initially letting slip that the earliest Libyan protests were organized by the LIFG [al-Qaeda affiliate Libyan Islamic Fighting Group, recognized as a terrorist organization by the UNSC], Al-Jazeera quickly changed its line to present a heavily filtered account portraying the events as "peaceful protests." To explain away the gunshot deaths of Libyan soldiers during the uprising, the Qatar-based network presented a bizarre scenario of 150 dead soldiers in Libya

---

[346] RT, "Video of abandoned Libya military base in Benghazi after days of fierce battles," Uploaded February 24, 2011, https://www.youtube.com/watch?v=t7-3wbyN_Ns

[347] Kareem Fahim and David Kirkpatrick, "Libyan Rebels Said to Debate Seeking U.N. Airstrikes," *New York Times*, March 01, 2011, http://www.nytimes.com/2011/03/02/world/africa/02libya.html See also Tony Cartalucci, "US Libyan Policy Zero Legitimacy," http://landdestroyer.blogspot.com/2011/03/us-libyan-policy-zero-legitimacy.html

[348] Nazemroaya, "Or Brother Leader."

having been executed by their officers for "refusing to fight." The mysterious officers then miraculously vacated their base disappearing into thin air while surrounded by angry protesters! Off the record, one American intelligence analyst called these media claims an "absurdity" and suggested instead the obvious: that the soldiers were gunned down in an armed assault by war-hardened returned militants from Iraq and Afghanistan.[349]

Even news agencies such as BBC were forced to concede their reports could not be confirmed and were based on "witness accounts." [350] These were the plethora of unconfirmed rumors contributing to the general war hysteria. This included imaginative canards about the distribution of Viagra for the purposes of rape, the storming of hospitals, and massacres at mosques. With apocryphal rumors the beating drums for war continued unabated.

But long after the smoke cleared in the aftermath of NATO's successful destruction of the Libyan state, the Belfer Center for Science and International Affairs at the Kennedy School of Government at Harvard issued a highly instructive and sobering report on what transpired in Libya.[351] The author of the report was Dr. Alan Kuperman, Associate Professor of Public Affairs at the University of Texas. He concluded that the allegation Qaddafi's forces engaged in wanton massacres precipitating the Libyan civil war—a narrative repeated and recycled *ad nauseam* by major news

---

[349] Yoichi Shimatsu, "Mideast Revolutions and 9-11 Intrigues Created in Qatar," New American Media, March 5, 2011,
http://newamericamedia.org/2011/03/mideast-revolutions-and-9-11-intrigues-created-in-qatar.php
[350] Jon Williams, "The difficulty of reporting from inside Libya," BBC, February 20, 2011,
http://www.bbc.co.uk/blogs/legacy/theeditors/2011/02/reporting_from_1ibya.html
[351] Alan Kuperman, "Lessons from Libya: How Not to Intervene," Policy Brief, Belfer Center for Science and   International Affairs, Harvard Kennedy School,
http://belfercenter.ksg.harvard.edu/publication/23387/lessons_from_libya.html?utm_source=feedburner&utm_medium=feed&utm_campaign=Feed%253A+belfer%252Fsecurity_nato+%28Belfer+Center+for+Science+and+International+Affairs+-+Security_NATO%29

organs and human rights organizations—was specious. Furthermore, it was the opposition who initiated violence to begin with. Dr. Kuperman observes:

> **Contrary to Western media reports, Qaddafi did not initiate Libya's violence by targeting peaceful protesters. The United Nations and Amnesty International have documented that in all four Libyan cities initially consumed by civil conflict in mid-February 2011—Benghazi, Al Bayda, Tripoli, and Misurata—violence was actually initiated by the protesters.** The government responded to the rebels militarily but never intentionally targeted civilians or resorted to "indiscriminate" force, as Western media claimed. Early press accounts exaggerated the death toll by a factor of ten, citing "more than 2,000 deaths" in Benghazi during the initial days of the uprising, whereas Human Rights Watch (HRW) later documented only 233 deaths across all of Libya in that period. [Emphasis added.]

In the hysteria and haste for war, the veracity of the prevailing narrative was never challenged. A chorus of pro-war advocates, including credulous leftist[352] in unison with neoconservatives[353] (with their proclivity for military intervention) eagerly promoted the pro-war propaganda of NATO and their dependent Libyan rebels. Many figures critical of the Iraq war and its spurious pretenses did not learn salutary lessons applicable to yet another "WMD moment." As Dr. Kuperman admonishes, those eager to intervene on humanitarian grounds need to "beware of both misinformation and rebel propaganda. If Western countries had accurately perceived Libya's initial civil conflict—as Qaddafi using discriminate force against violent tribal, regional, and radical Islamist rebels—NATO would

---

[352] Amy Goodman of Democracy Now!, author Juan Cole, commentator Cenk Uygur, Rachel Madow of MSNBC, and more.
[353] Stephen M. Walt, "What Intervention in Libya Teaches US About the Neocon-Liberal Alliance," *Foreign Policy*, March 11, 2011, http://www.foreignpolicy.com/posts/2011/03/21/what_intervention_in_libya_tells_us_about_the_neocon_liberal_alliance

have been much less likely to launch its counterproductive intervention."[354] Misinformation and mendacity kills.

Within the Obama administration, at the forefront disseminating lies to legitimize the assault on Libya was the State Department of Hillary Clinton. Recent revelations by the *Washington Times*, based on released recordings, show high ranking US officials in the Pentagon and in intelligence distrusted the narrative propagated by the Clinton State Department; it presented selective and tendentious information to Congress and other officials. An intelligence official explained to the *Washington Times* that the decision to bomb Libya was based on "light intelligence" and "speculative arguments."[355]

The Pentagon so distrusted Clinton's narrative that they went against protocol and established their own diplomatic channels to Libya. The American intermediary dispatched by the Joint Chiefs of Staff told the Qaddafi government in July 2011, "You should see these internal State Department reports that are produced in the State Department that go out to the Congress. They're just full of stupid, stupid facts." The Pentagon liaison explained that Army Gen. Charles H. Jacoby Jr., a top aide to then Chairman of the Joint Chiefs Adm. Mullen, "does not trust the reports that are coming out of the State Department and CIA, but there's nothing he can do about it." This was because "Mr. Obama privately informed members of Congress" that Libya " 'is all Secretary Clinton's matter,' [while] the nation's highest-ranking generals were concerned the president was being misinformed." In her career of public service Clinton has consistently been a bellicose personality eager for intervention.[356] Accordingly, she was one of the most vociferous voices pushing to

---

[354] Kuperman, "Lessons."
[355] Kelly Riddell, "Exclusive: Secret tapes undermine Hillary Clinton on Libyan war. Joint Chiefs, key lawmaker held own talks with Moammar Gadhafi regime," *Washington Times*, January 28, 2015,
http://www.washingtontimes.com/news/2015/jan/28/hillary-clinton-undercut-on-libya-war-by-pentagon-/?page=all
[356] Gary Leupp, "The Warmongering Record of Hillary Clinton," *Counterpunch*, February 11, 2015,
http://www.counterpunch.org/2015/02/11/the-warmongering-record-of-hillary-clinton/

attack Libya. In the aftermath of successful regime change, she blithely remarked: "We came; We saw; He [Qaddafi] died."

UNKNOWN SNIPERS

The tactic of using unknown snipers to instigate internecine conflicts and provide a media smokescreen for destabilization is a frequent tactic of the NATO bloc.[357] This adds further complication to the narrative. Russian investigative journalist Nikolai Starikov authored a book analyzing the role unknown snipers have taken in the destabilization of states targeted for regime change by the US and its allies. This tactic was used against states such as Romania, and Venezuela, where it was used in the 2002 CIA backed military coup against Hugo Chavez. The killing of 18 protestors in an opposition march to the presidential palace organized and backed by the US regime change apparatus—with the trite mainstream media line Chavez was "killing his own people"—provided a veneer of legitimacy to the coup. That unknown snipers are a tactic of the US regime change apparatus was attested by Chalmers Johnson, author of the bestseller *The Sorrows of Empire*.[358] In an interview Johnson remarks that the "methods of clandestine activities" to overthrow unwanted governments includes the use of "provocateurs" to get people to riot who will subsequently be killed by US sponsored snipers. Their deaths are blamed on the targeted government.[359] "We've used that ploy so many times from Jakarta to Caracas recently," remarked Johnson. "It's *insane* to believe [CBS news anchor] Dan Rather that innocent bystanders were shot by thugs of the Chavez regime," he adds.

---

[357] Gearóid Ó Colmáin, "Unknown Snipers and Western backed "Regime Change" A Historical Review and Analysis," Center for Research on Globalization, March 07, 2011, http://www.globalresearch.ca/unknown-snipers-and-western-backed-regime-change/27904

[358] eon3, "DECLINE of EMPIRES: The Signs of Decay," YouTube, January 22, 2008, https://www.youtube.com/watch?v=Q2CCs-x9q9U&feature=related

[359] See also Tony Cartalucci, *Subverting Syria*, Progressive Press, 2012, for the use of sniper provocateurs to overthrow the Thai and Syrian governments. Snipers also committed the massacre that brought down the Ukrainian government during the "Euromaidan" protests, see http://www.progressivepress.com/blog-entry/dirty-war-ukraine.

There is evidence this method was used in the Libyan operation. Al-Jazeera aired videos ostensibly showing peaceful "pro-democracy" protestors fired on by "Qaddafi's forces." In a common media deception tactic, the actual video was edited to give the appearance that security forces were killing them. The unedited version of the video available on YouTube shows pro-Qaddafi demonstrators with their characteristic green flags being shot by unknown snipers. With a one-sided narrative dominating throughout the disinformation campaign against Libya, it has been impossible to focus attention on the identity of these snipers.[360]

AL-JAZEERA FAKE TRIPOLI VICTORY

The media war against Libya reached its apex when it became a direct instrument of the NATO-rebel assault against Tripoli in the final battle for its control. In an article "The Libya Media Hoax: Fabricated Scenes of Jubilation and Euphoria on Green Square"[361] it was shown how al-Jazeera[362] manufactured a phony scene of rebel victory of Tripoli's Green Square to sow confusion in the Libyan people:

> Surpassing previous mass media fabrications, both in scale and boldness, yesterday morning's Al Jazeera mise-en-scène will surely go down in history as one of the most cynical hoaxes committed by corporate media since the manipulated pictures of Iraqis toppling Saddam Hussein's statue after the US invasion in 2003."

---

[360] Colmáin, "Unknown Snipers."

[361] Metro Gael, "The Libya Media Hoax: Fabricated Scenes of Jubilation and Euphoria on Green Square," Metro Gael, August 23, 2011,
http://www.globalresearch.ca/the-libya-media-hoax-fabricated-scenes-of-jubilation-and-euphoria-on-green-square/26155

[362] See Thierry Meyssan, "Wadah Khanfar, Al-Jazeera and the triumph of televised propaganda,"
Voltiarenet, September 26, 2011,
http://www.voltairenet.org/article171512.html for an exposé of the transformation of al-Jazeera from a respectable alternative news source to a partisan instrument of Qatar's foreign policy eager to assimilate into the power centers of Atlanticist globalization. This was done under the stewardship of Mahmoud Jibril, Prime Minister the TNC no less.

On the morning of August 22nd 2011, al-Jazeera aired a "live" report from Green Square in Tripoli, which claimed to show the capture of the Libyan capital by rebel forces. Scenes of jubilation and euphoria enveloped Al Jazeera's reporter Zeina Khodr as she declared: "Libya is in the hands of the opposition."

Gaddafi's sons were said to have been arrested, and more defections were announced. The Libyan capital was, we were told, now in the hands of the rebel forces. For many, it seemed a fait accompli. [Lizzie Phelan confirmed that Saif Qaddafi was still in the Green Square and he made an appearance to rally troops in the final defense of the country.]

In fact, the Al Jazeera pictures from Green Square were an elaborate and criminal hoax. The report had been prefabricated in a studio in Doha Qatar. This information had been passed onto Libyan intelligence and the Libyan people had already been warned about the Qatari psyops a couple of days previously on Rayysse state television.

The Al Jazeera hoax was intended to create the impression that Tripoli had fallen so as to break the Libyan resistance by creating panic and chaos in the Libyan capital...to provide cover for the massacres of civilians that would occur in the days following the declaration of rebel victory.

In other words, the media would provide cover for the war crimes and crimes against humanity that are necessary in order to subjugate the Libyan Jamhahirya to Western corporate interests.

Shortly after the Al Jazeera pictures were released, this author contacted independent reporter Lizzie Phelan in Tripoli. Miss Phelan was able to confirm from what she described as reliable sources that the al-Jazeera pictures were false.

By the end of the day, it emerged that all the twitter lies emanating from the criminals in the National Transitional Council were also, unsurprisingly, false. Gaddafi's sons had not been arrested, and the rebels were not in control of the city.

The Qatari al-Jazeera synthetic version of Tripoli was sloppily constructed with discrepancies between it and the actual Green Square, which included *sui generis* architecture dating back to the Roman Empire:

> [Pictures prove] that the producers of the Al Jazeera hoax are no Dutch masters, as the glaring discrepancies between the real Green Square in Tripoli and the Al Jazeera version are patently obvious. The differences between the architecture in Green Square in Tripoli and the pictures shown in Al Jazeera are well documented in the video below.

> While the Al Jazeera mise-en-scène is entertaining, the leading actress Zeina Khodr is unlikely to receive awards for her rather sluggish performance. She said her lines rather mechanically, as one who was not particularly enamored of the script, or perhaps it was the far-fetched aspect of the entire screen play that bothered her.

> This media hoax is another poignant example of the desperation of NATO, who have ruthlessly bombed a sovereign nation for 6 months and have so far failed to effect regime change. It also proves yet again the role of the corporate media in disinformation and war.

LEVERAGING SOFT POWER AND THE UN AS AN INSTRUMENT OF EMPIRE

The vast disinformation operation acted as preparation for justifying regime change, and in synergy with the newfangled soft power strategy of the Obama team. In accordance with a new soft-power doctrine, a key pillar of the anti-Libyan offensive was to use international organizations such as the UN (and related organizations) to legitimize aggression. An act of humanitarian imperialism, the Libyan war operation was framed under the RtoP doctrine. The bombing campaign was justified on "humanitarian" grounds. An Orwellian "humanitarian war" needs human rights violations as casus belli. To justify war requires the semblance of a humanitarian catastrophe. Thus, the Obama team required a big lie hysteria involving human rights violations by Libya to be presented at the UN. In this way, the operation was akin to the false WMD claims made by the Bush II regime. In another way, it was a stark shift from the Bush's tactics because during his tenure the US was

IV. The New Humanitarian Imperialism

critical of the UN Commission on Human Rights (UNCHR). In fact, the US even boycotted it prior to the Obama presidency. Contrary to this approach, the Obama team used it as a tool for regime change, engaging fully at the council. Whereas the Bush II regime saw the UN as a nuisance, Obama apparatchiks used it as an instrument to further its geopolitical objectives.

Illustrating this, in May of 2012, after the Libyan regime change operation succeeded, the efficacy of this approach was touted by Obama apparatchik Suzanne Nossel. Nossel, now executive director of Amnesty International (AI) (thus, exposing how compromised AI is as a watch dog of "human rights") was the former US Deputy Assistant Secretary of State for International Organizations. Here she held "responsibility for U.S. engagement at the UN Human Rights Council." Nossel, a member of the elite corporate sponsored Council on Foreign Relations (CFR) as "Visiting Senior Fellow for Global Governance," wrote a paper delineating how the US attained its objectives during its first years of participation at the UNHRC.[363] According to Nossel, this was the "story of how the United States and others turned around the Human Rights Council since joining the body in 2009." She offered "a case study on effective tactics for achieving U.S. policy goals through multilateral diplomacy and advancing human rights norms at the United Nations." Overall, Nossel finds that "due in significant part to vigorous, determined efforts by the United States, the Human Rights Council [showed] a newfound credibility as a human rights watchdog."

This "vigorous" and "determined effort" played out in a demonization campaign against Libya, which was built on a web of lies. One such example was during the UN's Universal Periodic Review of human rights on Libya published on January 4, 2011. Here, the UN report praised Libya's human rights record to the consternation of Nossel, who described the Council's report as "abhorrent," calling for a complete "redo."

---

[363] Suzanne Nossel, "Advancing Human Rights in the UN System," CFR, June 2012, http://www.cfr.org/international-organizations-and-alliances/advancing-human-rights-un-system/p28414

Acting under the framework of this Nossel doctrine to utilize the UN, the legitimization of the NATO bombing assault at the UNSC was dependent upon a vast disinformation campaign carried out by a coterie of so-called "human rights" organizations, think-tanks, and media. These organizations worked to justify intervention, propagating myths about the use of black African mercenaries, Libyan military jet attacks on civilians, and massacres by Qaddafi against civilians. In what would become "a self-fuelled cycle of misinformation" international news outlets quoted human rights organizations who would then base their claims on media reports. In short, the basis for the war against Libya was built on a cycle of fraud.

The UN's High Commission for Human Rights, which supervises the UNHRC, was also a driver of this cycle of fraud against Libya, setting the narrative for war. The Commission's head Navi Pillay played a straightforward role in this regard. Pillay frequently used phrases such as "press reports suggest," and unquestioningly accepted unfounded or hyperbolic claims of anti-Libyan Arab news agencies such as Qatar's al-Jazeera and al-Arabiya. These agencies were regurgitating claims of the Libyan opposition. Moreover, the information disseminated by these news outlets reflected the foreign policy of their patrons such as House al-Thani of Qatar, owners of al-Jazeera. With the caveat that "reports are still patchy and hard to verify," Pillay nonetheless concluded that "the Libyan leader [Qaddafi] must stop the violence now." She repeated the patently fraudulent claim that "tanks, helicopters, and military aircraft have reportedly been used indiscriminately to attack the protestors."[364] This was an act of malfeasance by an international public servant ostensibly acting impartially. Giving an interview to CNN from Davos, Switzerland — the confab of Atlanticist plutocrats to determine the course of the world economy — it remained an open question whether or not she was in fact an international public servant or acting in the interest of moneybags at Davos.

Another exacerbating circumstance was that Libya held no ambassador to the UN; its representatives defected, likely the sleeper agents of foreign powers. Despite not representing any government,

---

[364] "UN rights council recommends suspending Libya, orders inquiry into abuses," UN News Center, February 25, 2011,
http://www.un.org/apps/news/story.asp?NewsID=37626#.U-lkofldX4V

these two defectors were nonetheless permitted access to the UNSC to deliver anti-Libyan remarks, another act of malfeasance by the UN. Because Libya was unable to respond to the claims, it subsequently named the former foreign minister of Nicaragua Rev. Miguel D'Escoto Brockman as its permanent representative. His attendance at the UN was immediately blocked through the efforts of Susan Rice, America's UN ambassador, on the technicality that he was on a tourist and not a diplomatic visa to the US. Bereft of a representative, and not able to answer the charges brought against it, Libya faced a kangaroo court. The anti-Libyan operation was a merciless offensive on all levels including the UN. Brockman aptly accused Secretary-General Ban Ki Moon of betraying the Charter of the UN, adding that the UN was acting as "a lethal weapon of the empire."[365]

Equally crucial in lending credence to the anti-Libyan hysteria were NGOs in the orbit of the Western intelligence community. Although in this case they were ostensible "human rights organizations," this follows the pattern of the other regime changes in the "Arab Spring." In the anti-Libyan case, these "NGOs" acted as black propaganda outlets, censuring the Libyan Jamahiriya government for alleged human rights violations to justify the coming humanitarian imperialist attack. These groups presented fraudulent or hyperbolic claims against Qaddafi's government by presenting evidence of gross widespread human rights violations. The narrative which emerged at the UNHRC with the aid of these groups and Pillay was that Qaddafi is "killing his own people" in the eastern city of Benghazi and abroad. The specific claim made was that Qaddafi ordered Libyan state forces to kill 6,000 civilians in Benghazi and elsewhere.[366] These unproven but widely disseminated claims were the basis for the expulsion of Libya from the Human Rights Council and its referral to the UNSC.

One of the first "NGOs" to attack Libya at the UN — in tandem with the US funded Freedom House and the CIA's sidekick the NED — was UN Watch. This "NGO," created in 1993, acted decidedly from a pro-Israel position, and had informal ties to the US State

---

[365] Nazemroyah, "Or Brother Leader."
[366] Ibid.

Department. The organization was created by Morris Abram, then honorary President of the American Jewish Committee, a New York-based pro-Israel lobbying group. Morris was the US Permanent Representative to the UN in Geneva during the Clinton Administration. Israel desired to smash Libya to undermine the overall Arab position, and because of its support of militant Palestinian liberation groups.

In May 2010 Libya was elected to the UNHRC. Subsequently, UN Watch, US-funded Freedom House, a related organization FIDH, and more "NGOs," campaigned to remove Libya from the UNHRC. They succeeded in March 1, 2011 when the operation on the ground was already underway. Notably, this development was praised by the US ambassador to the UNHRC and in the House Foreign Affairs Committee, where Congressman Howard remarked, "Hillel Neuer [the head of] UN Watch [is] one of the strongest and most informed critics of the Human Rights Council." In making the decision to expel Libya, the UN's Periodic Review, which contrastingly praised Libya's human rights record, was not considered. Instead, the unfounded claim that Libya was killing civilians was. That Libya was expelled from the UNHRC also meant that they could not answer the calumny leveled against them.

One of the foremost sources for the "Qaddafi is killing his own people" hysteria was the Libyan League for Human Rights (LLHR). This "NGO" was led by its General Secretary Dr. Sliman Bouchuiguir. After presenting hysterical claims—emphasizing the Libyan Jamahiriyah was committing crimes against humanity in Geneva at the UNHRC—the LLHR was instrumental in sparking UN involvement in conjunction with the pro-Israel UN Watch and the omnipresent CIA "sidekick" the NED. LLHR lobbied and got 70 additional NGOs along with the NED—although only 25 of them claimed to be human rights organizations—to send letters to key international leaders, *inter alia*, calling on the UN High Commissioner of Human Rights to "monitor the situation and take action as needed." Most importantly, they called for an international response through the invocation of the RtoP doctrine. The parties addressed included US President Barack Obama, the EU's High Representative Catherine Ashton, and UN Secretary-General Ban-Ki Moon.

Upon further examination it is evident that the claims of the LLHR are not only dubious at best, but the LLHR was partisan and a highly compromised organization in the orbit of both Western intelligence and the Libyan opposition itself. In other words, the LLHR was the voice of the CIA, State Department, and the Libyan opposition. The LLHR was a member of the International Federation for Human Rights (FIDH), a French based organization tied to the NED—the CIA "sidekick" (see Chapter III)—that operated on the African continent. According to author Julien Theil, "The FIDH, has received direct funding, in the form of grants, from the National Endowment for Democracy for its programmes in Africa. In 2010, a NED grant of $140,186 (U.S.) was one of the latest amounts given to the FIDH for its work in Africa."[367]

On February 21, 2011 a joint communiqué was issued in an emergency session of the UN by the LLHR and the FIDH, demanding international action in Libya. One analyst's report: "They called for involvement by the International Criminal Court while [claiming] 400 to 600 people had died since 15 February 2011. This of course was approximately 5,500 short of their later claim that 6,000 people had been massacred in Benghazi. The joint letter also promoted the false view that 80% of Gaddafi's military force was composed of foreign mercenaries, something which over half a year of fighting was to show to be untrue. All these allegations were repeated in Bouchuiguir's statement to the 15th Special Session on 25 February, as was as the call to seize the Security Council, the ICC and to expel the Libyan Arab Jamahiriya from the Council."[368]

In an indispensable and revelatory interview, the LLHR's General-Secretary Dr. Sliman Bouchuiguir was forced to concede, in his words, "there is no evidence" to any of his organization's claims.

[367] Mahdi Darius Nazemroaya and Julien Teil, "America's Conquest of Africa: The Roles of France and Israel: Introduction by Cynthia McKinney," GlobalResearch.ca, October 06, 2011, http://www.globalresearch.ca/america-s-conquest-of-africa-the-roles-of-france-and-israel/26886

[368] "Universal Periodic Review of Libya: Was the case for R2P based on fraud?" Center for the Study of Interventionism, http://interventionism.files.wordpress.com/2012/03/libyauprfinal.pdf

When questioned on how the group of 70 NGOs he stewarded in Geneva could support the LLHR's claims, Buchuiguir responded that a network of close relationships was the basis. In his own words, "we rely on mouth to ear." In sum, these claims, accepted as truth by the "international community," were based on mere hearsay. Nazemroyah: "This is a mockery." Even Bouchuiguir candidly admitted, in "a court of law, they can't rely on mouth to ear." Nonetheless, it was sufficient for the UNSC to authorize military intervention.

In another revelatory interview, Mustafa Jalil of the TNC (Transitional National Council), who was then Minister of Justice in Qaddafi's government, admitted Qaddafi never gave the order to use force. At the time there was a consensus among ministers working in Qaddafi's government force would not be used during protests, he revealed.[369] This assessment is also reflected in the findings of the DIA (Defense Intelligence Agency) selectively dismissed by the State Department of Hilary Clinton.[370]

More thoroughly damning was that LLHR's claims were coordinated with the Transnational National Council (TNC) itself, the Libyan opposition organized and supported by Western powers that would assume power at their command. Some TNC members, he candidly admitted, were his friends. Additionally, no less than five executive members of the LLHR were part of TNC. Bouchuiguir revealed that individuals tied to the LLHR or holding membership included Mahmoud Jibril and Ali Tarhouni of the TNC. That Jibril was prime minister of the TNC reduces its trustworthiness to absurdity. Nonetheless, he was revealed as a chief source for the LLHR. Questioned on his source for allegations against Qaddafi, Bouchuigur remarked, "I got that [information] from the Libyan Prime Minister...on the other side [the Libyan opposition]. Mr.

---

[369] Saman Mohammadi, "Head Of Fake Libyan Revolution Admits Ghadafi Did Not Kill Protesters," Information Clearing House, May 22, 2014, http://www.informationclearinghouse.info/article38570.htm
[370] Gary Leupp, "The Warmongering Record of Hilary Clinton," *Counterpunch*, February 11, 2015, http://www.counterpunch.org/2015/02/11/the-warmongering-record-of-hillary-clinton/

Mahmoud [Jibril]." [371] The hysteria at the UN was incited by allegations coming directly from the opposition itself.

Tellingly, before playing the role of propagandist, Jibril was brought into the Libyan government of Qaddafi by his son Saif al-Islam to steward Western pushed privatization of Libyan industries; Tarhouni would become the minister of oil in the new post-Qaddafi regime. Groomed in the US and present at major meetings about regime change in Libya, Tarhouni was Washington's partner in Libya. As Minister of Oil and Finance, his first acts were privatization and handing over Libya's resources to the foreign corporations and governments of the NATO-Qatar assault against Libya.

The participation of these compromised figures in the LLHR severely discredits its narrative. Indeed, some anti-Qaddafi Western media candidly explained, the TNC, which these outlets were generally supportive of, had no commitment to truth throughout the civil war. The *New York Times* remarked: "[L]ike the chiefs of the Libyan state news media, the rebels feel no loyalty to the truth in shaping propaganda, claiming nonexistent battlefield victories, asserting they were still fighting in a key city days after it fell to Qaddafi forces, and making vastly inflated claims of his barbaric [acts]."[372] Of the TNC's own media channel, created though the aid of Qatar, the *Los Angeles Times* likewise explained, "It's not exactly fair and balanced media." The *Los Angeles Times* noted that news emanating from the TNC's station was filtered through sclerotic criteria that ennobled their cause.[373]

Bouchuiguir himself was of a dubious background. He was Western educated and wrote his PhD thesis at George Washington

---

[371] Forestgamertube, "Lies behind the 'Humanitarian War' in Libya: There is no evidence! (Part 1), NATO Crimes In Libya," October 11, 2011, https://www.youtube.com/watch?v=j4evwAMIh4Y

[372] David Kirkpatrick, "Hopes for a Qaddafi Exit, and Worries of What Comes Next," *New York Times*, March 21, 2011, http://www.nytimes.com/2011/03/22/world/africa/22tripoli.html?page wanted=all

[373] Mahdi Darius Nazemroaya, "The media misinformation campaign behind the war," Voltairenet, May 16, 2011, http://www.voltairenet.org/article169874.html

University under the auspices of Bernard Reich, a prominent pro-Israel political scientist who wrote a book about the US-Israel special relationship. Reich also touted the creation of a "New Middle East" favorable to Israel. Bouchuiguir's thesis, published as a book in 1979, was on "The Use of Oil as a Political Weapon: A Case Study of the 1973 Arab Oil Embargo." This thesis explored the use of oil as an economic weapon by Arabs. It is apparent Bouchuiguir drew heavily from Reich, who on October 23, 1973 provided testimony to the US Congress on "The Impact of the October Middle East War." Bouchuiguir's thesis has been referred to in US strategic circles.

Seizing on the lies of Bouchuiguir by quickly maneuvering at the United Nations Security Council, Western powers pushed for the authorization of a military assault with its tenuous humanitarian pretext. This time they moved far more quickly than the 2003 Bush-Blair drive to smash the Iraqi state, not giving pacifist resistance a chance to organize before the destruction of Libya would be a fait accompli. On the basis of Bouchuiguir's letter and unfounded propaganda, at most hearsay, the UNSC voted to sanction Libya and authorize a "no-fly zone." Under the RtoP doctrine—and with the acquiescence of Russia and China—UNSC Resolution 1973 was passed authorizing military intervention under the mandate to "protect civilians" by "all means."

Whether Russia naively assumed Western powers would act under the guidelines enumerated in the resolution, or if some other consideration was at play, is difficult to ascertain. It is worth noting this failure reportedly prompted the Russian ambassador to Libya to call Russian President Medvedev a "traitor." [374] China in these matters typically defers to the Russian position. NATO subsequently interpreted this as carte blanche to complete the destruction of Libya.

Hearsay from sources whose desire to serve Western interests was only outstripped by their alacrity to seize power, cannot provide the basis for initiating a brutal war, the deadly ramifications of which reverberate today. As pointed out by the Indian delegation at the

---

[374] Joshua Keating, "Did Russia's Libya Ambassador Call Medvedev a Traitor?" *Foreign Policy*, March 24, 2011, http://foreignpolicy.com/2011/03/24/did-russias-libya-ambassador-call-medvedev-a-traitor/

time, there was never an independent investigation or verification to the hysterical allegations made by the powers pressing for war at the UNSC.[375] In the words of Bouchuiguir himself, "there is no evidence." The UN—whose role is ostensibly to promote international peace and security while respecting the sovereignty of nations—provided legal legitimacy to the offensive. The UNSC sanctioned an act of international banditry and the complete destruction of a sovereign nation-state. By becoming an instrument of war, in this manner, the credibility of the UN as a force for peace and security was severely undermined. This was perfectly congruent with the new "soft power" emphasis of the Obama regime, vindicating this as a new strategy of empire.

But how was this possible? How could the UN whose stated mission is to ensure "international peace and security" become a "lethal weapon of the empire"? How could it fall prey to the intrigues of duplicitous Libyan opposition figures and nefarious NGOs, thus, vindicating the doctrine of Suzanne Nossel?

Firstly, the UN was under inept and corrupt leadership with the tenure of Secretary-General Ban Ki Moon. The current Secretary-General is increasingly partisan in the interests of NATO bloc powers. Moon has been implicated in charges of corruption, by no less than his own Under Secretary-General Inga-Britt Ahlenius, who was in charge of the UN Office of Internal Oversight Services (OIOS). Ahlenius, whose career has been renowned for integrity, drafted a 50 page report on the UN's finances and its use of funds in various services. Ahlenius pointedly declared to Moon, "Sir, your actions are unprecedented...you deserve more than just condemnation." Directed at Moon, the report declared, "your actions...lack transparency and violate audit regulations." "I am sorry to say that the Secretary-General steps into a phase of delinquency, where he is utterly collapsing, and one might say, from which he cannot be rescued," she lamented. The hapless Moon responded at first by silence and then censoring the report, recalling it from the official UN

---

[375] The Indian UN delegation contended that "The report of [the UN] Envoy and that of others had not yet been received. As a consequence, today's resolution was based on very little clear information." http://www.un.org/press/en/2011/sc10200.doc.htm#Resolution

website 2 days after it was published. Ahlenius followed this exposé by coauthoring a book with Swedish journalist Nialas Ekdal titled "Mr. Chance, the UN Deterioration Under the Direction of Ban Ki-Moon" continuing the theme of Moon's illicit disposal of public funds.[376]

More specifically, the heart is the successful weaponization of the RtoP doctrine at the UN, and the infestation of nefarious NGOs as a integral part of the UN's infrastructure. Fundamentally, it was reflected in the integration of the UN into the unipolar world power structure and American globalization. Ideologically, for American apparatchiks, critical to this process was the thesis of Jessica Mathews, an American establishment figure, then working at the elite corporate backed CFR (today President of the Carnegie Endowment for International Peace and member of the elite Atlanticist Bilderberg Group's steering committee). Mathews's triumphalist thesis "Power Shift,"[377] appearing in the 1997 January-February *Foreign Affairs*, was chosen by the CFR as one of their most influential to have appeared in 75 years of publication. Mathews's argument—which proceeded from the equally crucial and bombastic Francis Fukayama thesis [378] —was that the period of the 1648 Westphalian system of sovereign nation-states was becoming anachronistic. In its place a power was shifting to supranational organizations and NGOs with globalization paramount.

This process of bringing the UN in line with the thinking of Mathews and the "New World Order" began under the auspices of

---

[376] Hassan Hamadé, "CORRUPTION AT THE TOP: An Open Letter to the dishonorable Ban Ki-moon," Voltairenet, January 27, 2012,
http://www.voltairenet.org/article172532.html
[377] Jessica Mathews, "Power Shift," Council on Foreign Relations,
January/February 1997,
http://www.foreignaffairs.com/articles/52644/jessica-t-mathews/power-shift
[378] For the vast majority of American foreign policy apparatchiks the bombastic Francis Fukayama thesis of the "End of History" — the argument that the US achieved the highest form of human development imaginable—fundamentally undergirds their thinking. This implicitly also holds that those not in conformity with this superior system are morally wrong. The ramifications for this is the preclusion of a rational and balanced approach to international politics, and a priggish belief in American moral superiority.

Secretary-General Kofi Annan. In addition to his successful bureaucratic and managerial reforms, as Secretary General, Annan harmonized the UN with the unipolar world power structure and its byproduct of globalization. Annan's signature initiative was the "Global Compact." Ostensibly, "[on] the basis of a voluntary dialogue, businesses, unions and NGOs were brought together to discuss and commit to respect human rights, labor standards and the environment." In practice, this initiative, as noted by independent journalist *Thierry Meyssan*, undermined the power of the sovereign nation-state as an institution. Simultaneously, it bolstered the corporatist globalist power structure, thus, burying the spirit and letter of the original San Francisco Charter:

> In practice, the Global Compact did not yield the desired effect on the ground. On the contrary, it deeply distorted the nature of the UN by playing down the power of nation-states and emphasizing that of transnational corporations and of associations which are "non-governmental" only in name and which are covertly funded by the great powers. By promoting lobbies as partners of the United Nations, Kofi Annan buried the spirit of the San Francisco Charter. It is no longer a question of saving mankind from the scourge of war by recognizing the legal equality of nations large and small, but of improving the human condition by supporting the convergence between private interests.

> The Global Compact is a deviation from the nearly universally accepted logic that international law serves the common good, to a logic embraced only by the Anglo-Americans for whom the common good is a chimera and good governance consists in bringing together the largest number of special interests. Ultimately, the Global Compact has had the same effect as the charity galas in the US: to give oneself a good conscience by launching high-profile initiatives while condoning structural injustices.

> In that sense, the terms of Kofi Annan (1997-2006) reflect the reality of the historical period, that of a unipolar world subjected to the globalization of U.S. hegemony at the expense of nation-states and the peoples that they represent...

Peace has stopped being a concern for the UN since the unipolar world has its own policeman, the U.S.; thus the organization can concentrate instead on absorbing all forms of protest to better corroborate the global disorder and justify the progressive global expansion of U.S. hegemony.[379]

Moreover, Meyssan notes, this converged with the decades long strategy from the Reagan era onward (see Part III) to leverage "NGOs" as instruments of foreign policy and subversion under the guise of "democracy" promotion via the NED. Within this framework "the beneficiaries participate in the Global Compact, thereby bending the positions of the Nation-States which lack the means to fund their own lobbies." It is evident that the "reform" Global Compact infrastructure imposed by Kofi Annan at the UN was perfectly contiguous with the forthcoming soft power strategy of the Obama team, thereby setting the framework for the Libyan tragedy. This was especially pronounced because Global Compact "NGOs" were under the dominion of the American corporate-government colossus to begin with. And as Bouchuiguir commented, "all NGOs are acquainted."[380]

SOFT POWER AND THE SYSTEM OF ALLIANCES

The Obama "soft power" shift also indicated a tendency to emphasize alliances and vassals over exclusively American leadership. This was under the prescription of Assistant Defense Secretary Joseph Nye, Jr., "a smart strategy that combines hard- and soft-power resources—and that emphasizes alliances and networks that are responsive to the new context of a global information age." Obama apparatchik Suzanne Nossel elaborated this outlook further, offering that "US interests are furthered by enlisting others on behalf of U.S. goals, through alliances, international institutions, careful diplomacy, and the power of ideals." US strategy against Libya played out in precisely this way. This alliance strategy took shape in

---

[379] Thierry Meyssan, "Kofi Annan: black skin, white mask," Voltairenet, March 30, 2012, http://www.voltairenet.org/article173325.html
[380] Tony Cartalucci, "Lies Behind the 'Humanitarian War' in Libya: There is No Evidence!" Land Destroyer Report, October 19, 2011, http://landdestroyer.blogspot.com/2011/10/lies-behind-humanitarian-war-in-libya.html

the 'leading from behind" approach. This entails outsourcing geopolitical initiatives to allies—with them trumpeting at the forefront—while Washington discreetly provides necessary military or logistical assistance. In addition to NATO allies—with France and Britain, the most bellicose at the forefront—regionally, this included relying on allies such as Qatar to smash Libya.

The Gulf Arab states long rejected Libya's leadership in the Arab world, and despised Qaddafi, prompting Libya to shift focus to the African continent. Enmity between Qaddafi and Gulf states was personal. In 2004 Qaddafi was accused of plotting to assassinate Saudi King Abdullah and the two exchanged insults. Although he later made overtures for reconciliation with the Saudi King, Qaddafi charged he was "liar" "a British product and American ally." Meanwhile, King Abdullah chided Qaddafi: "Your lies precede you and your grave is in front of you."

But the foremost Gulf State relied on by the US to smash Libya was the Gulf emirate Qatar. The tiny Gulf emirate undertook an ambitious foreign policy since Sheikh Hamad bin Khalifa al-Thani deposed his conservative father in his 1995 bloodless coup. Qatar had long been an American protectorate with al-Udeid Air Base, nineteen miles southwest of its capital Doha, one of its most important airfields of the Gulf region, hosting United States Central Command. As time went on, it has increasingly sold its usefulness in American foreign policy. Its ambition skyrocketed with the advent of the US sponsored "Arab Spring." This is especially evinced in its sponsored news outlet al-Jazeera aiding in the destabilization's credence, and providing propaganda for the operation. Its other crucial vector of influence is the Muslim Brotherhood, the foremost Islamist organization which it sponsors. The MB's most influential cleric, Egyptian based Yusuf al-Qaradawi announced a fatwa for any able-bodied Libyan soldier to shoot and kill Libya's leader, Muammar Qaddafi. "Whoever in the Libyan army is able to shoot a bullet at Mr. Gaddafi should do so," Qaradawi declared, "to rid Libya of him."[381]

---

[381] Meredith Jessup, "Egyptian Muslim Brotherhood Cleric Orders Gaddafi Assassination," The Blaze, February 21, 2011,

Continuing its history of sponsorship of exiled Libyan opposition forces, Qatar supported the Libyan opposition in material terms. With its small air force, it was the only Arab state to enforce the UNSC approved "no fly zone." It would supply hundreds of troops on the ground in violation of the UNSC approved mandate[382] and supply the Libyan rebels with arms. [383] Qatar provided Libyan opposition with tens of millions of dollars in aid, military training, and more than 20,000 tons of weapons. Most of these weapons went directly to Islamist militias. According to the *Wall Street Journal*, when Tripoli finally fell to rebel forces the chief of staff of Qatar's forces Maj. Gen. Hamad Ben Ali al-Attiyah was present along with the infamous Abdul Hakim Belhaj, reputed Libyan Islamist militant leader who became military commander of Tripoli.[384] As a testament to the centrality of Qatar to the operation, when asked in an interview on al-Jazeera how much Qatar spent to support the Libyan revolution, the Qatari Prime Minister retorted, "It's a lot. It cost us a lot." [385] Indeed, welcoming Qatari's Hamad al-Thani to the White House, Obama told the press: "We would not have been able, I think, to shape the kind of broad-based international coalition that includes not only our NATO members, but also includes Arab states, without the Emir's leadership."[386]

---

http://www.theblaze.com/stories/2011/02/21/egyptian-muslim-brotherhood-cleric-orders-gaddafi-assassination/

[382] Ian Black, "Qatar admits sending hundreds of troops to support Libya rebels," *Guardian*, October 26, 2011,
http://www.theguardian.com/world/2011/oct/26/qatar-troops-libya-rebels-support

[383] Ian Black, "Libyan rebels receiving anti-tank weapons from Qatar," The Guardian, April 14, 2011,
http://www.theguardian.com/world/2011/apr/14/libya-rebels-weapons-qatar

[384] Sam Dagher, Charles Levinson, and Margaret Coker "Tiny Kingdom's Huge Role in Libya Draws Concern," *Wall Street Journal*, October 17, 2011,
http://www.wsj.com/articles/SB100014240529702040023045766270009227 64650

[385] Blake Hounshell, "The Qatar Bubble," *Foreign Policy*, April 23, 2012,
http://www.foreignpolicy.com/articles/2012/04/23/the_qatar_bubble

[386] "Remarks by President Obama and Emir Hamad bin Khalifa al-Thani of Qatar After a Bilateral Meeting," The White House: Office of Press Secretary,

This included the Arab League, another multilateral institution, to lend legitimacy to the operation to destroy Libya. Secretary of State Hillary Clinton cited Arab League approval of military intervention as justification to undertake a "no fly zone" against Libya. Libya was turning away from the Arab world and focusing on the African continent, thereby making the completely ignored African Union a relevant institution. In conjunction with Qatar, Saudi Arabia, long at odds with Qaddafi, is reported to have played a role in this regard. Although the kingdom would be uneasy about undermining its partner Egypt, who depended on Libya, it may have acquiesced to get blessing for its intervention in neighboring Bahrain. According to the *Asia Times*, a full 22 member endorsement of a "no fly zone" against Libya by the Gulf-dominated Arab League never happened. Of 22 full members, only 11 were present, and the Arab League secretary general Amr Moussa was keen to demonstrate his usefulness to Washington to become next president of Egypt.[387]

Lebanon was also a factor in securing the anti-Libyan resolution at the UN. Under the government of President Michel Suleiman it proceeded against Libya by cosponsoring the "no-fly Zone" resolution. Notably, the Lebanese militant group and Iranian proxy Hezbollah took a stand in support of Qaddafi's ouster—a position in alignment with the US. As explained by Professor Idris Samawi Hamid, the rationale is Qaddafi's rumored complicity in the murder of prominent Shiite cleric Imam Sayyid Musa Sadr. This apocryphal narrative led many Shiites to hold him in opprobrium. [388] The

April 14, 2011, https://www.whitehouse.gov/the-press-office/2011/04/14/remarks-president-obama-and-emir-hamad-bin-khalifa-al-thani-qatar-after-

[387] Pepe Escobar, "Exposed: The US-Saudi Libya deal," *AsiaTimes*, April 2, 2011, http://www.atimes.com/atimes/Middle_East/MD02Ak01.html

[388] See Profesor Idris Samawi Hamid, "A Revolutionary Spirit," Information Clearing House,

http://www.informationclearinghouse.info/article29471.htm While Hezbollah and partisans of Iran claim Qaddafi is the culprit behind Sadr's death there is no concrete evidence Qaddafi was behind his killing. The Lebanese organization he helped to found Amal remained coy, stating they did not know the culprit but looked forward to ascertaining the truth. To begin with, Qaddafi had nothing to gain from killing Sadr. On the contrary,

accusation came from partisans of Iran and Hezbollah, and not Amal the Lebanese organization Sadr founded.

NATO'S ISLAMIST EXTREMIST ALLIES

The Libyan regime change scenario additionally relied on an alliance with proxies on the ground. It is self-evident that the rebel forces staging an uprising against Qaddafi were not defenseless civilians but an armed force. More paradoxically for US officialdom's propaganda narrative, they were armed forces allied to al-Qaeda — putatively targets and enemies of the US in its so-called "war on terror." Despite the paradox, this was no aberration in policy. Author Peter Dale Scott explains in *Asia-Pacific Journal*, "al-Qaeda was a

---

an act such as this would contradict his own ideologically Nasserist underpinnings. Most likely, the forces that brought Iran and Hezbollah to power were behind his killings. See Rick Gladstone, "The Shah of Iran, the Islamic Revolution, and the Mystery of the Missing Imam," *New York Times*, January 14, 2016, http://nytimes.com/2016/01/15/world/middleeast/iran-shah-reza-pahlavi-shiite-cleric-moussa-al-sadr.html Strategically, to this bloc his death was a boon. Sadr and the militia he founded Amal — like Qaddafi — were Nasserist (i.e. pan-Arab nationalists) in orientation. This was expressed in their founding constitution (See Afwajamal Media Network, http://www.afwajamal.com/english/?page_id=57) In fact, Sadr worked under the authority of a Nasserist organization in ecumenical work. This is evinced in his efforts in Lebanon to affirm Levantine Alawia as being within the scope of Twelver Shi'ite Islam. "So it is interesting to note by what higher authority Musa al-Sadr claimed to act in the matter of the Alawis. His initiative, he declared, was part of his ecumenical work on behalf of the Islamic Research Academy, a Nasserist appendage of Al-Azhar." See Martin Kramer, "Syria's Alawis and Shi'ism," MartinKramer.org, http://www.martinkramer.org/sandbox/reader/archives/syria-alawis-and-shiism/ While Amal was Nasserist and pan-Arab, Iranian proxy Hezbollah was Islamist and bolstered the position of non-Arab Persian Iran. Hezbollah and Amal eventually engaged in fierce internecine combat for leadership of Lebanon's Shiite community with both offering differing visions. The Islamist Iranian backed Hezbollah emerged transcendent over Amal.

covert U.S. ally" in interventions in the Balkans and Libya "rather than its foe."[389] He notes the parallels:

> U.S. interventions in the Balkans and then Libya were presented by the compliant U.S. and allied mainstream media as humanitarian. Indeed, some Washington interventionists may have sincerely believed this. But deeper motivations – from oil to geostrategic priorities – were also at work in both instances...There have been other interventions in which Americans have used al-Qaeda as a resource to increase their influence, for example Azerbaijan in 1993. There a pro-Moscow president was ousted after large numbers of Arab and other foreign mujahedin veterans were secretly imported from Afghanistan, on an airline hastily organized by three former veterans of the CIA's airline Air America. (The three, all once detailed from the Pentagon to the CIA, were Richard Secord, Harry Aderholt, and Ed Dearborn.) This was an ad hoc marriage of convenience: the *mujahedin* got to defend Muslims against Russian influence in the enclave of Nagorno-Karabakh, while the Americans got a new president who opened up the oilfields of Baku to western oil companies.

> The pattern of U.S. collaboration with Muslim fundamentalists against more secular enemies is not new. It dates back to at least 1953, when the CIA recruited right-wing mullahs to overthrow Prime Minister Mossadeq in Iran, and also began to cooperate with the Sunni Muslim Brotherhood.

> That the U.S. would support al-Qaeda in terrorist atrocities runs wholly counter to impressions created by the U.S. media. Yet this on-going unholy alliance resurrects and builds on the alliance underlying Zbigniew Brzezinski's 1978-79 strategy of provocation in Afghanistan, at a time when he was President Carter's National Security Adviser.

Also worth noting, in the late 1990s a plot to assassinate Qaddafi involving al-Qaeda was revealed by British MI-5 agent David Shayler.

---

[389] Peter Dale Scott, "Bosnia, Kosovo, and Now Libya: The Human Costs of Washington's On-Going Collusion with Terrorists," Asia-Pacific Journal, http://japanfocus.org/site/make_pdf/3578

In *The Forbidden Truth,* Shayler and a group of authors reported that British intelligence agency MI6 paid al-Qaeda the equivalent of $160,000 to help fund an assassination attempt against Qaddafi.[390]

US strategy once again conformed to this tendency with the 2011 Libyan operation. In the heart of the rebellion, the northeastern Cyrenaica region, which includes the cities Benghazi, Dernah, and Tobruk, Islamist extremism was prevalent. With very little information available at the time about the Libyan opposition, other than glib singing of tomorrows of "democracy," one important study providing insight on this population center was a December 2007 West Point study examining the backgrounds of *jihadi* guerilla fighters under the banner of al-Qaeda. The northeastern corridor that includes the cities of Dernah, Tobruk, and Benghazi emerges as a key world center of suicide bombers. In this regard, Dernah even outpaced Riyadh, Saudi Arabia, sending one fighter into Iraq per 1,000 to 1,500 of its population. West Point authors Joseph Felter and Brian Fishman explain Saudi Arabia took first place in absolute numbers of *jihadis* sent to combat the United States and other coalition members in Iraq during the time in question. Libya, less than one fourth as populous, took second place. Saudi Arabia sent 41% of fighters. Felter and Fishman noted, "Libya was the next most common country of origin, with 18.8% (112) of the fighters listing their nationality stating they hailed from Libya." "Libya contributed far more fighters per capita than any other nationality," the report noted.[391]

At the time, the *Asia Tribune* commented, "[A]larmingly for Western policymakers, most of the [*jihadi*] fighters came from eastern Libya, the center of the current uprising against Muammar el-Qaddafi. The eastern Libyan city of Darnah sent more fighters to Iraq than any other single city or town, according to the West Point report. It noted that 52 militants came to Iraq from Darnah, a city of just

---

[390] See History Commons, "1996: British Intelligence and Al-Qaeda Allegedly Cooperate in Plot to Assassinate Libyan Leader" http://www.historycommons.org/context.jsp?item=a96libya#a96libya
[391] Dr. Webster G. Tarpley, "The CIA's Libya Rebels: The Same Terrorists who Killed US, NATO Troops in Iraq," Tarpley.net, March 24, 2011, http://tarpley.net/2011/03/24/the-cia%E2%80%99s-libya-rebels-the-same-terrorists-who-killed-us-nato-troops-in-iraq/

80,000 people (the second-largest source of fighters was Riyadh, Saudi Arabia, which has a population of more than 4 million). Benghazi, the capital of Libya's provisional government declared by the anti-Qaddafi rebels, sent in 21 fighters, again a disproportionate number of the whole."[392]

This high concentration of extremists in northeastern Libya is related to its prevalence of Islamic fundamentalism. The West Point study explained, "The vast majority of Libyan fighters that included their hometown in the Sinjar Records resided in the country's northeast, particularly the coastal cities of Darnah 60.2% (52) and Benghazi 23.9% (21). Both Darnah and Benghazi have long been associated with Islamic militancy in Libya, in particular for an uprising by Islamist organizations in the mid-1990s. The Libyan government blamed the uprising on "infiltrators from the Sudan and Egypt" and one group—the Libyan Fighting Group (jama-ah al-libiyah al-muqatilah)—claimed to have Afghan veterans in its ranks. The Libyan uprisings became extraordinarily violent."

As al-Jazeera let slip, this Islamist extremist group, also referred to as Libyan Islamic Fighting Group (LIFG), was the leading edge in initiating the February 2011 rebellion against Qaddafi. As described by the International Business Tribune:

> The LIFG is a radical Islamic group which has been fighting small scale guerrilla warfare against Gaddafi for almost a decade. Much of the LIFG leadership came from soldiers who fought against the Soviet forces in Afghanistan, as part of the *Mujahedeen*. Since the beginning of the uprising reports said that some of the LIFG has joined the TNC rebel movement on the ground, and many accused the fighters of having links to al-Qaeda, which the LIFG has since denied.

> Previously however, the LIFG had stated that its ultimate goal is to install an Islamic state inside Libya, which given the fact that many of its fighters are now on the side of the TNC is

---

[392] Daya Gamage, "Libyan rebellion has radical Islamist fervor: Benghazi link to Islamic militancy, U.S. Military Document Reveals," *Asian Tribune*, March 17, 2011, http://www.asiantribune.com/news/2011/03/17/libyan-rebellion-has-radical-islamist-fervor-benghazi-link-islamic-militancyus-milit

quite worrying. However as the LIFG is reported to have a fighting force of no more than a few thousand men, it is believed it will not be able to cause much trouble within the opposition.[393]

This group, providing an institutional basis for the rebellion, was a branch of al-Qaeda. On November 3, 2007 LIFG merged with al-Qaeda to form its North African branch, Al-Qaeda in Islamic Maghreb or AQIM. A 2008 statement attributed to al-Qaeda chief Ayman Zawahiri confirmed this merger.[394] The self-styled "Emir" of LIFG Abu Layth al-Libi, a later senior al-Qaeda commando, declared: "It is with the grace of God that we were hoisting the banner of jihad against this apostate regime under the leadership of the Libyan Islamic Fighting Group, which sacrificed the elite of its sons and commanders in combating this regime whose blood was spilled on the mountains of Darnah, the streets of Benghazi, the outskirts of Tripoli, the desert of Sabha, and the sands of the beach." The West Point study emphasized that "Libyan factions (primarily the Libyan Islamic Fighting Group) are increasingly important in al-Qa'ida. The Sinjar Records offer some evidence that Libyans began surging into Iraq in larger numbers beginning in May 2007. Most of the Libyan recruits came from cities in northeast Libya, an area long known for *jihadi*-linked militancy."

That al-Qaeda was at the center of the rebellion against Qaddafi was confirmed in an interview with one of the rebel commandos. In a London *Telegraph* article "Libyan rebel commander admits his fighters have al-Qaeda links," it was revealed that Libyan rebel commando and LIFG member Abdel-Hakim al-Hasidi, commander of the Dernah Brigades, admitted he personally recruited "around 25" men from the Dernah area in eastern Libya to fight against coalition

[393] Haddadi, "Does the Transitional Council Really Represent Libyan Democracy and Opposition to Gaddafi?" *International Business Times*, July 20, 2011, http://www.ibtimes.co.uk/does-the-transitional-council-really-represent-libyan-democracy-and-opposition-to-gaddafi-183738
[394] "Libya releases scores of prisoners," Al-Jazeera, April 09, 2008, http://www.aljazeera.com/news/africa/2008/04/200861502740131239.html

troops in Iraq for al-Qaeda.[395] Some, he remarked, "were on the front lines in Adjabiya [to fight Qaddafi]." "Mr al-Hasidi insisted his fighters "are patriots and good Muslims, not terrorists, and are fighting against the invader." During the 2011 uprising, al-Qaeda issued a call for supporters to back the Libyan rebellion, which would lead to the imposition of "the stage of Islam."

When Tripoli finally fell to NATO-Qatari and rebel forces, the de facto emir and founder of LIFG, Abdel-Hakim Belhaj, emerged as the military dictator of Tripoli. Belhaj led the highly trained "Tripoli Brigade" which stormed Qaddafi's fortress of Bab-al-Aziziyah. As explained by the *Asia Times*, "the so-called Tripoli Brigade [was] trained in secret for two months by US Special Forces. This turned out to be the rebels" most effective militia in six months of tribal/civil war."[396] Being the most battle-hardened warriors, many key rebel leaders were of this same coloration: "Hardly by accident, all the top military rebel commanders are LIFG, from Belhaj in Tripoli to one Ismael as-Salabi in Benghazi and one Abdelhakim al-Assadi in Derna, not to mention a key asset, Ali Salabi, sitting at the core of the TNC."[397] Another personality was Sufian bin Qumu who "escaped from a Libyan prison, fled to Egypt and went on to Afghanistan, training at a camp run by Mr. [Osama] bin Laden."[398] Leaked files revealed Qumu as a LIFG member, and Osama Bin Laden's occasional chauffeur in Sudan. [399] NATO's SACEUR

---

[395] Praveen Swami, "Libyan rebel commander admits his fighters have al-Qaeda links," *Telegraph*, March 25, 2011, http://www.telegraph.co.uk/news/worldnews/africaandindianocean/libya/84 07047/Libyan - rebel-commander-admits-his-fighters-have-al-Qaeda-links.html

[396] Pepe Escobar, "How al-Qaeda got to rule in Tripoli," *Asia Times*, August 30, 2011, http://www.atimes.com/atimes/Middle_East/MH30Ak01.html

[397] Ibid.

[398] Rod Nordland and Scott Shane, "Libyan, Once a Detainee, Is Now a U.S. Ally of Sorts," *New York Times*, April 24, 2011, http://www.nytimes.com/2011/04/25/world/guantanamo-files-libyan-detainee-now-us-ally-of-sorts.html?_r=0

[399] "Former Gitmo prisoner recaptured as suspect in assault on US consulate in Libya," RT, April 15, 2013, http://rt.com/news/bengrazi-consulate-assault-arrest-857/

(Supreme Allied Commander of Europe) General Stavridis conceded there were "flickers" of al-Qaeda in the rebellious forces against Qaddafi.[400] The facts belie this disingenuous characterization.

In a revelatory study released in 2014 by the center-right Accuracy in Media group, it was reported the US willingly facilitated a large shipment of weapons to al-Qaeda in Libya to combat Qaddafi. The report was conducted by analysts, former CIA officials, and included a study of 85 Freedom of Information Act documents from the Department of Defense, State Department, FBI and CIA, as well as information from insiders privy to the flow of weapons in Libya, the Maghreb, and Africa. Its focus was on al-Qaeda branch Ansar al-Sharia's 2012 Benghazi attack, in which US Ambassador to Libya Christopher Stevens was killed, and how it could have been prevented. The conclusion is that tacit collusion with al-Qaeda in 2011 led to Stevens's death. As reported by the UK's *Daily Mail*, this US support facilitated an estimated $500 million in weapons to al-Qaeda militants:

> The Citizens Commission on Benghazi, a self-selected group of former top military officers, CIA insiders and think-tankers, declared Tuesday in Washington that a seven-month review of the deadly 2012 terrorist attack has determined that it could have been prevented – if the U.S. hadn't been helping to arm al-Qaeda militias throughout Libya a year earlier.

> "The United States switched sides in the war on terror with what we did in Libya, knowingly facilitating the provision of weapons to known al-Qaeda militias and figures," Clare Lopez, a member of the commission and a former CIA officer, told Mail Online.

> She blamed the Obama administration for tacitly approving the diversion of half of a $1 billion Qatari arms shipment to al-Qaeda-linked militants.

---

[400] Adam Entous, Keith Johnson and Charles Levinson, "Amid Libya Rebels, 'Flickers' of al Qaeda," *Wall Street Journal*, March 30, 2011, http://online.wsj.com/news/articles/SB1000142405274870455990457623111 72563565048?mg=reno64wsj&url=http%3A%2F%2Fonline.wsj.com%2Farticl e%2FSB10001424052748704559904576231172563565048.html

"Remember, these weapons that came into Benghazi were permitted to enter by our armed forces who were blockading the approaches from air and sea," Lopez claimed. "They were permitted to come in. ... [They] knew these weapons were coming in, and that was allowed...

"The intelligence community was part of that, the Department of State was part of that, and certainly that means that the top leadership of the United States, our national security leadership, and potentially Congress – if they were briefed on this – also knew about this." The weapons were intended for Gaddafi but allowed by the U.S. to flow to his Islamist opposition.[401]

In sum, what was framed as a pro-democracy protest in Libya was yet another violent uprising against Qaddafi, albeit in this instance supported by al-Qaeda mercenaries and fanatics. As a testament to this, following the NATO/rebel victory in Libya, in the heavily Islamic Benghazi, heart of the rebellion, the *Telegraph* reported al-Qaeda's Islamic flag was proudly waved over the Benghazi courthouse.[402] "The flag, complete with Arabic script reading 'there is no God but Allah' and full moon underneath, was seen flying above the Benghazi courthouse building." "Vice.com also reported that Islamists had been seen driving around the city's streets, waving the Al Qaeda flag from their cars and shouting 'Islamiya, Islamiya! No East, nor West.' The revelation came just days after it emerged that rebels in Libya have imposed Sharia law in the some parts of country since seizing power. Mustafa Abdul-Jalil, chairman of the National

---

[401] David Martosko, "Benghazi attack could have been prevented if US hadn't 'switched sides in the War on Terror' and allowed $500 MILLION of weapons to reach al-Qaeda militants, reveals damning report," *Daily Mail*, April 22, 2014, http://www.dailymail.co.uk/news/article-2610598/Group-US-switched-sides-War-Terror-facilitating-500-MILLION-weapons-deliveries-Libyan-al-Qaeda-militias-leading-Benghazi-attack.html#ixzz3A95ArBl6
[402] "Libya: Al Qaeda flag flown above Benghazi courthouse," *Telegraph*, November 01, 2011, http://www.telegraph.co.uk/news/worldnews/africaandindianocean/liby a/8861608/Libya-Al-Qaeda-flag-flown-above-Benghazi-courthouse.html

Transitional Council, said Islamic Sharia law would be the 'basic source' of legislation in free Libya." Complacent news outlets attempted to downplay this display of Islamism as an isolated incident, but as explained by the conservative *National Review*, what emerged in Benghazi was a sea of al-Qaeda flags. Pictorial evidence attributed to Reuters in both the *New York Times* and an Arabic-language internet forum Muslm.net demonstrated the Benghazi waterfront engulfed in al-Qaeda flags. *Vice*, which was on the ground, confirmed the presence of the al-Qaeda flag.[403] Videos also showed a parade of the flags.[404]

Implicitly, a byproduct of tacit cooperation with al-Qaeda was a discrediting of the official American foreign policy script. On the one hand, fighting and drone bombing in Afghanistan and Pakistan was justified by the threat of al-Qaeda, in the process unilaterally killing hundreds of innocent Pakistani and Yemeni civilians (largely not covered by the corporate media). Conversely, the US was supporting and supplying rebel forces with elements of al-Qaeda in Libya bolstering their presence in the region.

NATO'S "HUMANITARIAN" BLOODBATH
AND THE ANNIHILATION OF SIRTE —
SAME FATE CITED TO AWAIT BENGHAZI

NATO's direct intervention in Libya was framed under the pretext of protecting civilians. In the aftermath of UNSC Resolution 1973, no such actions to protect civilians were carried out. The opposite occurred. NATO proceeded with a ruthless bombing campaign to topple Qaddafi's regime and any allied resistance completely. NATO acted as the Air Force for rebel fighters. Brushing aside the enumerated restrictions of the UN mandate, NATO and Qatar provided weapons, special forces on the ground to direct anti-Qaddafi rebels and mercenaries, carried out targeted assassinations, and bombed civilian population centers and vital infrastructure that

---

[403] Sherif Elhelwa, "AL QAEDA PLANTS ITS FLAG IN LIBYA," Vice News, October 27, 2011, http://www.vice.com/read/al-qaeda-plants-its-flag-in-libya

[404] "Al-Qaeda Flags Are Raised in a Pro-Shari'a Rally in Libya," MEMRI TV, October 25, 2011,
http://www.memritv.org/clip/en/0/0/0/0/252/0/3171.htm

had no military utility. These actions contradicted both the spirit and letter of UNSC Resolution 1973, itself of dubious legality. NATO was given the mandate to protect civilians, but with NATO leaders—from Hillary Clinton and Barrack Obama to William Hague and David Cameron—repeatedly declaring that "Qaddafi had to go," it was manifest that the *terminus ad quem* was regime change. Examining the often contradictory, but revelatory, statements of NATO leaders, inexorably leads to this conclusion. President Obama remarked that he "made it clear that Qaddafi had lost the confidence and the legitimacy to lead, and I said that he needed to step down from power."[405] Elaborating further Obama stated the US would work "with other nations to hasten the day when Qaddafi leaves power."[406] Similar statements from Western leaders were frequent. Additionally, then Secretary of State Hillary Clinton later revealed the US representative to Tripoli Christopher Stevens had covertly worked to recruit insurgents to overthrow the government of Qaddafi. If regime change rather than the protection of civilians was the goal, civilian deaths would be a corollary. Indeed, later questioned by the *Washington Times*, State Department officials confirmed regime change was their objective.[407]

Dr. Kuperman's outline in his authoritative report for the Belfer Center at Harvard shows NATO's actions support this conclusion:

> The conventional wisdom is also wrong in asserting that NATO's main goal in Libya was to protect civilians. Evidence reveals that NATO's primary aim was to overthrow Qaddafi's regime, even at the expense of increasing the harm to Libyans. NATO attacked Libyan forces indiscriminately, including some in retreat and others in Qaddafi's hometown of Sirte, where they posed no threat to civilians. Moreover, NATO continued to aid the rebels even when they repeatedly rejected government cease-fire offers that could have ended the violence and spared civilians. Such military assistance

---

[405] "Remarks by the President in Address to the Nation on Libya," Whitehouse.gov, March 28, 2011, http://www.whitehouse.gov/the-press-office/2011/03/28/remarks-president-address-nation-libya

[406] Forte, *Sirte*, 83.

[407] Riddell, "Secret Tapes," *Washington Times*.

included weapons, training, and covert deployment of hundreds of troops from Qatar, eventually enabling the rebels to capture and summarily execute Qaddafi and seize power in October 2011.[408]

At the announcement of the UNSC approval of a "no fly zone," it was apparent that the record of NATO in carrying out humanitarian imperialism would be repeated in Libya. The bloodletting would not end or be mitigated but increase. The objective of regime change rather than the rescue of civilians entails a crippling of the state's ability to resist, including through the use of terrorism. This entails deliberately terrorizing and attacking civilian populations to prompt their acquiescence or surrender as a part of overall strategy. It included targeting pre-selected civilian infrastructure such as the Great Man-made River, civilian airports, government buildings, factories, and radio stations, supposedly because they are centers of "propaganda," deleterious to civilians.

NATO's previous engagement in a humanitarian framed war in the former Yugoslavia is instructive. It bombed bridges, schools, hospitals, radio stations, and power plants, with weapons that included highly indiscriminate cluster bombs. [409] These were all NATO's pre-selected "legitimate military targets." In one such example a children's hospital in Belgrade was the subject of a NATO bombing attack, singled out as a strategic target. NATO acknowledged this attack but claimed it did not attack the area holding newborn babies. NATO did however attack the hospital's power generator, for all purposes destroying the hospital and its incubators that held newborn babies. This, as a result, killed many children.[410]

---

[408] Kuperman, "How Not to Intervene."

[409] Richard Norton-Taylor, "Minister admits cluster bomb tally unknown," *Guardian*, May 26, 2008, http://www.theguardian.com/uk/2008/may/27/military.armstrade?guni=Article:in%20body%20link

[410] Prof. Michel Chossudovsky, "Libya: The Objective of 'Humanitarian Bombing' is Death and Destruction," Global Research, March 25, 2011, http://www.globalresearch.ca/libya-the-objective-of-humanitarian-bombing-is-death-and-destruction/23945

NATO followed this pattern in Libya and engaged in atrocities against civilians and infrastructure. In addition to attacking the GMR, the Jamahiraya Satellite Channel was bombed by NATO to contain the flow of disseminating information. A concrete factory and cultural center in al-Khams were bombed after the announcement that civilian sites would be attacked.

Soon after bombing raids began reports emerged of civilian deaths caused by NATO. The top Vatican official in Libya reported in late March that 40 civilians were killed by Western forces in Tripoli. "The air strikes are meant to protect civilians, but they are killing dozens of civilians," Bishop Giovanni Innocenzo Martinelli, apostolic vicar of Tripoli, explained to Reuters. "In the Tajoura neighborhood, around 40 civilians were killed, and a house with a family inside collapsed," he stated. Living conditions in Tripoli deteriorated daily with increasing food shortages and long waits for bread and fuel with the city under NATO blockade.[411]

In Zlinten another large scale massacre took place. According to independent journalist Mahdi Darius Nazemroyah, reporting from inside Libya, as a direct result of NATO's deliberate targeting of residential areas and civilian infrastructure, 85 people were killed, including 33 children, 32 women, and 20 men. NATO included a second round of bombing against homes once local residents arrived to rescue victims. This is called "double-tapping." Colonel Lavoie of NATO claimed it had solid intelligence these areas were "military bases." As demonstrated by photographic and film evidence, the areas attacked were residential and farmhouses. The purpose of this attack was to clear the way for the road to Tripoli. The clans in this area claimed they would stand against the Western-backed TNC.[412] Even the TNC-sympathetic BBC reporters on the ground described a

---

[411] "40 civilians dead in Tripoli strikes: Vatican official," *New York Post*, March 31, 2011, http://nypost.com/2011/03/31/40-civilians-dead-in-tripoli-strikes-vatican-official/

[412] Mahdi Darius Nazemroaya, "Breaking News: NATO Massacres of Civilians Aimed at 'Cleansing' the Libyan People's Resistance Photographic Evidence of NATO War Crimes," Global Research, August 10, 2011, http://www.globalresearch.ca/breaking-news-nato-massacres-of-civilians-aimed-at-cleansing-the-libyan-people-s-resistance/25966

poignant scene. They witnessed 2 dead children and 2 dead women. Amidst the rubble-filled aftermath:

A photocopied version of Ernest Hemingway's The Old Man and the Sea lay in the rubble. Next to it were school books, their pages fluttering in the light breeze.

A policeman picked through the remains of the house. He slid the door of a refrigerator lying on its back to one side. Inside was a melon, and some bags of beans.

Nearby a sofa and a bed lay broken and covered in dust. There were other signs of normal life: a teddy bear, a football.

They witnessed the wounded from NATO's attack as well:

There was 15 year -old Salwa Jawoo. Her name was on some of the school books at the scene - I found her in Zliten hospital.

Her face was scarred - she had a broken shoulder.

She said she was sitting outside her home when the first missile struck. It was the second one that injured her.

"There was no military camp. We were just living there. Why did they attack us?" she asked.

"My mother died, and my two sisters," she added, with a sigh. A tear ran down her cheek as she spoke. Her grief was genuine.

So, too, was the sorrow of Ali Mufta Hamed Gavez. His wife - also in the hospital - had her leg amputated after being wounded.

Next door in the mortuary the stench was overwhelming -- body bags laid strewn across the floor.[413]

NATO carried out another massacre against civilians in Tripoli at the home of Maj. Gen. El-Khweldi el-Hamedi, who was by many accounts elderly and retired. According to the *New York Times*, "The family's account, partly confirmed by rebels, claimed that the strikes

---

[413] "What really happened in Libya's Zlitan?" BBC, August 11, 2011, http://www.bbc.co.uk/news/world-africa-14486170?print=true

IV. The New Humanitarian Imperialism   189

killed 13 civilians and wounded six more. Local anti-Qaddafi fighters corroborated the deaths of four of those killed — one of the general's daughters-in-law and three of her children." "On Sept. 25, a smaller but similar attack destroyed the residence of Brig. Gen. Musbah Diyab in Surt, neighbors and his family members said. General Diyab, a distant cousin of Colonel Qaddafi, was killed. So were seven women and children who crowded into his home as rebels besieged the defenses of some of the Qaddafi loyalists" last holdouts, witnesses said."[414] Following these NATO attacks and many others, thousands of people came to funerals. Nonetheless, these were dismissed by corporate organs such as the *Wall Street Journal* as Qaddafi "propaganda" because the contents of the coffins were not exposed. There are many other reports of similar attacks carried out by NATO where civilians and civilian areas were deliberately targeted.

The culmination of NATO's direct intervention to enact regime change was perhaps "Operation Siren," NATO's plan for the final seizure for Tripoli. This operation included the direct involvement of NATO Special Forces including in the area of planning — a direct contravention of UNSC Resolution 1973. Britain's *Telegraph* reported: "MI6 officers based in the rebel stronghold of Benghazi had honed battle plans drawn up by Libya's Transitional National Council (TNC) which were agreed 10 weeks ago." [415] "For weeks, military and intelligence officers have been helping the rebels plan their coordinated attack on the capital, and Whitehall sources have disclosed that the RAF stepped up raids on Tripoli on Saturday morning in a pre-arranged plan to pave the way for the rebel advance," the *Telegraph* added. The paper explained the plan was

---

[414] C. J. Chivers and Eric Schmitt, "In Strikes on Libya by NATO, an Unspoken Civilian Toll," *New York Times*, December 17, 2011, http://www.nytimes.com/2011/12/18/world/africa/scores-of-unintended-casualties-in-nato-war-in-libya.html?pagewanted=all&_r=0
[415] Gordon Rayner, Thomas Harding and Duncan Gardham, "Libya: secret role played by Britain creating path to the fall of Tripoli," *Telegraph*, August 22, 2011, http://www.telegraph.co.uk/news/worldnews/africaandindianocean/libya/8716758/Libya-secret-role- played-by-Britain-creating-path-to-the-fall-of-Tripoli.html

enacted after "RAF Tornado GR4 aircraft attacked a key communications facility in south-west Tripoli as part of the agreed battle plan." The British Foreign Minister William Hague explained that "non-lethal" aid was provided to rebel forces to facilitate the assault including advanced telecommunications equipment and 1,000 sets of body armor and night vision goggles. Independent journalist Thierry Meyssan reported on the ground in Tripoli:

> On Saturday evening, at 8pm, when the hour of Iftar marked the breaking of the Ramadan fast, the NATO command launched its "Operation Mermaid Dawn" against Libya.
>
> The Sirens were the loudspeakers of the mosques, which were used to launch Al Qaeda's call to revolt against the Qaddafi government. Immediately the sleeper cells of the Benghazi rebels went into action. These were small groups with great mobility, which carried out multiple attacks. The overnight fighting caused 350 deaths and 3,000 wounded.
>
> The situation calmed somewhat on Sunday during the course of the day.
>
> Then, a NATO warship sailed up and anchored just off the shore at Tripoli, delivering heavy weapons and debarking al-Qaeda *jihadi* forces, which were led by NATO officers.
>
> Fighting started again during the night. There were intense firefights. NATO drones and aircraft kept bombing in all directions. NATO helicopters strafed civilians in the streets with machine guns to open the way for the *jihadis*.
>
> In the evening, a motorcade of official cars carrying top government figures came under attack. The convoy fled to the Hotel Rixos, where the foreign press is based. NATO did not dare to bomb the hotel because they wanted to avoid killing the journalists.
>
> At 11:30pm, the Health Minister had to announce that the hospitals were full to overflowing. On Sunday evening, there had been 1300 additional dead and 5,000 wounded.

NATO had been charged by the UN Security Council with protecting civilians in Libya. In reality, France and Great Britain have just re-started their colonial massacres.[416]

Nazemroyah of Global Research reporting from Tripoli confirmed this scenario and that NATO carpet-bombed Tripoli to pave the way for the rebel seizure of control.

Overall, there exists no comprehensive analysis of the civilian death toll caused by NATO's direct intervention,[417] but Human Rights Watch (HRW), itself generally aligned with NATO interests,[418] offered a minor critique by sampling a modicum of data. On May 14, 2012, after the NATO operation had already succeeded in smashing the Libyan state, HRW released, "Unacknowledged Deaths: Civilian Casualties in NATO's Air Campaign in Libya."[419] HRW's 82 page report revealed NATO's assault in Libya resulted in the death of at least 72 civilians, with 24 children among that number. In truth, this data presented by HRW understates the death toll caused by NATO, is not comprehensive, and relies on the most obvious samples of

---

[416] Thierry Meyssan, "NATO Slaughter in Tripoli: 'Operation Mermaid Dawn' Signals Assault by Rebels" Al Qaeda Death Squads," Voltairenet, August 21, 2011, http://www.globalresearch.ca/nato-slaughter-in-tripoli-operation-mermaid-dawn-signals-assault-by-rebels-al-qaeda-death-squads/26118

[417] NATO refused to cooperate with the UN commission or HRW on its actions in Libya despite operating under a UNSC mandate. As explained by Vijay Prishad, "The scandal here is that NATO, a military alliance, refuses any civilian oversight of its actions. It operated under a UN mandate (Security Council Resolution 1973) and yet refuses to allow a UN evaluation of its actions. NATO, in other words, operates as a rogue military entity, outside the bounds of the censures and sanctions of democratic society." See Vijay Prishad. NATO in the Dock on Libya Bombing," *Counterpunch*, May 15, 2012, http://www.counterpunch.org/2012/05/15/nato-in-the-dock-on-libya-bombing/

[418] Keane Bhatt, "The Hypocrisy of Human Rights Watch," February 5, 2014, ncla.org, http://www.globalresearch.ca/the-hypocrisy-of-human-rights-watch/5367940

[419] "Unacknowledged Deaths: Civilian Casualties in NATO's Air Campaign in Libya," Human Rights Watch, May 14, 2012, http://www.hrw.org/reports/2012/05/13/unacknowledged-deaths

NATO atrocities out of 10,000 sorties carried out. Nonetheless, it is instructive if extrapolated to understand NATO's overall approach during its UNSC authorized assault.

By perpetuating the rebel instigated conflict, NATO prolonged the civil war, thereby leading to more civilian deaths. Kuperman's authoritative interpretation:

> When NATO intervened in mid-March 2011, Qaddafi already had regained control of most of Libya, while the rebels were retreating rapidly toward Egypt. Thus, the conflict was about to end, barely six weeks after it started, at a toll of about 1,000 dead, including soldiers, rebels, and civilians caught in the crossfire. By intervening, NATO enabled the rebels to resume their attack, which prolonged the war for another seven months and caused at least 7,000 more deaths.

By all indications, when Qaddafi's forces engaged in battle against the violent rebel uprising, discriminate force was used to narrowly target them and avoid civilian casualties. Dr. Kuperman argued in the pages of the *Boston Globe* at the time, "President Barack Obama grossly exaggerated the humanitarian threat to justify military action in Libya. The president claimed intervention was necessary to prevent a 'bloodbath' in Benghazi." [420] Human Rights Watch, he explained, "released data on Misurata, the next-biggest city in Libya and scene of protracted fighting, revealing that Moammar Khadafy is not deliberately massacring civilians but rather narrowly targeting the armed rebels who fight against his government." In the other cities at least partially liberated from rebel control, such as Zawiya, a similar pattern was followed. "The best evidence that Khadafy did not plan genocide in Benghazi is that he did not perpetrate it in the other cities he had recaptured either fully or partially—including Zawiya, Misurata, and Ajdabiya, which together have a population greater than Benghazi."

In Misurata, a city among the most inflamed with violence, early fighting demonstrated a discriminate use of force by Qaddafi's forces,

---

[420] Alan J. Kuperman, "False pretense for war in Libya?" *Boston Globe,* April 14,
http://www.boston.com/bostonglobe/editorial_opinion/oped/articles/201 1/04/14/false_pretense_for_war_in_libya/

not a deliberate targeting of civilians. The evidence of a HRW report states that of 949 people wounded in the rebellion's start only 30 were civilian women or children... meaning that Qaddafi's forces focused narrowly on combatants." Qaddafi's actual execution of the war against the rebellion belies the Western hype and justification:

> During that same period, only 257 people were killed among the city's population of 400,000 — a fraction less than 0.0006 — providing additional proof that the government avoided using force indiscriminately. Moreover, Qaddafi did not perpetrate a "bloodbath" in any of the cities that his forces recaptured from rebels prior to NATO intervention — including Ajdabiya, Bani Walid, Brega, Ras Lanuf, Zawiya, and much of Misurata — so there was virtually no risk of such an outcome if he had been permitted to recapture the last rebel stronghold of Benghazi.

In sum, the hysterically hyped humanitarian catastrophe and Rwanda-style genocide supposedly imminent in Libya and Benghazi — short of a NATO military intervention — was a sham. Qaddafi directed his forces against violent rebels who initiated violence and subversion to begin with.

Indeed, rather than preventing this type of scenario, NATO facilitated such an outcome replete with widespread war crimes by rebel forces. This occurred in fervently pro-Qaddafi or anti-NTC cities where no threat to civilians could have existed. NATO relentlessly bombed and facilitated rebel assaults. The NATO aided rebel attack on Sirte, birthplace of Colonel Qaddafi and wellspring of pan-Africanism, typified this approach. In fact, perhaps the apex of NATO's killing spree in Libya was the utter annihilation of Sirte. Paradoxically, the ultimate fate of Sirte was the same fate Obama and NATO bloc leaders stated was obviated in Benghazi through military intervention. NATO and Obama claimed they were preventing a massacre in Benghazi, but through NATO such an outcome occurred in an utterly devastated Sirte. Rebel forces pursued what amounted to a scorched earth policy of wanton destruction. Following rebel capture of the city massacres of Qaddafi supporters were widespread.

NATO was at a loss to provide a pretext for the destruction of Sirte because it was a pro-Qaddafi city, as the British *Telegraph* reported, "staunchly loyalist." Moreover, there was "no sign of an internal uprising" as "civilian areas are filled with volunteers for Gaddafi." In Sirte was a people defending their homes from external attack. The otherwise unsympathetic *New York Times* alluded to this fundamental reality in Sirte, asking how could the allies "justify air strikes if, as seems to be the case, loyalists forces enjoy widespread support in the city and pose no threat to civilians."[421] Tripoli, the Libyan capital was similarly a bastion of Qaddafi support, as demonstrated by large rallies festooned with Qaddafi Green Revolution flags, far outstripping demonstrations against him.[422]

NATO repeatedly bombed Sirte even after Qaddafi's government was toppled, without justification. The rebel assault on Sirte was entirely dependent on NATO air strikes and support. As one rebel insurgent remarked to Reuters, "This could not have happened without NATO. They gave us big support." In late August, when the rebel siege of Sirte escalated, NATO's spokesman could not adequately explain how NATO strikes were protecting civilians.[423]

With many NATO direct air strikes against Sirte, civilians were the primary victims. Separate independent investigations highlighting NATO's attack on Sirte are instructive. The Independent Civil Society Mission to Libya, an organ of the Arab Organization for Human Rights, the Palestinian Center for Human Rights, along with the International Legal Assistance Consortium, discovered a massacre committed by NATO air power. In interviews with witnesses, they found that in "a western residential area in Sirte which was one of the last holdouts of Qaddafi supporters... a NATO

---

[421] Kareem Faheem and David Kirkpatrick, "Rebel Advance Halted Outside Qaddafi's Hometown," *New York Times,* March 28, 2011, http://www.nytimes.com/2011/03/29/world/africa/29libya.html?pagewanted=all

[422] See for example 108Morris108, "HUGE PRO GADDAFI RALLY in Tripoli - Raw Footage," July 01, 2011, http://www.youtube.com/watch?v=jWzNhk3zv4U

[423] Karin Laub, and Paul Schemm, "Libya Rebels Pledge Assault on Qaddafi Stronghold," AP, August 30 2011, http://usatoday30.usatoday.com/news/world/story/2011-08-30/Libyan-rebels-demand-Algeria-return-Gadhafi-family/50185014/1 Cited in Slouching Towards Sirte.

attack resulted in the deaths of 57-59 individuals," at least 47 of them civilians.

An on-site investigation corroborated this account, and other unrelated witnesses confirmed this atrocity. Amnesty International, which supported the NATO operation, also confirmed this atrocity with a similar account, stating: "(AI) was told by residents in Sirte that on September 14, 2011 NATO strikes killed several members of al-Gaddafi forces, as well as more than 40 civilians, most of whom had rushed to the scene after the first vehicle was struck."[424] In another instance, NATO carried out an air strike on an apartment building, killing three women and four children, claiming that it was a "command and control" center. AI remarks that "if this civilian house was targeted because it was believed [a Libyan military commander] was present, NATO should have made sure it had information on the presence of any civilians there. The fact that at least seven civilians were in the home should have been reason enough to cancel or delay the attack out of concern that it would have been disproportionate."[425] Mahmoud Zarog Massoud was one of many civilian victims of NATO's indiscriminate bombing. The *New York Times* gave an account of his personal ordeal:

> On a recent afternoon, Mahmoud Zarog Massoud, his hand swollen with an infection from a wound, wandered the broken shell of a seven-story apartment building in Surt [Sirte], which was struck in mid-September. His apartment furniture had been blown about by the blast.
>
> He approached the kitchen, where, he said, he and his wife had just broken their Ramadan fast when ordnance hit. "We were not thinking NATO would attack our home," he said.
>
> Judging by the damage and munitions' remains, a bomb with a delayed fuze struck another wing of the building, burrowed into another apartment and exploded, blasting walls

---

[424] "LIBYA: THE FORGOTTEN VICTIMS OF NATO STRIKES," Amnesty International, March 2012, http://amnesty.org.pl/uploads/media/Libya_NATO_FINAL_report_march_2012.pdf
[425] Forte, *Sirte*, 102.

outward. Debris flew across the courtyard and through his kitchen's balcony door.

His wife, Aisha Abdujodil, was killed, both her arms severed, he said. Bloodstains still marked the floor and walls.[426]

Indiscriminate strikes by NATO betray a willingness to execute civilians without warning on the mere arbitrary suspicion of a "command center." Such are NATO's "rules of engagement."

From the rebel perspective, the conquest of Sirte was punitive, an act of vengeance. With rebels adopting the logic that residents of Sirte had "chosen to die," they unleashed a fusillade of available firepower in their arsenal. "[We] want to save our fighters and not lose a single one in battles with Qaddafi's forces. In the end, we will get Sirte, even if we have to cut water and electricity and let NATO pound it with airstrikes," rebel spokesman for the Benghazi based rebels Mohammed al-Rajali bellowed. [427] Making good on their threats, the rebels—with NATO assistance—maintained a siege of the city while residents were deprived of food, water, electricity, fuel, and medicine. The *Australian* reported: "Long lines of civilian vehicles were seen leaving after a night punctuated by NATO air attacks. Forces fighting for the National Transitional Council (NTC) added their own artillery and mortar rounds at regular intervals. Civilians, many looking scared or sullen, said that conditions inside Sirte were 'disastrous.' "[428] The *Australian* also quoted a civilian fleeing the carnage in Sirte:

> "They have hit all kinds of buildings: schools, hospitals," he said, referring to NATO airstrikes.
>
> He said he could not distinguish between NATO and NTC attacks but believed it was a NATO bomb that destroyed part of his home on Saturday. NATO said it hit a number of

---

[426] Chivers, Smitt, "Unspoken Civilian Toll."

[427] "U.N. Warns Libya Is Short of Water, Fuel, Medicine," AP, September 02, 2011, http://www.foxnews.com/world/2011/09/02/un-warns-libya-is-short-water-fuel-medicine/

[428] Tom Coghlan, "Sirte civilians accuse NATO of genocide," *The Australian*, September 27, 2011, http://www.theaustralian.com.au/news/world/sirte-civilians-accuse-nato-of-genocide/story-e6frg6so-1226147923376

military targets including a rocket launcher, artillery, and three ammunition stores.

Another resident said: "NATO bombing is killing civilians. Where is the United Nations? Where is the Muslim world to stop this genocide of the people of Sirte?"

The man, who gave his name as Mohammed Ali Alum Sekily, said six members of his family had been killed, but declined to give details. An eight-day-old baby brought out in one car was born on the beach, the family said.[429]

The arsenal of weapons unleashed by rebel forces to pummel Sirte into submission were indiscriminate in nature and impermissible under international humanitarian law. As NATO continued with large bombing, rebel forces unleashed an unmitigated wave of artillery, heavy mortar, grad rockets, machine guns, and tank fire. The BBC reported "Sustained tank and mortar fire has been targeting Sirte and there are huge columns of smoke across the city...many buildings [are] struck and on fire."[430] Residents fleeing the chaos remarked to Reuters "they're shelling constantly. There's indiscriminate fire within individual neighborhoods."[431] Even the anti-Qaddafi BBC explained, "This is almost a scorched earth policy." "Sirte is being systematically destroyed block by block. Fighting is intense, incredibly destructive and almost mind-numbing." The reporter added, "Retribution in Sirte. Some NTC fighters deliberately burn houses in Qaddafi's home town."[432]

The UNHRC's own International Commission of Inquiry on Libya confirmed the punitive and indiscriminate nature of the rebel's assault against Sirte. It reported the use of heavy weapons by rebel

---

[429] Ibid.

[430] "Libya NTC forces take most of Gaddafi stronghold Sirte," BBC, October 7, 2011, http://www.bbc.co.uk/news/world-africa-15210806 Cited in *Slouching Towards Sirte*.

[431] Jospeh Logan, "Libya's NTC retakes airport in Gaddafi home town," Reuters, September 29, 2011,
http://mobile.reuters.com/article/topNews/idUSTRE78S2ME20110929?irpc=932

[432] Forte, *Slouching Towards Sirte*, 95.

forces "was so widespread as to be clearly indiscriminate in nature."[433] It explained that with the assault on Sirte "the scale of the destruction there and the nature of the weaponry employed indicated that the attacks were indiscriminate," making it a documented war crime.

The NATO supported rebel atrocities in Sirte did not end with the use of heavy firepower. The *New York Times* reported, "It was the anti-Qaddafi forces who endangered civilians they suspected of having sympathies for a dying government." Subsequent to rebel control of Sirte, documented massacres took place under NATO's protection. In one such case 53 pro-Qaddafi supporters were slaughtered by rebels in a hotel. Under the rebel's odious logic, Sirte's residents "chose death." HRW explained "the hotel is in an area of the city that was under the control of anti-Gaddafi fighters from Misrata before killings took place." HRW called upon the NTC to investigate the massacre. It stated: "We found 53 decomposing bodies, apparently Gaddafi supporters, at an abandoned hotel in Sirte, and some had their hands bound behind their backs when they were shot." [434] HRW's emergencies director stated "this latest massacre seems part of a trend of killings, looting, and other abuses committed by armed anti-Gaddafi fighters who consider themselves above the law."[435] These lawless massacres were directly facilitated by NATO, and would not have been possible without NATO air strikes and guidance. In the aftermath of Sirte's utter annihilation, a similar fate awaited other anti-NTC cities such as Bani Walid. Overall, with NATO's air strikes against civilian populations, and their facilitation of rebel atrocities, the West guided a large-scale wanton killing spree.

The extent of rebel forces' merciless onslaught did not end in places such as Sirte or Bani Wallid. There was also a racist component to the rebels' assault with ethnic cleansing to extirpate black Libyans and peoples of black African descent. In addition to

---

[433] "Report of the International Commission of Inquiry on Libya," OHCHR.org
[434] Abayomi Azikiwe, "QADDAFI LYNCHED BY US-NATO," *The Illegal War on Libya*, (Clarity Press, 2012).
[435] Ibid.

the widespread targeting black Libyans [436] —legitimized by the "African mercenaries" canard—the primarily black Libyan city of Tawergha, located south of Misurata, was ethnically cleansed by rebel forces. This small city of 31, 250 was emptied of its entire population by vindictive militias from neighboring Misurata. *McClatchy* reported:

> What happened to the residents of Tawergha appears to be another sign that despite the rebel leadership's pledges that they'll exact no revenge on supporters of deposed dictator Moammar Gadhafi, Libya's new rulers often are dealing harshly with the country's black residents.
>
> According to Tawergha residents, rebel soldiers from Misrata forced them from their homes on Aug. 15 when they took control of the town. The residents were then apparently driven out of a pair of refugee camps in Tripoli over this past weekend.
>
> "The Misrata people are still looking for black people," said Hassan, a Tawergha resident who's now sheltering in a third camp in Janzour, six miles east of Tripoli. "One of the men who came to this camp told me my brother was killed yesterday by the revolutionaries."
>
> On Tuesday, Amnesty International issued a report on human rights issues in Libya that included claims that the rebels had abused prisoners, conducted revenge killings and removed pro-Gadhafi fighters from hospitals.[437]

The *Wall Street Journal* also revealed the carnage and extent of the racist animus driving rebel militias:

---

[436] For example see "Mounting Evidence of Rebel Atrocities in Libya Video clips depict summary executions, lynching of an alleged mercenary and a beheading. Black African prisoners are singled out for abuse." April 20, 2011, http://pjmedia.com/blog/mounting-evidence-of-rebel-atrocities-in-libya/
[437] David Enders, "Empty village raises concerns about fate of black Libyans," McClatchy, September 13, 2011,
http://www.mcclatchydc.com/2011/09/13/123999/empty-village-raises-concerns.html

Now, rebels have been torching homes in the abandoned city [of Tawergha] 25 miles to the south. The *Wall Street Journal* has witnessed the burning of more than a dozen homes in the city Col. Gadhafi once lavished with money and investment. On the gates of many vandalized homes in the country's only coastal city dominated by dark-skinned people, light-skinned rebels scrawled the words "slaves" and "negroes."

"We are setting it on fire to prevent anyone from living here again," said one rebel fighter as flames engulfed several loyalist homes.[438]

Andrew Gilligan of the London *Telegraph* provided more insights on the racist nature of the rebels' forced expulsion of native Blacks in Tawergah: "And as so often in Libya, there is also a racist undercurrent. Many Tawargas, though neither immigrants nor Gaddafi's much-ballyhooed African mercenaries, are descended from slaves, and are darker than most Libyans. Along the road that leads into Tawargha, the Misurata Brigade has painted a slogan. It says, 'the brigade for purging slaves [and] black skin.' "[439] Black Libyans and Tawergans were subject to arbitrary arrests once inside refugee camps and even inside of hospitals, Amnesty International reported.[440] Relatives of people subjected to such arrests explained in makeshift refugee camps near Tripoli that they refrained from going outside for fear of arrest. Amnesty witnessed firsthand such incidents:

On 29 August, Amnesty delegates saw a Tawargha patient at the Tripoli Central Hospital being taken by three men, one of them armed, for "questioning in Misratah." The men had no

---

[438] Sam Dagher, "Revenge Feeds Instability in Libya," *Wall Street Journal*, September 13, 2011, http://online.wsj.com/news/articles/SB1000142405311190353280457656486 1187966284

[439] Andrew Gilligan, "Gaddafi's ghost town after the loyalists retreat," *Telegraph*, September 11, 2011,http://www.telegraph.co.uk/news/worldnews/africaandindianocean/libya/8754375/Gaddafis-ghost-town-after-the-loyalists-retreat.html

[440] "Tawarghas must be protected from reprisals and arbitrary arrest in Libya," Amnesty International, September 7, 2011, http://www.amnesty.org/en/news-and-updates/tawarghas-must-be-protected-reprisals-and-arbitrary-arrest-libya-2011-09-07

arrest warrant. Amnesty was also told that at least two other Tawargha men had vanished after being taken for questioning from Tripoli hospitals.

Even in the camps, the Tawarghas are not safe. Towards the end of last month, a group of armed men drove into the camp and arrested about 14 men. Amnesty spoke to some of their relatives; none knew of their fate or whereabouts. Another woman at the camp said her husband has been missing since he left the camp to run an errand in central Tripoli, about a week ago. She fears he might be have been detained.[441]

The response of the Western backed TNC to this expression of virulent racism by rebel militias was not condemnation, but to offer carte blanche. "Regarding Tawergha, my own viewpoint is that nobody has the right to interfere in this matter except the people of Misrata." "This matter can't be tackled through theories and textbook examples of national reconciliation like those in South Africa, Ireland and Eastern Europe," the TNC chairman added as a crowd cheered on while chanting "Allahu Akbar," or "God is greatest."[442] NATO again not only notably failed to protect civilians, it facilitated their deaths, displacement, and dispossession in an odious forced expulsion. The tragedy and racist assault that befell black Libyans such as those in Tawergha was directly facilitated by NATO's rampage in Libya. Without NATO support the rebel campaign of blood vengeance was inconceivable.

---

[441] Ibid.
[442] Sam Dagher, "Revenge Feeds Instability in Libya, Rebels Burn Abandoned Homes in Loyalist Town as a Transitional Government Leader Stands By; 'Tawergha Is No More' " *Wall Street Journal*, September 13, 2011, http://online.wsj.com/news/articles/SB1000142405311190353280457656486 1187966284

PART FIVE: CONCLUSIONS.
REALISM OVER ROMANTICISM

The genuine revolution is characterized by positiveness
and self-confidence. It does not content itself with reacting, by
always focusing on the enemies, and enumerating their evils,
baseness and crimes. The genuine revolution is that which first
and foremost [regards] itself [as] the foundation and the great reality,
and believes that imperialism and the external things are
a consequence of inner weakness.
— Michel Aflaq

In the final appraisal, the mainstream narrative surrounding the
wave of uprisings against status quo autocratic Arab regimes is false.
The idea that romantic Arab youth activists, or even local armed
opposition for that matter, alone initiated the attempt to topple their
governments is a myth. Even the notion that they were co-opted,
later collaborated, or were rescued by foreign powers seeking to
"ride the wave," so to speak, is equally specious. The so-called "Arab
Spring" that swept through the MENA region was, in truth, a wave
of destabilizations sponsored from its beginning by Washington and
its allies through "civilian-based power," supplemented with its
classic reliance on death squads, militias, and "air power" where
needed.

With the onset of *multipolarity*, the US moved for regime change
against both enemy and increasingly recalcitrant vassal states to
ensure the emerging multipolar world order would be set on *its*
terms. Additionally, although a new cadre emerged with the onset of
the Obama regime, the status quo imperative to secure Israel
remained. The Obama administration introduced new techniques of
projecting power. Whereas the second Bush administration was
blunt and bellicose, the Obama team acted more indirectly and
surreptitiously, often relying on local proxies and ambitious regional
powers such as Qatar and Turkey.

In Egypt this took the form of "civilian-based power" in the
foreground. Meanwhile, in the background a military coup called for
and facilitated by Washington unseated its erstwhile ally Hosni
Mubarak. This was closely followed by leaning on its historical

partners in the Muslim Brotherhood. In Libya the US leveraged soft power, and relied on its classic irregular warfare scenarios, once again allying itself with Islamist militants, tribal militias, mercenaries, and death squads to topple a secular leader Muammar Qaddafi. This was supported by NATO's brutal intervention tipping the balance in favor of its proxies. Bereft of powerful Western support, the Libyan rebels would have been quickly routed within a few weeks, and normalcy restored to the country.

In any case, for the Arab world, the romantic illusions of "democracy" and "dignity" — platitudes sold by the West — were shattered, and much of the region degenerated into the breakdown of the state and society. This was the chaotic self-fulfilling prophecy of "Lebanonization," unleashing the forces of sectarianism and balkanization. In the major states where regime change succeeded — Egypt and Libya, for example — the process accelerated. Egypt saw inter-confessional tensions between Coptic Christians and Muslims following the seizure of power by the Western-backed Muslim Brotherhood; Libya most palpably was reduced to the status of an outright failed state. There are painful, but nonetheless immediately salutary lessons for would-be Arab youth revolutionaries, the primary participants on the ground. Rather than credulously accepting vacuous ideals offered by self-interested Western powers, the outlook of *realpolitik* (politics of realism) is more instructive and practical. Following a wave of foreign-sponsored "revolutions" that swept Europe, Germany's Otto Von Bismarck — exemplar of statecraft in the 19th century — remarked that the age of romantic idealism was over; the future would be decided not by romantic notions or assemblies, but through *blood and iron*. It is incumbent upon the would-be revolutionaries of the Arab world and beyond to come to a similar conclusion. Ultimately, having a repressive, authoritarian, or autocratic state is better than having *no state* at all. In reality, political reforms cannot exist without a functioning national state. This is the fundamental condition all considerations are subordinated to.

That the common denominator of the successful and progressive modern Arab revolutionary movements, Ba'athism and Nasserism, is the critical component of pan-Arab nationalism is instructive. Seeing the inherent threat of Arab nationalism to imperialism, the West and

Israel used myriad means—assassinations, economic warfare, bellicose threats, vilification, mendacity, political Islam, and ultimately direct war—to undercut and ultimately destroy Arab nationalism. Contravening this sound guiding principle of their predecessors, today's Arab youth allowed themselves to become the malleable plaything of foreign powers to undercut the overall Arab position, and ultimately to unleash regional conflagration to smash Arab states. Such an eventuality would have been anathema to a Michel Aflaq or a Gamal Abdel Nasser. Because of prevalent nihilism, the belief in nothing—a phenomenon by no means limited to the MENA region—Arab youth were made dupes of these foreign machinations to perpetuate neocolonial exploitation. Without firm principles and beliefs, you lose the ability and direction to dictate your own future; instead, your future is dictated by a self-aggrandizing other.

The aftermath of NATO's regime change scenario in Libya, central case study of this book, illustrates these conclusions most palpably and tragically. The result of NATO toppling the Libyan state under Qaddafi with the aid of tribal militias and Islamist compradors is now hell on earth. The Libya of today is a no man's land where no one is safe—not even the new rump state's head of state, nor Arab or even Western diplomats. Drugs are rampant and the country is ruled by rival militias and warlords who continue to clash, with scores dying daily. The rump state and parliament left by NATO is a non-entity, and most people have foregone participation in the country's parliamentary elections. Thus, the liberal platitudes of the West readily swallowed by Arab youth are a sham. This reality is evinced by the West's indifference to the outcome of what they have wrought throughout the region: utter chaos. To posterity, let the Fall of the Arab Spring be a warning.

ABOUT THE AUTHOR

Christopher L. Brennan graduated *magna cum laude* and Phi Alpha Theta from Mercy College in Dobbs Ferry, NY with a degree in history. A maverick independent political analyst and activist based in New York City, his articles have appeared in the *Center for Research on Globalization* and *Counterpunch*.

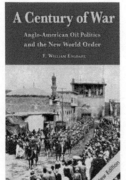

Three by Michel Chossudovsky

Towards a World War III Scenario: The Dangers of Nuclear War. The Pentagon is preparing a first-strike nuclear attack on Iran. 103 pp, $15.95.

The Global Economic Crisis: The Great Depression of the XXI Century, by Prof. Chossudovsky, with a dozen other experts. 416 pp, $25.95.

The Globalization of Poverty and the New World Order. Brilliant analysis how corporatism feeds on poverty, destroying the environment, apartheid, racism, sexism, and ethnic strife. 401 pp, $27.95.

Two by Henry Makow

Illuminati: Cult that Hijacked the World tackles taboos like Zionism, British Empire, Holocaust. How international bankers stole a monopoly on government credit, and took over the world. They run it all: wars, schools, media. 249 pp, $19.95. *Illuminati 2: Deception & Seduction*, more hidden history. 285 pp, $19.95

History

Two by George Seldes, the great muckraking journalist, whistleblower on the plutocrats who keep the media in lockstep, and finance fascism. *1,000 Americans Who Rule the USA* (1947, 324 pp, $18.95) Media concentration is nothing new! *Facts and Fascism* (1943, 292 pp, $15.95) How our native corporatist élite aimed for a fascist victory in WW2.

Two by Prof. Donald Gibson. *Battling Wall Street: The Kennedy Presidency.* JFK: a martyr who strove mightily for social and economic justice. 208 pp, $14.95. *The Kennedy Assassination Cover-Up.* JFK was murdered by the moneyed elite, not the CIA or Mafia. 375 pp, $19.95.

Two by Stewart H. Ross. *Global Predator: US Wars for Empire.* A damning account of the atrocities committed by US armed forces over two centuries. *Propaganda for War: How the US was Conditioned to Fight the Great War* Propaganda by Britain and her agents like Teddy Roosevelt sucked the USA into the war to smash the old world order. 350 pp and $18.95 each.

Afghanistan: A Window on the Tragedy. An eloquent photo essay on life amidst the ruins of war. 110 pp, $9.95.

Enemies by Design: Inventing the War on Terrorism. A century of imperialism in the Middle East. Biography of Osama bin Ladeen; Zionization of America; PNAC, Afghanistan, Palestine, Iraq. 416 pp, $17.95.

The Iraq Lie: How the White House Sold the War, by former Congressman Joseph M. Hoeffel. Bush Lied about WMD — and went ahead with war. $14.95

The Nazi Hydra in America: Suppressed History of a Century by Glen Yeadon. US plutocrats launched Hitler, then recouped Nazi assets to erect today's police state. Fascists won WWII because they ran both sides. "The story is shocking and sobering, and deserves to be widely read." – Howard Zinn. 700 pp, $19.95.

Inside the Gestapo: Hitler's Shadow over the World. Intimate, fascinating Nazi defector's tale of ruthlessness, intrigue, and geopolitics. 287 pp, $17.95.

Sunk: The Story of the Japanese Submarine Fleet, 1941-1945. The bravery of doomed men in a lost cause, against impossible odds. 300 pp, $15.95.

Terrorism and the Illuminati, A 3000-Year History. "Islamic" terrorists are tentacles of western imperialism. 332 pp, $16.95.

Troublesome Country. Throughout its history the US has failed to live up to our guiding democratic creed. 146 pp, $12.95.

Psychology: Brainwashing

The Rape of the Mind: The Psychology of Thought Control, Menticide and Brainwashing. Conditioning in open and closed societies; tools to defend against torture or social pressure. Classic by Dr Joost Meerloo, survivor of Nazism and McCarthyism. 320 pp, $16.95.

The Telescreen: An Empirical Study of the Destruction of Consciousness, by Prof. Jeffrey Grupp. How mass media brainwash us with consumerism and war propaganda. Fake history, news, issues, and reality steal our souls. 199 pp, $14.95. Also by Grupp: ***Telementation: Cosmic Feeling and the Law of Attraction***. Deep feeling is our secret nature and key to self-realization. 124 pp, $12.95.

Conspiracy, NWO

Corporatism: the Secret Government of the New World Order by Prof. Jeffrey Grupp. Corporations control all world resources. Their New World Order is the "prison planet" that Hitler aimed for. 408 pp, $16.95.

Descent into Slavery. How the banksters took over America and the world. The Founding Fathers, Rothschilds, the Crown and the City, world wars, globalization. 310 pp, $16. Also by Des Griffin: ***Fourth Reich of the Rich***, 316 pp, $16.

Dope Inc.: Britain's Opium War against the United States. "The Book that Drove Kissinger Crazy." Underground Classic, new edition. 320 pp, $12.95.

Ecology, Ideology and Power by Prof. Donald Gibson. Ulterior motives of the reactionary elite pushing population and resource control. 162 pp., $14.95

Final Warning: A History of the New World Order by D. A. Rivera. Classic, in-depth research into the Great Conspiracy: the Fed, the Trilateral Commission, the CFR, and the Illuminati. 360 pp, $14.95.

How the World Really Works by A.B. Jones. Crash course in conspiracy. Digests of 11 classics like *Tragedy and Hope, Creature from Jekyll Island*. 336 pp, $15.

Killing us Softly: *the Global Depopulation Policy* by Kevin Galalae, 146 pp., color. The Why and How of the covert, indirect war on the people. $15.95.

The Money Power: Empire of the City and Pawns in the Game. Two classic geopolitics books in one. The illuminist Three World Wars conspiracy: to divide us on ethnic and political lines to conquer humanity. 320 pp, $16.95

The Triumph of Consciousness. The real Global Warming and Greening agenda: more hegemony by the NWO. 347 pp, $14.95.

Conspiracy: False Flag Operations

9/11 on Trial: *The W T C Collapse.* 20 proofs the World Trade Center was destroyed by controlled demolition. 192 pp, $12.95.

Gladio, NATO's Dagger at the Heart of Europe: *The Pentagon-Mafia-Nazi Terror Axis.* The blood-red thread of terror by NATO death squads in Europe, from WW2 to the present. 490 pp, $25.

Conspiracies, Conspiracy Theories and the Secrets of 9/11, German best-seller explores conspiracy in history, before tackling competing theories on 9/11. 274 pp, $14.95.

Grand Deceptions: Zionist Intrigues. The Neocon World Order, from Herzl, to the world wars, Bolshevism, 9/11, Al-Qaeda, and media tyranny. 177 pp., $13.95.

In Search of the Truth: *An Exposure of the Conspiracy,* by Azar Mirza-Beg. A portrait of our times, society and religion, and the threat we face. 208 pp, $17.

JFK-911: 50 Years of Deep State., by Laurent Guyénot. The Greater Israel strategy behind the JFK and 9/11 murders. 238 pp, $15.95.

Subverting Syria: *How CIA Contra Gangs and NGO's Manufacture, Mislabel and Market Mass Murder.* Syrian "uprising" is a cynical US plot using faked news, provocateurs, opportunists, mercenaries, and Wahhabi fanatics. 116 pp, $10.00.

Terror on the Tube: Behind the Veil of 7/7, an Investigation, by Nick Kollerstrom. The glaring evidence that all four Muslim scapegoats were completely innocent. 7/7 clinched the assault on our rights. 3rd ed, 322 pp, $17.77.

The War on Freedom. The seminal exposé of 9/11. "Far and away the best and most balanced analysis of September 11th." – Gore Vidal. 400 pp, $16.95.

Truth Jihad: *My Epic Struggle Against the 9/11 Big Lie.* Kevin Barrett's profound and humorous autobiographical testament. 224 pp, $9.95.

Coming Soon

A Prisoner's Diary, by Hussain Mohammed Al-Amily
ISIS is US: *How the CIA and Friends Created the Terror Monster.*
The New World Order in Action: *from the Middle East through Greece to Ukraine,* by Takis Fotopoulos.

E-Books

9/11 Synthetic Terror; Barack Obama Unauthorized Biography;
Gladio; Grand Deceptions; In Search of the Truth; Iraq Lie; JFK-911;
Just Too Weird; Killing Us Softly; Myth of the Arab Spring;
Nazi Hydra; Subverting Syria; Surviving the Cataclysm; Target: China.

17138547R00124

Printed in Great Britain
by Amazon